Reviews of *A Fish Out Of Water*

Today most people view Alaska from the deck of a cruise ship or from the busy gift shop-filled streets of the coastal ports. But if they look beyond the vendors hawking whale watching or helicopter flightseeing excursions, and walk around the back streets, they might get a glimpse of an earlier, rougher Alaska, where men and their families mostly scratched out a hardscrabble living from the sea or the forest.

It is this rough life that Arlene Lochridge has reconstructed from the candid (some so candid that the writer destroyed them) diaries of her Aunt Hazel, who traveled to the Ketchikan area of Southeast Alaska in the 1940s with her husband, Carl, to make a living trolling in their boat for salmon.

Together with family and historical photographs of the period, the author has put together a book that offers a gritty and very readable view of an earlier Alaska – tiny wilderness outposts, rough and tumble towns, and a remarkable woman dealing with a full plate of challenges.

Joe Upton
Author of *Alaska Blues*
and other books about Alaska

A FISH OUT OF WATER perfectly captures the bygone era of America's last frontier – Alaska in the 1940s – through the eyes of one gutsy lady.

Tom Thompson
President, Anacortes Museum Foundation

A fascinating window into life as a commercial fisherwoman in the '40s. The historical references to the Alaskan landscape and the nature of fisher people at that time reinforce my knowledge of the history of Alaskan fishing.

Corey Arnold
Crewmember, *Deadliest Catch*
on the Discovery Channel

A wonderful time capsule of Southeast Alaska is in the collected diaries, and many historical photos embellish this courageous fisherwoman's hard life in the 1940s. I loved it!

Chris Arnold
"The Alaskan Photographer"
Homer, Alaska

A Fish
Out of Water

Arlene Lochridge

BOOK PUBLISHERS NETWORK

Book Publishers Network
P.O. Box 2256
Bothell • WA • 98041
PH • 425-483-3040
www.bookpublishersnetwork.com

10 9 8 7 6 5 4 3 2 1

Printed in the United States of America

LCCN 2010901603
ISBN10 1-935359-31-2
ISBN13 978-1-935359-31-9

Editor: Julie Sandora
Cover Designer: Laura Zugzda
Typographer: Stephanie Martindale

Special Thanks

I would like to express my deep affection and appreciation to my brother, Alan Chamberlain, for his collaboration and unwavering support. This book would not have been possible without his saving of Hazel's diaries. Also thanks to Linda, Jeff, and Amy Chamberlain, Alan's family.

Contents

Acknowledgments

I wish to extend my profound gratitude to John Michals, my copy editor/writer/advisor and jack-of-all trades for his enthusiasm and dedication to this work.

I would like to acknowledge Isabelle Corlett, my graphics/technical consultant, for her invaluable expertise and her cheerfulness.

To Richard Van Cleave, Senior Curator of Collections, Ketchikan Museums, many thanks for Alaskan historical research and collaboration. He contributed generously of his time, regional knowledge, and enthusiasm.

Deep respect and appreciation are given to Joe Upton, a talented writer and author of several books about Alaska, for his suggestions, guidance, and gracious review.

To the board of the Anacortes Museum Foundation of Anacortes, Washington—thanks for the use of the troller drawing and description.

I am greatly indebted to my endorsers for their sincere faith in the value of this work: Joe Upton, Tom Thompson, Chris Arnold, and Corey Arnold.

Loving thanks are given to my great friends and relatives who tenderly edited, critiqued, and offered encouragement when I needed it: Edna Sahm (my neighbor and fellow author), Paul and Betty Lochridge, Glen and Ruth Chamberlain, Gordon and Earlene Bundy, Bob and Barbara Ramirez, Veleta and Romeo Camozzi, Karen and Nolan Nelson, Chuck and Shirley Dawson, Anthony Magenet, Chris Arnold, Joyce Boosey, Kay Galyean, Bernie Blaney, Marilyn Brossard, Bev Cole, Karen Portillo, Melvie Maigaard, Ed Carli and Don Belding.

I also wish to pay tribute to the members of my two writing groups: **Works in Progress** *of Escondido and* **Davina's Writer's Connection** *of Rancho Bernardo.*

Most of all, I am full of love and intense gratitude for the Lochridge and Ogden clan—Steve, Karen, Kevin, Kelsey, and Kory – my family. They've endured my rants and ravings forever, it seems. Thanks!

More than anyone else, however, Frank, my husband, provided unwavering and absolute support. This project would never have been completed without his love and generosity. He's my guy!

Introduction

My Aunt Hazel never murdered my Uncle Carl. After reading her diaries, I am amazed at her restraint.

Carl was a 54-year-old ex-baseball player turned chicken farmer when he and my aunt first met.

Maybe it was too much of a comedown in career for Carl—going from pro athlete to poultry grower—or maybe it was the consequence of his Norwegian genes. But for some reason, Carl convinced himself that he should undertake a new, rugged lifestyle—commercial fisherman in Alaska. That was bad enough. Much worse was that he, through some emotional magic, influenced Hazel to not only marry him, but to join him in this envisioned adventure.

How he managed that baffles our family even today. At the time, my aunt was a 40-year-old Seattle socialite and successful career woman. During the decade prior to her marriage to Carl, Hazel directed an organization of more than 600 professional women. Yet this tall (5'11"), attractive, athletic divorcee set-aside family, friends, and profession in order to help her new-found soulmate undertake an exotic enterprise.

The pair purchased a modest, used 40-foot trolling boat named the Olympic. And on June 26, 1940—two days after exchanging vows—the newlyweds voyaged north. They sailed not into the proverbial tropical sunset, but rather to an alien—and mostly frozen—Alaskan territory.

Seven frustrating years later their escapade ended with Hazel returning to Seattle alone. In the interim, the couple had good times and bad—but more bad than good. I imagine that for my aunt, repatriation to Seattle must have been an approximation of being released from purgatory and inducted into heaven.

It's difficult, living in today's society, to appreciate the hardships and desolation one would have endured in the Alaska of the 1940s. Hazel and Carl—with no more angling experience than trout fishing in a mountain stream—went into the wilds to undertake an existence for which they were ill prepared. That sounds to me like one definition of insanity. Especially when it's done voluntarily.

I'd love to know more about how Hazel and Carl survived their years of Alaska. I get glimpses into their lives from her diaries, but only glimpses. And even some of those observations and insights are incomplete or absent. You will notice—how can you not—that there are few entries for the year 1945. They don't exist. They did, but Hazel deliberately destroyed them. And she hid all of the diaries while she was alive, saying that they were too private to share. **"I bared my soul in those books, and you can read them when I'm dead,"** *she told me. And she kept her word; her collection of booklets became a bequest to my brother and me.*

I'm glad to have Hazel's detailed accounts; they tell me much that I never knew about my aunt. But also, tantalizingly, they raise more questions than they answer.

Nonetheless, I am fascinated by the Alaska portion of my aunt's life. So much so that I thought it worthwhile to share her diaries—and some of my ruminations about them—with other readers. Hazel's notes are a kind of educational time capsule. They are also a reminder that not all of World War II was fought on the battlefields of Europe, Africa, or the Pacific. Some hardships were suffered closer to home.

I confess, I'm not sure if I should view my aunt as being heroic, stoic, or some combination. But however she is to be judged, I admire her. Perhaps I idealize her, because although I write about her now with an adult's mind, I recall her with a child's wonder. At the time Hazel was living the life recorded in her journals, I was just a young girl. And Hazel was an exciting, enigmatic figure who occasionally came to visit. I had no idea then what feminine courage and pioneer-woman's spirit existed within her.

My aunt had a dedication to spouse and a willingness to sacrifice that perhaps is lost in some of today's society. But you should decide that for yourself. I have transcribed Hazel's diaries, added some reminiscences (my own and those of other family members), and blended in some history, to provide perspective.

As a tribute to my aunt, I offer you, "**A Fish Out of Water**."

From Seattle Socialite ...

To Commercial Fisherwoman

Part I
1940

A Fish Out of Water

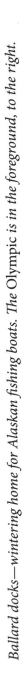

Ballard docks—wintering home for Alaskan fishing boats. The Olympic is in the foreground, to the right.

Getting There
Seattle to Ketchikan

🐟

6/26—Wed.
Ballard Locks to Port Townsend

[Note: Ballard—a Scandinavian-influenced neighborhood of Seattle—is a wintering home for hundreds of Alaskan fishing boats. See photo on facing page.]

Went to Ballard Fishermen's Festival last nite with Mother and Dad. Annual event where our pastor blesses the fishermen. Blessing was: "There are ships that will not sail again. There are fishermen who will go down to the sea no more. Yet, go in Christian faith and—confidently and courageously—experience God's blessing and peace upon your labors. God be with you. Amen."

Didn't sleep all night. Thinking about Mother and Dad. Both had tears in their eyes. Know they're worried. Can't believe we're doing this at ages 40 and 54. Fishing in Alaska. So far away. Left Ballard Standard Oil Dock at 10:30. Thru locks at 11 a.m., Port Wells—noon.

Point No Point—1:00. I got sick. Hope this isn't something that will happen often. Port Townsend—3:30. Anchor trouble. Carl got it figured out before long.

6/27—Thurs.
Port Townsend to Nanaimo, B.C.

Left Port Townsend at 6:45. Richardson *[dock with small store and gas]* on Lopez Island at 10:30. Left at 11:00. Crossed International Line at 2:00. First casualty—dishpan upset on floor. What a mess! Dodd Narrows—8:15 p.m. No trouble, very smooth. First dinner tonite while boat was running. Arrived at Nanaimo at 9:00 p.m. Could not buy any milk. Tied up to junk barge.

6/28—Fri.
Nanaimo to Departure Bay

Up at 4:30. Breakfast and dishes washed, bed made and ready to leave at 6:00 a.m. Had to wait for Customs to open. Canadian officer came aboard and required us to seal our guns. There is a $400 fine in Canada if caught with unsealed firearms. *[Four hundred dollars in 1940 was an unbelievable amount of money! The sealing of guns, according to Canadian Customs officials, typically would mean putting firearms into a locked container, then attaching an adhesive seal to that container in such a way that the seal would have to be broken to open the container. The person transporting firearms into Canada would, upon entering Canadian jurisdiction, go to a Customs office and have the guns sealed. Then, when the person with the firearms was about to leave Canadian jurisdiction, he would go to the nearest Customs office and show officials that the seal was unbroken (thus proving that the firearms had not been accessed while in Canada). If the seal had been broken, the firearms owner would be fined.]* Had to buy 5 new charts. Left Nanaimo at 2:00 p.m. Went up the beach and loaded rocks for ballast. Anchored boat in stream and loaded rocks in buckets from bank onto the deck and into the hold (about 2 tons) till our good ship *Olympic* was trim. A back-breaking job—took several hours. Now ready for the high seas and Seymour Narrows. Thence to a cannery in Departure Bay to make a few minor repairs and to repair pike pole that I broke earlier. Pumped out bilge; was surprised at the amount of water. (Henry had pumped it out Tuesday nite before we left Seattle.) At 9:00 p.m. one of the Japs came along and asked us to move as they were expecting a new barge—so we had to re-tie the boat again.

6/29—Sat.
Departure Bay to Seymour Narrows (4:30 a.m. to 8:30 p.m.)

Left Departure Bay at 4:30. Soon as we got into the Straits of Georgia, was so ruff the dishes bounced around and clothes fell off hooks. Too ruff to wash dishes. Got sick and had to go to bed till 11:30 when it calmed down. Then Carl went to bed while I steered the boat—no one around, miles from land—rather a "little" feeling. 2:00 p.m. calm as glass. Arrived at Seymour Narrows at 8:30. Too late to go thru. *[The treacherous currents give the safest passage during a relatively brief period of high tide, and they had missed it.]* Tied up to a float at Menzie's Bay—much bother with tires *[used as bumpers]* and what-not. Carl decided it wasn't such a good place so moved to other side of dock. A couple guys came along and said we had to go back to other side of the dock as they were expecting a boat to come in soon. At 10:00, we were finally tied up for the night. Passed many Indian fishing boats and villages between Cape Mudge and Seymour Narrows.

Sat.Jun.29   16 hrs.

Departure Bay to Seymour Narrows
(Menzie's Bay)   4:30a.m.to 8:30 p.m

Left Departure Bay at 4:30. As soon
as we got out into the Straits of
Georgia, it was so ruff (dirty water)
the dishes bounced around and clothes
fell off the hooks. Too ruff to wash
the dishes-- and I got sick, and had
to go to bed till 11:30 when it calmed
down. Then Carl went to bed while I
steered the boat--no one around--miles
from land--rather a "little"feeling.
p.m. as calm as glass. Arrived at
Seymour Narrows at 8:30. Toolate to
go thru so tied up for the night at
Menzie's Bay, to a float, much bother
with tires and what-not. Carl decided
it wasn't such a good place so we
moved to the other side of the dock.
But a couple of guys came along and
said we would have to go back to the
other side of the dock, as they were
expecting a boat to come in soon. At
10 p.m. we were g finally tied up for
the night. Passed many Indian fishing
boats and villages between Cape Mudge
and Seymour Narrows.

Original from 1940 diary.

6/30—Sun.
Menzie's Bay to Alert Bay—70 miles

```
Left Seymour Narrows (Menzie's Bay) at 7:30 in
order to go thru the Narrows at high-water slack.
The Narrows very ordinary—a few whirlpools. Heard
this could be a tricky area.
```

[Hazel and Carl apparently had no idea of the dangers they passed through so casually. Seymour Narrows is a three-mile-long section of Discovery Passage in British Columbia. Most of it is less than a half-mile wide, and during tidal ebb and flow periods, currents are so fierce that even whales wait for slack tide before pushing through together.

[There have been multiple shipwrecks—one as recent as 1981—in the Narrows. One-hundred-nineteen ships—including a U.S. warship—have sunk in the Narrows, with a loss of 114 lives.

[Famed explorer Captain George Vancouver called the Narrows "one of the vilest stretches of water in the world." Scientists agree with his assessment, calculating that the waterway is one of the most turbulent natural channels on Earth.

[There is a slim window of opportunity for safe passage—about one-half hour of high tide—when tidal currents subside. At other times they reach speeds up to 15 knots and generate whirlpools down both sides of the strait.

[In addition to rip currents and whirlpools, another hazard was an underwater mountain that rose to within nine feet of the surface. This jagged rock formation—known as Ripple Rock—also created treacherous vortices. The dangerous projection was blasted away in 1958. Twenty-seven months of tunneling and engineering work preceded the actual blast, which was the largest non-nuclear explosion ever set off in the world. (To watch the actual video of this blast, google "Ripple Rock Explosion" and you will see it on You Tube.)

[Even after the removal of Ripple Rock, navigating the Narrows is still considered a hazardous undertaking.]

Saw our first eagle. If we don't catch enough fish, we can catch eagles—$1.00 bounty. Mountains have snow on tops. Dull gloomy day. Started to rain about noon. Passed a Prince Rupert Ship, *Princess Adelaide*, and couple of other boats that we couldn't read their names. Ran on a reef—Earl's Ledge—as we were eating lunch. Carl yelled for help, and a couple of guys came out to help. Didn't seem to be any damage, so we went on. A small leak developed later, so decided to stop at Alert Bay for repairs. Got there at 7:30 all in one piece, with Carl pumping out bilge most of the way. Milk is 15 cents/qt.; bottles 10 cents. Will not take U.S. bottles.

7/1—Mon.—Dominion Day
Alert Bay, B.C.

Up at 7:30. This is a Canadian holiday—Dominion Day—same as our 4th of July. Washed clothes. Wind blowing very hard. Many Indians here and a lot of Chinese and Japs—very few white people. Passed an Indian cemetery with many totem poles. Walked along main drag today—lots of "licensed premises" signs, which mean "beer tavern" in America. No movie in this town. Salmon sells for 4 cents/lb. Beer 25 cents/glass. Had to wait for high tide at 10 p.m. before we could get the boat up on the ways. *["Up on the ways" means up on a type of drydock—a place to repair boats. The fishermen stay/live on their boats while "on the ways," even if the boat is there for several days. The boat goes on and off the drydock at high tide. Synonyms for "ways" are "cradle" or "grid."]*

7/2 to 7/4—Tues.–Thurs.
Alert Bay

On ways at Sharpe Shipyards. Got off cradle July 4th. Copper painted, replanked for worms, and cemented nail holes. *[Copper painting reduced the presence of barnacles, which slows the boat down and causes more fuel to be used. It also discouraged the infestation of woodworms.]* Tide not in far enough, so have to wait here for a higher tide at 12 tonight. The wind is blowing like the devil in this man's town. Walked down to see *Princess Norah* dock. Saw Ruth Johnson hanging on the arm of a young man. What next?!

7/5—Fri.
Alert Bay to Safety Cove—76 miles (5:30 a.m. to 6:30 p.m.)

Left Alert Bay at 5:30 for Queen Charlotte Sound. Many islands and channels before we got there. At 11:00 a.m., reached the sound. Weather good for a while, but soon began to get ruff. Such ground swells and sideswipes! Dishes fell off shelves and broke—everything slid off the shelves. Carl was all for turning back, but I said no, let's go on. *[What a trooper!]* Saw an eagle swoop down and grab a fish just in front of the boat. Soon after, I got sick and had to go to bed. Carl hung on to the wheel to keep from sliding around. The boat dipped and rolled so that I thot we would never get out of it in one piece! This lasted till 4:20. Nothing to eat—too ruff. Ran into lots of gill netters. Carl thot one was stalled and went over to help him—but he was only pointing for us to keep away from his net! He was quite upset with us. After we reached an inlet away from the ocean, water calmed down and was smooth. We began to feel like humans once more. Arrived at Safety Cove at 6:30—beautiful little cove about ½ mile wide. Steep rocks on each side, all wooded heavily with fir trees. A little dock with a house and gas station—a Standard Oil Co. man and wife live here. Soon after we arrived, 3 trollers from Alaska came in on their

way back to Seattle—no fish, <u>so</u> <u>they</u> <u>said</u>. Herman
off the *Wild Bill* of Everett *[city in Washington State]*
came over and went thru all our charts with us.
He marked the best way to go and places to stay
overnite. He stayed till 2:30 a.m. Saw many gill
netters in the deep water with nets, corks, and
flags. Ran over one net. Guess we'd better pay more
attention to what we're doing.

[Pages are missing from 7/6 through 10/17.]

Ketchikan in the '40s

🐟

[With a population of six thousand, Ketchikan was home mainly to hard-workin', hard-livin' lumbermen, miners, and fishermen. It was a sin city, full of prostitution, gambling, venereal disease, and rampant drunkenness. The U.S. House of Representatives charged it with conditions of vice and crime such as could not be matched elsewhere on the continent. Congressmen called Ketchikan the worst "pesthole" in America. It didn't take my Uncle Carl long to fit right in.

[L. Ron Hubbard, author and founder of Scientology, spent a long winter in Ketchikan, not by choice. He shared some of his remembrances about Ketchikan decades later with a class he was teaching. "They have here in Ketchikan the only stream in the world where the fish and the fishermen go up to spawn. It's a red-light district called Creek Street. It stretches up around the curve, a very beautiful little stream. But the buildings have trap doors—most of Ketchikan is built over water. The fishermen—it's mostly fishermen who come there—have time off and money. They come from their boats by skiff and climb a ladder (depending on the level of the tide) up to the trap doors. The fishermen wear rather heavy rubber boots. If they fall into the water, the boots fill and the fishermen sink. When police find a fisherman drowned or floating in the straits, without anything in his pockets, they look him over and decide: "Hmmm. Suicide!"

[Two hundred or more prostitutes plied their trade on Creek Street. Vice was not just defiant in Ketchikan, it was arrogant. Dolly Arthur, bordello proprietress, said, "When they're here, all they talk about is fishing. When they're out fishing, all they talk about is Creek Street." Dolly's bordello is a museum today, popular with tourists.]

Creek Street, circa 1940. (Photograph from Ketchikan Museums.)

[I can't help but wonder what was going through Hazel's head when she realized that "this" would be her new home. Did she know anything about Ketchikan before moving there? Did she have doubts about her decision to give up her comfortable life in Seattle for this so-called adventure? She surely was going to be a "fish out of water" in Ketchikan in 1940.]

10/18—Fri. Alaska Day

[Alaska Day is a legal holiday observed on October 18. It is the anniversary of the formal transfer of the Territory of Alaska from Russia to the United States in 1867.

[You might consider some of the geographic context of this vast state. Alaska is the coldest, largest (twice the size of Texas), least populated, and in some ways, most esoteric of the fifty states. Alaska's landmass is

one-fifth that of the continental United States—so big that it sprawls across four time zones. If Alaska were superimposed onto the contiguous United States, it would span from Georgia to California and from the Canadian border to Mexico.

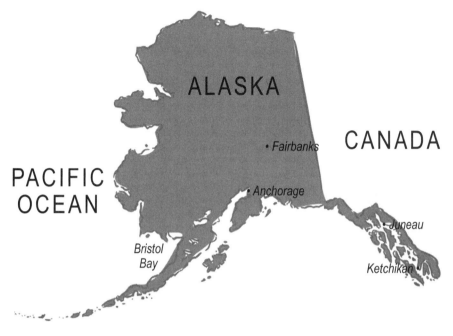

[The present-day population of this enormous state is only about 680,000— barely enough for one passable-size city. By way of comparison, Texas currently has an estimated twenty-four million residents.

[During the 1940s—the years of concern in this manuscript—Alaska had not even achieved statehood status. And it counted its population as less than seventy-three thousand souls.

[In the '40s, Ketchikan was the salmon capital of the world and the world's largest canning center—packing millions of pounds of salmon, cod, herring, and halibut. Five species of salmon were found in Ketchikan—king (Chinook), silver (coho), pink (humpie), sockeye (red), and chum (dog).]

Our First Fishing Season

[Author's note: A map of the fishing grounds can be found on the inside of the back cover.]

Skowl Arm

Carl and Walt worked on gurdies *[winches]*, marked line. Walt tried generator, but it didn't work. Carl traded a new battery for 2 loaves of bread, a lb. of coffee and couple slices of Walt's deer meat he got from the watchman. Rained hard all day. Carl and I carried water for Walt and us. *[The boats did not have running water.]* Played poker after dinner. Broke fastener on oven door.

10/19 & 20—Sat. and Sun.

Bad weather—rain, foggy and blowy. *[October is typically Ketchikan's rainiest month.]* Couldn't fish. Walt brot fried bacon and pot of coffee over; I made pancakes. Carl and Walt worked all day on anchor system. Took bath in rubber tub. Had to heat water on stove. Quite an ordeal just to take a bath.

10/21—Mon.
Skowl Arm to Kassan Bay

Started fishing in Skowl Arm at 8:00. Pretty good weather—cold, some rain and some sunshine. Not very ruff. Hit a big log—scary. Our best fishing day so far. Caught 6 mild cures, all red. No scrap fish. *[See glossary for fish types.]* Fished till 4:00, then made a run for Kassan Bay. Pretty ruff when we got out beyond the light of the lighthouse. "Happy," the buyer, was not here—gone to Ketchikan. The *Igloo* was already here and had informed all and sundry about us. Walt anchored, and we tied up to him for the nite. Wind blew and rained all nite. Carl, Walt, and I worked on gear after supper. 122# of large reds.

10/22—Tues.
Kassan Bay to Skowl Arm

Bad day—wind and rain. Got up late. Waited for "Happy" to come back before we left. He got in at 11:30. Sold him 122# of large reds. He will go to Ketchikan in 10 days again, and then we'll get our money. We left at 12:30. Pretty ruff—rolled and dived a lot, got back to Skowl Arm at 2:00, and tied up to float. Asked watchman to eat with us. Walt brot stew and butter. We bought 1 loaf raisin bread, 2 loaves whole wheat, and 2 apple pies from "Happy." Gave one loaf to the watchman because he gave Carl rope and me magazines.

10/26—Sat.
Skowl Arm to Ketchikan

Left here at 5:30 with Walt Henning. Got to Troller's Cove at 7:00. *Winnie B* had left, so we went rite on to Ketchikan. Started to get ruff as soon as we left Patterson Island. Everything fell over and fell off. Radio fell off wall and down steps—waves came up over top of the boat. Skiff nearly fell overboard. Lost two tires overboard. By time we got to Guard Island, it quieted down. As soon as we reached the channel, we stopped to wash our fish (which were 3 days old). Ate pearls of wheat that I had cooked before we got to Skowl Arm Light. Tied up at New England Fish Co. at 11:15. Sold fish for $17.42. Then tied up at Thomas Basin. *[Thomas Basin was the* Olympic's *homeport and dock. It was one of two small boat harbors in Ketchikan at the time. Today it is a stone's throw from the cruise-ship dock.]* Got our laundry that had been at Harbor Hardware for over two weeks. *[Harbor Hardware was located across the street from the entrance to Thomas Basin.]* Got mail. After we got cleaned up, Walt and us ate dinner at Holland Café. Tried to keep up with Carl and Walt on their beer (with wine), but I got sick instead. Should know better than try to compete with the two of them! Bought groceries and gear. Walt and us had a lunch on our boat at midnight. *[Lunches and dinners get mixed up during fishing season.]* Carl took our radio to the repair shop to see what the damages were.

10/27—Sun.
Ketchikan

Got up late. Carl gave some of his rocks *[ballast]* away. Picked up our radio—nothing wrong—$1.50 for over-haul. It works better than ever. *[Hazel and Carl had one of the better radios among the fishermen. Friends often came to their boat to listen to programs—especially the news.]*

10/31—Thurs.
Skowl Arm

Carl worked on herring spoons *[spoons are shiny lures designed to wobble when pulled through the water]* this morning. Changed them all to the way Walt has his. Left float at 9:30. Fished all day and only caught 2 small ones. A good day, flat and lots of sunshine. Wrote letters to Mother, Zellah, Dorothy and Lillian. Tried to carve out a pumpkin without Carl seeing me. After dinner, I went outside and held it up to the window. Big Ole and Walt were here. Carl and I went up to see the watchman and took the pumpkin along, also the letters to be sent on the mail boat tomorrow. The tide was so low we had about 99 steps to climb up the ladder. *[At Thomas Basin, the difference between the lowest and highest tides on any given day is nearly twenty feet.]* Came here 2 weeks ago today.

11/4—Mon.

Overslept. Got up at 7:30. Ready to leave at 8:30. Wind, rain, and blowing—pretty ruff. Towards noon it calmed down and was nice rest of the day. Caught 8 fish. Fished till dark. Best day so far!

102#	mild cure @ .25	$25.50
24#	small red @ .11	2.64
35#	white @ .10	3.50
		$31.64

11/5—Tues.—Election Day, 8:30 to 5:30

First frost. Ice in bait bucket and tub. Lots of snow on top of hills. Cold, but bright with sunshine. Fished all day—caught 3 fish.

```
62#     red @ .25              $15.50
8#      small @ .11               .88
                                $16.38
```

Saw a sea lion on Kassan Point.

[Most of the world's sea lions live along Alaska's vast coastline. There are believed today (2009) to be about sixteen thousand across the Bering Sea off Russia's coast.]

11/6—Wed.
BIGGEST FISH SO FAR!!

Fished all day. Very cold. Cold North wind. Smooth water. Caught 4 fish. One weighed 47#. Carl and I had our picture taken with it in our arms. Walt was here for dinner. Expect to go to Ketchikan tomorrow morning. As the mail boat will not be here till Friday, the watchman gave me back my letters so I can mail them myself.

```
102#    @ .25                  $25.50
20#     @ .10                    2.00
                               $27.50
```

On the back of these photos it states that the fish weighed 52#, even though the diary says 47#. The pictures were sent to Hazel's parents and her sister, Zellah. Apparently Hazel couldn't resist the exaggeration. Don't all true fishermen exaggerate?

11/7—Thurs.

Bad wind, blew all nite. Could not fish today. Lots of snow on mountains and frost here. Sunshine all day. Washed clothes. Dried stiff like board—had icicles on them. Carl and Walt went hunting—no luck. Made an applesauce cake. Awful cold, nearly froze all night.

11/8—Fri.
Skowl Arm to Ketchikan, 7:30 to 12:00

Left at 7:30. Everything covered with ice—even on bay itself (on account of so much fresh water.) *[The freezing point of salt water varies, based on the amount of salt in the water. Ocean water freezes at around -2ºC, or 28.4ºF. Fresh water freezes at 0ºC, or 32ºF.]* Not very ruff, only in places. Got to Ketchikan at noon. New England Fish Co. isn't buying any more fish. Went back to city dock. Bought 81 gals. of gas at Standard Oil Co. Sold fish to Oxenberg Bros. for $119.02. Tied up at Thomas Basin. Picked up mail and bought Carl some 50% wool underwear—2 suits for $6.50. Bought groceries and hardware. Ate dinner at Blue Fox. Saw Walt on our way home. He had a bottle of rum. He and Carl drank too much rum, as usual.

Hunkerin' Down for an Alaskan Winter

[It is winter that most defines Alaska. Winter in Alaska has its own beauty—the moonlit darkness, the silvery snow, the star-studded sky, the lacy, shimmering sheets of green and red ionosphere known as the Aurora Borealis, or Northern Lights. Beauty notwithstanding, however, no living thing can survive in Alaska unless it is adapted—via natural selection or man-made equipage—to the extraordinary cold. Summer days in Alaska can go as high as a hundred degrees Fahrenheit, but then winter temperatures fall to as low as eighty degrees below zero. Also, winter in parts of Alaska can last nine months or more. That's one reason that Alaska once was known as "Seward's Icebox." And why the state is both under-populated and under-explored even today.]

11/9—Sat.
Ketchikan

Put *Olympic* on ways at 10:30 a.m. Snowed all day, about 2 inches. Carl took rowboat and went off and left me high and dry all day. *[She's stuck on the boat up on the drydock!]* He brought Walt and Ray and his Indian girlfriend over in evening. Carl

bot a bottle of whiskey, which we drank up. Walt
dropped a bottle of rum overboard. It landed on a
plank, and at low tide he went in after it! Carl
got pretty well lit.

11/11—Mon.—Armistice Day

*[Armistice Day is the anniversary of the symbolic end of World War I
on November 11, 1918. It commemorates the armistice agreed between
the Allies and Germany. The date is a national holiday in many allied
nations to commemorate those members of the armed forces killed during the war. After World War II, it was changed to Veterans' Day in the
United States. Although Armistice Day was in honor of World War I,
Veterans' Day is in honor of veterans of every war that the United States
has fought.]*

Eleanor Moeser *Quaker Box* came to see us this a.m.
before I had the dishes washed. Went up to see
the parade at 11:00. Thirty-six boats—led by the
Coast Guard. *[Interesting that the Armistice Day Parade was a boat
parade and not one of floats upon trucks or floats pulled by cars, as one
normally sees in such celebrations. Ketchikan is located on an island, so
this makes sense. Very few people owned cars, as they had to be shipped
in on a steamer and were very costly.]* At 2:00 the Shriners,
School Band, CCC Boys, and a few others were in
parade *[on land, I assume]*. We ate dinner at the Stedman. Came home and Carl bought gin and mixer.
Later Walt and Ray came over. Carl told them to
go home! Expect to go to Skowl Arm tomorrow.

*[The Civilian Conservation Corps (CCC) was a work-relief program for
young men from unemployed families. Established on March 19, 1933,
it was under the direction of U.S. President Franklin D. Roosevelt—part
of Roosevelt's New Deal legislation. Its intent was to combat poverty and
unemployment caused by the Great Depression. The CCC was a popular
New Deal program among the general public. It operated in every U.S.
state and several territories. The young men went to camps for six-month
periods, where they were paid to do outdoor construction work. The*

enrollees worked forty hours a week and were paid thirty dollars a month (roughly equivalent to $425 in 2009 dollars). They were required to send twenty-five dollars a month home to their families.]

11/12—Tues.

Rained and wind blew all day, so couldn't leave. Had my hair cut today. Bought Carl a membership in Alaska Liars Club. Also ordered him slippers from Montgomery Ward Co. for Christmas. The stove gas-line broke when Carl went to fill the gas tank. Had to get Burke *[handyman]* to come down and fix it.

11/15—Fri.

Weather still too bad to leave. Walt went to Mt. Point to hunt. Got stuck on the rocks, so we had to go down and pull him off. Ruff weather, too. Went to see *The Marines Fly High*. Ran into Harold. Had a beer with him at the Stedman Bar. Then Carl and I went to Hollond's—danced, came home at 10:30.

11/19—Tues.

Bad weather. The Pritchers' boy—Ralph—was smothered in a fire on his boat at Juneau. (Don't know how the fire started.) Went over and called on them tonight—they were quite distraught, of course. *[Boat fires and explosions were frequent happenings—fishermen's most-feared dangers. Boats in the '40s were powered by gasoline and were mostly made of wood, adding to the fire risk.]* Wrote to Mother.

11/23—Sat.

Bought new stove and pipe ($16.25) for downstairs. Didn't get it up till about 6:30. Had to borrow wood from the *Admiral*. *[Old-timers were emphatic that only wood or coal was fit fuel to heat a boat. However, many fishermen converted their stoves to oil because chopping wood and keeping coal on a small boat was a lot of trouble.]* Funeral for Ralph Pritcher at 2:30. One of the pallbearers didn't show up so they asked Carl to be one. Stayed up till 2:30 drying clothes. George Haack came to see about Carl's water-cooled engine.

11/24—Sun.

Got up late. Nice weather till about noon, then wind and rain again. We dug out all the parowax in the window frames and poured black tar paint to stop the leaks. Cleaned and rearranged all clothes and groceries downstairs. Married 5 months ago today.

11/26—Tues.

Left Seattle 5 months ago today. Put plastic cement in the leaks—guess we got them all stopped at last. Very bad day—wind, rain and very high tide. Stayed on boat all day. Washed curtains and made a new one for the front window below. Ed Carter gave me a jug of loganberry wine.

11/29—Fri.

Washed woodwork upstairs. Got letters from Mother and Ella. Carl got one from Bothell, telling of the $800.00. *[Carl's father had recently sold the family chicken ranch in Bothell, Washington. Both Carl and his brother, Orie, received periodic checks from the sale.]* Carl bot me new shoes for Christmas. Ed Carter invited us for Christmas.

11/30—Sat.

Carl bought 2ⁿᵈ sack of coal. Bought $12.00 of groceries. Went to Sons of Norway dance. Met Lame Ole, who wants us to join. *[Sons of Norway is a fraternal organization representing people of Norwegian heritage in the U.S. and Canada. Ketchikan was a clannish town—in the '40s at least. Scandinavians tended to stick together—doing their drinking in certain bars or spending their time at the Sons of Norway. Other ethnic groups kept to themselves. The merchants and professional people frequented the Elks Club, and the commoners lived it up at the Eagles and Moose Lodges. And of course, the church-going community frowned on the bar crowd altogether.]* Carl bought a quart of wine on way home.

12/1—Sun.

Made a stew in Harold's kettle. Went for a walk. Came home, had dinner and wrote letters. At 10:45, Carl went out for a walk. I went to bed at 12 but didn't sleep. Got up at 4 a.m. to hunt for Carl. Met the prowler car, and he took me around to look for Carl. At 5 a.m. two men brot him home—drunk as a skunk. He had spent $20.00! *[Twenty dollars might not sound like much now, but in 1940 it would buy eighty glasses of pub beer. Even in ten-ounce glasses, that's eight hundred ounces, or <u>more than six gallons of beer</u>! Since Carl didn't die of alcohol poisoning that night, he either drank something harder—like whiskey, another of his favored beverages—or he had help with the drinking, or both.]*

12/6—Fri.

Carl fixed over the shelves in our clothes closet. Added two more shelves and put a round rod instead of the square one. He also received his overcoat from Bothell and two 80% wool union suits *[long underwear]*. Got letters from Mother and Katy. Went to Townsend Club—dance and eats cost us 65 cents. Took couple chances on a quilt. Got home at 12:30.

[According to Richard Van Cleave at the Ketchikan Museum, the Townsend Club was a group working for social good. They had a great effect on the formation of the Social Security system. This system was later extended to include dependents, the disabled, and other groups. Responding to the economic impact of the Great Depression, five million old people in the early 1930s joined nationwide Townsend clubs. The club was promoted by Francis E. Townsend to support his program demanding a two-hundred-dollar monthly pension for everyone over the age of sixty.]

12/9—Mon.

Cleaned cupboards, washed woodwork, and scrubbed floors. Bought 1 doz. Christmas cards for $1.00, also 58 cents of wool to crochet some slippers for Carl. Very foggy day. Carl had a new damper put in the heater—20 cents. Addressed Xmas cards and wrote notes. Went to Red Cross and got more knitting.

12/15—Sun.

Finished and mailed all my 25 Xmas cards. Had my first good tub bath. Carl bored some holes in the partitions and between shelves. After dinner Carl and I went to hear Sumrall, the lecturer and evangelist. *[Dr. Lester Sumrall (1913-1996) was one of the most colorful preachers of the twentieth century. Few evangelists had seen so much of the world as Lester Sumrall had witnessed—and given witness to. He began traveling in 1934 to more than 110 countries, preaching the gospel. He penned over 130 books and is known as the father of Christian television.]*

12/18—Wed.

Have sore throat. Guess I'm getting a cold. Got 6 Christmas packages. Mother sent: overnite cookies, chocolate cookies, peanuts, 2 dishtowels, 3 hotpads, 2 hankies for Carl, and 2 for me. Zellah sent: 5 pint jars of jam and jelly, and some little cookies from Alan. Lillian sent: red wool mittens for me, blue wool mittens for Carl, a plum pudding, a jar of jam, and peanuts. Ella sent: red wool scarf for me, 2 hankies, and 2 hankies for Carl, pkg. of Lipton's tea, 2 cans of cookies (homemade), a piece of fruitcake, and 2 pkgs. of gelatin. Katy sent: red wool sweater from all 3 girls, bath towel and 2 washcloths to match, apron, and hanky. From Mrs. Hewith: 2 glasses of jelly, potholder, dishcloth, 3 hankies for me, 2 dishtowels, scrub brush, sox for Carl, 2 hankies for Carl, a hand towel, and a box of candy.

12/20—Fri.

Bad day. I've got a bad cold and feel rotten. Seems worse today—on my chest. Carl cut out the beam over the steps. Red Irwin came by and called out to Carl that if he would come over he'd give him 2 cans of deer meat. In about ½ hour Carl went over to his boat and came back with 2 cans of deer meat, 1 doz. lemons, a bag of apples, and 2 pkgs. of barley. Karl Hansen came down and invited us up for evening.

12/21—Sat.

Still bad weather. Carl put in 2 extra shelves near gas tank at head of bed and another one at foot of bed for magazines. (I worry about the gas tank being so close to our heads.) Bought 2# butter for 75 cents, 2 tomatoes, and a head of lettuce for 27 cents. Carl and I went over to call on Mr. Irwin and gave him a pint of our precious canned chicken. Mrs. Pritcher invited us to the Yacht Club for cards in evening. Played cards and danced, had a lunch, got home after one o'clock. *[The "Yacht Club" was a float house (wanigan) attached to the docks/ floats of Thomas Basin. It was a popular meeting place and dance hall for the fishermen.]*

Winter 2008. The Ketchikan Yacht Club, formed in the 1940s, still meets in their wanigan in Thomas Basin. Can't you picture what it looked like about seventy years ago? Note that many fishing boats have left for the winter. (Photograph and information from Richard H. Van Cleave.)

12/22—Sun.

Nice day, so we called Hansens and decided to go after Xmas trees. Got to their house about 1:45. The 2 Carls left immediately. Mrs. Hansen and I stayed home. Took my knitting. Had dinner when men got back. Carl bot $1.15 of whiskey—curses! Put up our tiny tree when we got home and worked on decorations till after 12. Tree decorations consist of tin foil from prune cartons, cigarette packages, and gum wrappers. I also used bits of tinsel ribbon from our Christmas packages, cotton from a Kotex pad, and silver paper from gift wrappings. *[Quite resourceful, I would say.]*

12/24—Tues.

Beautiful sunshine, but very cold. Lots of frost that never melted in the sun. Mr. and Mrs. Burnett, Mr. and Mrs. Pratt, and Mrs. Buckbee came calling in early p.m. All had been drinking some. Carl tacked up evergreens on front of boat. Finished trimming tree. Bot some silver rain *[tinsel?]* and some candy canes for tree. I made some fudge, an apple pie (the best one so far), and some date bars. Harold Hansen and 2 of his pals came in late afternoon. Brought us a drink. Carl and I went calling on Pritchers, Haacks, and Burnetts. Invited us to come to Yacht Club tonite and play cards. Carl got $2.00 from Ray on his Thanksgiving raffle and bought a pint of whiskey. He was 45 min. late for dinner, and I got mad. Went to Yacht Club, and Mrs. Burnett got smart and bawled Carl out for talking too much while we were playing Bingo. Carl got mad and walked out after one game of pinochle with Mr. and Mrs. Burnett and Mrs. Pritcher. I left too to look for Carl. Came home to boat, and he was not there. Finally found him at Arctic Bar with a couple of drunks. *[During the 1950s, the Arctic Bar collapsed and washed under the Ketchikan Creek Bridge during an unusually high tide and flood in Ketchikan Creek.]* Carl and I managed to leave together and went to P.O. and got 2 Xmas cards and a pkg. from Grace B. She sent Buddy Squirrel salted peanuts and bottle of hand lotion.) Home about 11:30—ate lunch and went to bed but not to sleep. Talked and drank, etc. till 5:30 a.m.

12/25—Wed.—Christmas Day

Inquired about phoning to Mother for Xmas—only $4.70 for 3 min.!! *[In one of the rare instances of prices going down, a three-minute long-distance call today might cost as little as three cents. Hooray for technology!]* Very cold, lots of frost on everything. Went to Shamrock at 6:00 to wait for Ed to get thru work. His wife is about ½ darkie all right, but she was very nice and a very good cook. Another woman and a man were also there. Turkey, 2 kinds of dressing, potatoes, gravy, macaroni, bread, celery, olives, radishes, cheese, fruitcake, and coffee. Stayed till 1:30.

12/26—Thurs.

Didn't do much today. Ate too much last night. Carl is still celebrating Xmas. I didn't leave the boat all day. Ed Carter came down about 8:00. He got sleepy, and he and Carl both laid down on the bed and slept. Carl finally came up and played cards with me. Ed slept till 9:30. Woke up with a thud; he was supposed to meet his wife at 9:15.

12/27—Fri.

Several Xmas cards and letters. Wrote letter to Mother. Carl gone all day—still celebrating. Was supposed to come back to the boat at 7:45 and go to show with me, but I didn't leave till 8:20, and he didn't come. Saw Wallace Berry in *20 Mule Team*. Went to Shamrock on my way to the show, and there he was—drinking beer. Got home from show at 11:45—no Carl. At 2:15 or so, he and Ed came home, drunk. Ed left right away and Carl and I had a lovely scene all nite long. I threatened to leave him if he didn't stop drinking.

12/28—Sat.

Carl was gone all afternoon. Big "Ole" came and stayed for 2 hours. Rained hard most of the day. Carl came home at 4:30 and went right to bed. I went for a walk and to the Library. Bot some squash and 2 doz. eggs. Mrs. Pritcher and Mrs. Burnett came by at 8:30 and wanted us to go to the Yacht Club and dance, but Carl was in bed—dead to the world. Took bath and went to bed at 10:30.

12/29—Sun.

12 noon before we got up. Nice sunshine but very cold. Carl and I went for a long walk to the Indian village near Mt. Point. Took some pictures of totem poles. Cooked noodles and chicken. Listened to President's speech. Things are heating up in Europe. Pretty scary. Finished Red Cross sweater.

Ketchikan has the world's largest collection of standing totem poles. Native tribes use totem poles to tell stories, commemorate events, and pay tribute to tribal or family members or leaders.

12/30—Mon.

Sunshine, but very cold. Went for long walk to Ward's Cove. Came home, had dinner, and then went to see *My Favorite Wife*. Seagulls ate most of our red snapper.

12/31—Tues.—New Year's Eve

Snow on ground and still snowing when got up. Big party at Yacht Club for 5 p.m. supper. Pritcher and I went in together on the chili. 16 people for supper. Played cards, danced, and had a few drinks. Lots of boats at the Basin blew their horns at midnight. (Guess it's a tradition here.) Got home at 2:45. So ends our first year of married life on a boat. Not very romantic. It's the nertz. *["It's the nertz" was one of Hazel's favorite expressions to convey dissatisfaction—with almost anything. Nertz is slang for nuts.]*

Part II
1941

Life on the *Olympic*

A Description

[By way of explanation, here is a photo and some facts about Hazel and Carl's Olympic—how it was set up and operated. Look closely; see Hazel standing at midship, beside the cabin. She was five feet eleven inches, so she gives a sense of scale.

[This is how I remember the Olympic. It was a forty-foot salmon troller. A size comparison of the living space today would be a twenty-six-foot motorhome—approximately two hundred square feet. The boat had two levels. The lower level had the galley with an oil cook stove and the sleeping area. They slept in sleeping bags. There was no bathroom—they used a pot. They bathed in a rubber tub after heating water on the stove. The upper level had a dinette area—large table with a built-in bench. Steering of the boat was done on this level.

[The boat had a coal heater and oil lamps. Electricity was available only when the boat was operating or plugged in at the dock. It had no running water. They depended mostly on rainwater, which was caught in gutters and ran into a water tank, or barrel. When docked, they could get water by bucket from a hose or spigot. When out fishing for several days and needing water, they headed for nearby land, got in the skiff, rowed ashore, and hauled water from a stream.

[The boat had no two-way radio, fathometer, autopilot, or other electronics. Radar for fishing vessels was unheard of at that time. They navigated by compass and use of charts.

[To give a hint of my aunt's character, it helps to consider items she took with her on the boat. Hazel had a typewriter. She typed these daily diaries and numerous letters to family and friends. She also typed knitting instructions and recipes for her fellow fisherwomen. My aunt had a treadle sewing machine. She sewed curtains for the Olympic's windows and portholes, as well as blackout curtains for many boats. She tailored hand-me-down clothing using her machine. Hazel had a mandola, a stringed musicial instrument related to the mandolin. She entertained Carl and others with her musical ability. A camera, presumably a box camera, was another of Hazel's possessions. She faithfully recorded her experiences with it. Most of the photos included in this book are ones that she took. Film and processing were expensive in the '40s—processing had to be sent out. However, that was important to her. Hazel's possessions were definitely atypical of fishermen of that time and place.]

1/3—Fri.

Still snowing. Heater stove smoked and puffed all day—disgusting. Went to Townsend Club in p.m. Carl and I and one other woman were appointed to count votes. Carl made a speech afterwards. Served chili and crackers for 10 cents.

1/4—Sat.

Carl worked on engine all day, fastening the engine bed. He tore out plugs between ribs up in front end of boat. I washed clothes. Red snapper for dinner. Went to the Erickson's at 7:30. Mr. and Mrs. Pratt took us. Mrs. Burnett caused a scene just before we left. Host and hostess were drunk. Ten people were there. Much to eat. Played pinochle. Got home at 2 a.m.

1/7—Tues.

Rain and more rain! Baked bread and cinnamon rolls. Mrs. Pritcher came and told us there was a place near them to tie up, so we hurried and moved. Had to break ice all around the boat. Took Carl all the rest of the day to get tied up, lights connected, etc. Went over to Pritchers' about 5 p.m. He was at a meeting at the Yacht Club. Took my cinnamon rolls.

1/8—Wed.

Rain, rain, rain! Sick of it. Finished Carl's white sweater. He didn't say a word about it, of course. Still have a pain in my neck and head. Carl worked on the scuppers. *[Scuppers are holes in the boat's side to carry water overboard from the deck.]* Karl Hansen came down and wanted us to come up and play pinochle tonight, but we can't go on account of Mrs. Iffert's invitation. We'll go tomorrow night. Carl helped

Mrs. Craft fill her oil tank. Mrs. Iffert had wild blackberry pie.

[Ketchikan has the heaviest average rainfall in North America and is the fourth wettest spot on earth. Therefore, it measures its rainfall in feet, not inches. They receive 13.5 feet annually, which is 162 inches. It rains an average of 228 days each year. Like many towns in Alaska, Ketchikan refers to rain as "liquid sunshine."]

1/9—Thurs.

Rain and wind. Letters from Zellah and Bothell. Returned Red Cross sweater and got more wool for a red one. Bot ingredients for our pills *[some type of home remedy]*. Inquired at Montgomery Wards about a job. *[When fishing season ended, the fishermen worked at various jobs to supplement their incomes.]* Wrote a letter to Zellah and sent Mother a duplicate. Went to Karl Hansen's in p.m. and played cards. Carl seems to be getting a bad cold. Doped him up good with lemon, soda, and aspirin *[early version of Alka-Seltzer]*. Had to take a taxi home from Hansens' because it was raining so hard—25 cents. 5 sacks of coal = $5.25.

1/10—Fri.

Bad day—rain and wind. Carl's cold seems to be better. Was taking a nap when Alice Haack and baby came to call. I asked them to stay and eat dinner with us. Carl went up to their place and left a note on the door for George to come and eat with us. Had meatballs and gravy, potatoes, corn and plum pudding. Carl was mad at me because I gave them our good pudding. After dinner we played pinochle and "the old she-bitches called everything a misdeal when they lost" (these are Carl's words, not mine). Their young son is a big nuisance—very spoiled.

1/11—Sat.

Ruth Iffert came to call just as we finished break-fast—while Carl was sitting on the pot! She stayed for about an hour. This is the morning after Carl used me as a "wagon" in his dream, and I had to get up in the middle of the night and change his pajamas and put towels in the bed. Bot groceries: butter—40 cents, bread—20 cents, carrots and broc-coli—26 cents. Carl bot 1 pint of whiskey—$1.00. Made Zellah's mahogany cake, and it stuck to the bottom of the pan. Carl had too much to drink today—again! We went to the Moose Dance—35 cents each *[held by the local branch of the Loyal Order of Moose]*.

1/12—Sun.

We slept till noon. Carl went up to see Ed's wrecked car. Plans to start repairing it Monday a.m. Carl borrowed $1.00 from Ed for a bottle of whiskey. We called on the *Ada*. They were eating; did not ask us in.

1/19—Sun.

Nice day. Harold and a pal of his came before we had finished breakfast. He had a bottle of whiskey. Getting sick of Harold. Bad influence on Carl. Ruth Iffert called about 1 or so. Invited us up for waffle supper. Mrs. Pritcher is still sick with the flu. We saw Leif Sather on the street; he has been drafted. *[In September 1940, the U.S. Congress passed the Selective Service Act. The nation's first peacetime draft, it called for the registration of all male citizens from twenty-one to thirty-five years of age. Carl didn't have to register; he was too old.]*

1/20—Mon.

Nice sunshine. Letters from Mother, Zellah, and 3 others. Carl fixed oven door on stove and cleaned out all the soot. Went for a long walk.

1/23—Thurs.

Cold and frosty. Mrs. Pritcher asked us over for clam chowder. Made Zellah's 7-min. frosting, and it turned out good. After dinner we went to Covell's party. About 25 there. We danced some square dances. Carl bot some whiskey to the tune of $2.25! Ericksons' and us went up to the Shamrock after the party (1:45 a.m.).

1/24—Fri.

Didn't get up till 12:15! While eating breakfast, Mrs. Burnett came over to invite us to dinner tonight. When Mrs. Burnett came, the door was frozen shut, and we couldn't get it open. (Carl wasn't here.) I tried to open the other door and pulled off the handle! It was the nertz. Very cold today—ice all around the boats.

1/25—Sat.

Very cold with an icy wind. Carl's cold is worse. Coughed and sneezed all nite. He was mad at me and wouldn't talk all day. I would not go to the Moose dance on account of Carl's grouch. Mr. Whitehead gave us a dishpan of clams. Wrote 5 letters.

[Hazel wrote and received many letters during her years in Alaska. This was an important part of personal communication (part of the lifestyle, though people didn't think in those terms back then). Public telephone calls—especially long-distance calls—were very costly ($4.70 for three

minutes to Seattle). Calls were also inconvenient, especially from a fishing boat in Alaska. There were no cell phones, much less e-mail and Internet. (None of those had even been created then.) Telegrams were also very expensive and used only for emergencies.

[We don't write letters any more. We dash off e-mail and text messages. We send our love into the world as ephemeral electrons. It won't clutter our closets, so guess our children won't have to sort through it when we die. It's efficient, it's convenient, and it's fast. But in just one click, it's gone or the technology can become obsolete. There will be no more written diaries such as these. Sad.]

1/26—Sun.

Snowed all nite—2 or 3 inches all over boat. Carl shoveled it all off before breakfast. Started to rain and wind blew very hard. Carl and I took a taxi (40 cents) to Lantermans for dinner.

2/2—Sun.—Ground Hog Day

Sun in the early morning, but it soon turned to wind and rain. Cooked beans in pressure cooker. Carl and I went for a walk. Saw a troller submerged. Looked like it had had a fire. Gave me a sick feeling—could've been us. Cooked dinner for the Pritchers as she is still sick.

2/10—Mon.

Raining. Took Carl to the doctor, much against his will. Not much wrong with him. Gave him a tonic. Letters from Orie and Zellah. I had a bad headache all day—too much diesel oil fumes, I guess. *[This was the first time the word "diesel" was mentioned. Hazel always talked about purchasing gas. Perhaps the boat ran on diesel.]* Carl worked on the generator all day.

2/12—Wed.

Carl wrenched his back yesterday working on bow poles, and now he is all stiff and sore. Rubbed some Watkins liniment on him and used the electric pad. Got a catalog from Ward's.

2/14—Fri.

Letters from Zellah and Orie—also valentine from Ella. The $90.00 check arrived at the bank today. Paid Pritcher $2.00 for lites, 40 cents for eggs and also paid Burke 50 cents. Orie wants Carl to come back to Bothell and settle up things in regards to sale of chicken ranch. Karl and Eva Hansen walked down to our boat. Carl and I went to the steamship companies to see about steerage rates. $21.00 is the cheapest. *[Steerage is the part of a ship providing accommodations for passengers with the cheapest tickets. The accommodations were usually on the lowest decks and with only the most basic of amenities.]*

Carl Settles Ranch Affairs

2/19—Wed.

Carl filled the cook stove tank this morning. He
worked all day scraping and painting with copper
paint. It didn't do his back any good. Went up
town and bought Carl's ticket *[for trip to Seattle]*. Went
down to dock to see Carl off. Found 35 cents on
the dock. Carl's ship, the *Prince Rupert*, left
at 11 p.m. The steerage passengers looked like
thugs. Very cold nite.

2/21—Fri.

Very cold—frost on all windows—drips on ceiling
and ice in bay. Slept cold all nite. Still having trouble with cook stove. The gang was at the
wanigan and insisted that I come over and eat.
Mrs. Pritcher is ill with quinsy *[sore throat]*.

Hazel and Carl sitting on the wanigan with friends.

2/22—Sat.—Washington's Birthday

Scrubbed woodwork and painted till 3 and then went up to Eva's for waffles and little pigs. Mrs. Pritcher is still in bed. Loaned her my electric pad—now suppose I'll freeze tonight. On way home, met Harold with his arm in a sling. Said he broke it—slipped on ice. Darned old stove still won't work. Wish Carl was here to fix it. Had a bath.

2/24—Mon.

Still cold and frosty. Asked George Haack to come over and look at stove. Painted all day. Bot a red turban and some things at 10-cent store. Went to First Aid class.

2/26—Wed.

Cold and frosty. Carl left one week ago today. Mailed letter to him. Washed from 8 to 10, took a bath, and washed my hair. Started to snow about noon and snowed all day. Went to First Aid class in 3 inches of snow. At 10:15, when I came home, there was 4 inches on boat. Shoveled it all off before I went to bed at 12:00. *[Imagine doing this difficult work at midnight! Hazel was aware that shoveling snow off the boat was necessary as the weight could cause the boat to sink. In the winter of 2008, Richard Van Cleave, Senior Curator of Collections, Ketchikan Museums, reported that a boat in Thomas Basin had sunk due to the weight of the snow.]*

2/27—Thurs.

2 letters from Carl—one from Prince Rupert and one from Vancouver. Got mixing bowls from Ward's. Snow still on ground—cold and frosty. Still painting woodwork. So lonesome without Carl. Went to bed at 9 and read for about one hour. Bot eggs from Vernie.

3/1—Sat.

Went to P.O. and got the last of the Ward's order. Had to send food chopper back and the brown leather tacks. Painted all day. Bot canned goods. Also fur moccasins for Alan's birthday and a doll for Arlene. Sewed curtains out of oiled silk for 2 rear windows in galley. Ruth came at 6:15 when I was in such a mess and asked me to help with a dinner at the church Tuesday nite. Bertie Pratt came over after me at 7:30 to come and play cards at the Yacht Club. Got home at 12:15 and sat up till 2:30 making the curtains for the portholes. Ironed the starched clothes.

3/5—Wed.

Carl gets in tonite on *Prince Rupert*! Got up early and finished painting the cans. Cleaned and scrubbed. Went to meet the boat at 8:45, but it didn't get in till 9:30. Bot a magazine and sat in the Hotel and read till the boat arrived. Carl was loaded down with his bag, sack of clothes, and a box of jelly. We sat up and talked till 1:30.

3/6—Thurs.—Alan's birthday (6 years old)

Rained most of day. Carl had the Express man bring down his trunk and a box of machinery – $4.71 in excess baggage! Kotex from Ward's arrived today. *[Interesting that Hazel ordered Kotex from the catalog. It probably was cheaper by bulk. In Hazel's later years, I remember once asking her what she considered the greatest invention during her lifetime. The word "Kotex" immediately sprang from her mouth. She said it came out right after her high school years (about 1920) and that women were wildly excited about it—but discreetly, of course. She once purchased one for a nickel and was chastised by her mother for her senseless waste of money.]* Lots of callers to see Carl: Bertie Pratt, George Haack, Harold Hansen, Pritcher. Carl bot some gin and a mixer, and we had a few drinks. Played some pinochle and went to bed. Talked and talked! Got up at 11:30 and had cheese sandwiches and hot water.

Blackout

3/7—Fri.

Tonite is the "Blackout" in Seattle. *[A blackout in this context doesn't mean an electrical outage; it means that no building, including houses, could show any lights at night. The idea was to prevent enemy bombers (Japanese or German) from using city lights as navigational or targeting aids.]* Carl worked all day putting things away—getting coal and kindling. Rained part of day, then sun came out. Letter from Zellah. Went to Townsend meeting with Mrs. Pritcher. *Sonsies* were there, too. Carl got mad at me because I danced with that tall musician. Also had to dance with "Speed."

3/8—Sat.

Carl worked on gurdie gearshift. We both have very bad colds. I went to bed in afternoon. Carl broke his mother's mirror when he went to nail it up. He felt bad about it—remembered her using the mirror for many years.

3/11—Tues.

Nice day. Spent $8.50 at Harbor Hardware—paint, wire, nails, etc., and a water can for $1.40. Got the meat grinder and the leather tacks from Ward's. Eva came for dinner. Mr. Pritcher sick today. Mrs. Pritcher came over and played cards with us. At 10 p.m. Carl and I walked home with Eva. Stopped at the Arctic on way back. Met Leif, the cook, and Carl was mad at me all over again.

3/12—Wed.

Got up early. Carl took the leads, wire, and fire extinguisher up town. He is still drinking. Brot home a pint of whiskey, and I hid it. Didn't go to First Aid class on account of Carl's condition. I painted inside of oven, stovepipe, and exhaust pipe with heat-resisting aluminum. *[Sounds as if Hazel does more than her share of the work.]* Carl was out till 11:30 with his beer pals. Bot 5 sacks of coal.

3/13—Thurs.

The leads and wire were delivered early this morning, at 9 a.m. Carl and I went after the fire extinguisher; it had a plugged hose. *[It was very important to keep the extinguisher in good working condition due to high danger of boat fires and explosions.]* Came home and washed clothes. Machine shop finally finished the job on the gearshift—$3.75. Carl was too drunk to work on it. He drank all day and got meaner and meaner. This drinking business is getting old! Sent clothes to laundry—big things only. Made cupcakes. Bot bread, butter, and an oven thermometer. "Mac" from Schwaubachs was here for a while—so drunk! At 4:15 I walked out on Carl—went to Library and read till 7:00. Then went to show and got home at

10:15. Karl Hansen sent word for us to come up, but Carl S. (my Carl) didn't tell me till the next morning. He never knows what he's doing when he drinks. Can't depend on him for anything.

3/15—Sat.

Bot a new mirror. Carl put up his sailfish pictures. Mrs. Burnett asked us over to a card party tonite. Ruth came at 5:15 and insisted we come for dinner tomorrow, but Carl said no. Too much work to do.

3/19—Wed.

Coast Guard came aboard for inspection and to ask us to join the "Auxilliary," so we went to the office and joined. Carl bot a new light fixture for the mast lite. Worked on it for a couple of hours—high up on the ladder—in the rain. After our dinner went over to the Haacks to see the baby's pictures. They were eating T-bone steaks and French fried spuds. Typed sweater directions from Mrs. Pratt's book and also some recipes for Vernie and Alice.

3/25—Tues.

Nice day with sunshine. Cleaned house and wrote letters to Mother and Zellah, and Juanita Johnston with 60 cents for Red Cross book. Typed knitting directions for Vernie and me, also some recipes. Made oatmeal cookies. Carl aluminum painted all day. Went for a walk in evening and stopped at Marine Bar and Arctic Bar. Came home and both took baths.

Starting to Fish

3/26—Wed.
Ketchikan to Meyers Chuck

[Meyers Chuck is located forty miles northwest of Ketchikan. "Chuck" is a Chinook-jargon word applied to a saltwater body that fills at high tide. This particular natural, well-protected harbor has long been shelter for fishing boats caught in the stormy waters of Clarence Strait. In the 1940 census, there were 107 people living at Meyers Chuck. By 2005, the population had dwindled to 21.]

Frosty and foggy. Left at 8:30 for cold storage plant. While Carl got ice and bait, I bot groceries. *[Prior to having access to ice for purchasing, fishermen had to chip ice from icebergs or glaciers to fill their holds.]* Left at 9:40. Beautiful sunshine and smooth water. Arrived at 3 p.m. Went for walk all around town. Cleaned spoons and put new hooks on them.

3/27—Thurs.

Up at 5:30—ready to leave at 7:15. Beautiful day—smooth, sunshine, and some fog. Carl had an awful time getting the lines out. Caught 2 fish—one fiddler *[small fish]* and one 9½# red. Also lost one. About 10 a.m. the wind began to blow, and by 11 it was pretty ruff. I got sick again! Everything started to roll around, so Carl said we had better quit. By then it had begun to rain. Got back to the float at 11:30. Much rain from then on—all day. Beautiful snow capped peaks all around us. Scenery here in Alaska is pretty spectacular most of the time. Went for a pail of water and stopped at store.

3/30—Sun.

Rain, hail, and wind at 4 a.m. Decided not to go fishing. But at 6 a.m., the *Lydia A*, tied up next to us, decided to go out. Carl had to get up and re-tie the boat. So then we both got up. By this time, it was a beautiful day, but most of the boats did not go out. Mrs. McDermott, from the *JoJo*, Carl, and I went for a walk at 3 p.m. Called on the school teacher and family. Came back to boat and Mr. McD. and son came over for a while. Carl and I played pinochle. *JoJo* and the *Aksala* are leaving at 2:30 a.m. for Ketchikan. One boat had a 70# halibut.

4/1—Tues.

Up at 4:30—fished till 5:30. Buyer came back at 4 p.m. Nice day, smooth water. Began to rain about 8 and continued till about noon. Only caught 2 fish today, and got a 30# halibut. Dogfish just about drove us nuts. *[Dogfish are small sharks that will latch onto almost anything put in the water, including human hands.]* Quit early. Sold 119# salmon and 30# halibut to buyer. Had a bath.

4/7—Mon.

Left at 5:45. Rain and wind. Fished Vixen Inlet till 10—no bites. Then went to Union Bay—no bites. So started back to Meyers Chuck at noon. Began to get ruff. We rolled some—a S.E. wind was blowing. As we reached Lemesurier Point, it got much worse. Waves came up over the bow, and the wind was a regular gale. Couldn't turn into M.C. as we would be in the troff *[trough]* and would roll over! So kept going, but made little headway. Both of us were scared stiff—didn't know what to do, and the wind blew harder all the time. Dishes, water, food, and what-have-you all over the floor. Carl wanted to turn around and go back, but was afraid we'd get in a troff and roll over. Finally we came to a place that looked smoother than the rest, so he turned us in a hurry. We rolled, but we made it! Started back to Union Bay, and it was not as ruff. *[When a boat is caught "in the trough" with its side to the sea, it can roll over. Waves can overwhelm the boat and swallow it whole, or punch lights out, break windows, and knock out the command center, leaving it vulnerable to the next wall of water that comes along. With most waves, the boat rises with the wave. However, an occasional rogue wave can bury a boat.]* Decided to anchor in Vixen Harbor. Had to go very slow, as we did not know our way in. Finally at 2:30 p.m., we anchored. Then it began to "willy"—such awful gusts and rain! *[A "willy" or "williwaw" is a sudden violent squall blowing offshore from a mountainous coast.]* It blew and rained all nite long. There were about 15 boats anchored too. Such a day—I hope we don't have that to experience again.

[According to John Falk, Adventure *magazine, August/September 2009, rogue waves have been the stuff of seamen's lore for centuries. The mere phrase conjures up visions of a mountain of seawater rising out of the mist without warning and swallowing the mightiest of ships. But by one definition, a rogue is simply any wave that's double the size of a sea's "significant wave height" (which itself is defined as the mean of the three highest waves in the water).]*

4/8—Tues.

Began using "B-Y's" today. *[B-Y Formula #18 was used for seasickness.]* Carl had to pull both anchors by hand. Up at 5:30. Good weather, smooth water. So left at 5:45. Fished till about 2:00. Had 4 fish. Began to get ruff so we decided to go to Meyers Chuck at once. It was ruff off of Lemesurier Pt. again—almost like yesterday—but we made it—3:30. Packer got back at 8 p.m. with 12 letters for us. *[Joe Upton explains in* **Alaska Blues** *that packers, or tenders, are boats that move among the fishing fleet. They are usually older and longer boats that hold iced fish acquired from several fishing boats. Since many times the fishing areas are far from the canneries, fishermen prefer to sell their fish out on the fishing grounds, rather than keep the fish on board and take them to town after the fishing period is over. The packers also bring mail, groceries, and other supplies with them. (Liquor and cigarettes were popular items with Carl.)]*

4/9—Wed.

Up at 6—couldn't sleep on account of wind and rain—blew all day long and part of nite. Sat around all day and read magazines. One boat went out between squalls but soon came back. Toward dark, some of the boats moved in toward shore and put out shorelines. Carl didn't think it would be necessary as the wind wasn't quite as bad as the night before. So he put the other anchor out, and we went to bed. The willys were awful while they lasted.

4/10—Thurs.

Up at 5, as usual, and fishing at Meyers Chuck. *[Usually the first hour of daylight is best for king salmon fishing, thus explaining why Hazel and Carl rise so early.]* Smooth water and sunshine, but a cold North wind. Fished till 11:30 and only had 4 fish, so we came in. *Prudence* gave us a jar of deer meat. Carl bot bait, gas, and rock salt.

4/11—Fri.—Good Friday

Fished Meyers Chuck from 5:45 to 9:15 and only caught one small white. Water smooth for an hour or so but then got ruff—wind and rain—so we pulled in the leads and went to Vixen Harbor and Union Bay. Only caught one small red and a fiddler, which we ate. Anchored in Vixen Harbor at 4:45, and weather was much better. Carl had an "accident" last nite. Got up to use the pot, and missed. So I had to scrub the floor and wash his pajamas!

4/14—Mon.

Wrote insurance letter re: $25.00 and hung it on the P.O. door—too early for them to be up. Left M.C. at 6:20 and fished U.B. and Vixen till 11:30. Carl lost a 45 lb. lead as he was taking up the lines. Anchored at Vixen. Had much trouble with the anchor system. Went after water. Carl and *Nira* went hunting, and I went "oaring." *Nira* and Stringer came in late. Had them over for fish stew and a game of pinochle.

4/17—Thurs.
Union Bay

Up at 4:30. Fished here all day. Caught 91 lbs. Saw a huge whale about 200 yards in front of boat—rolled over 3 times and then dove down—came up again several minutes later a long ways off. Fished till 7:45. Got caught on a reef and lost line, leaders, and lead. Heard the drunk man with the D.T.'s yelling all nite.

4/19—Sat.

Up at 4:30. Fished till 11:45—no bites and no luck. Buyer got back at 8 p.m. We got film, pork steaks, and mail. Got a picture of Arlene and Alan. They're getting big. Wrote 6 letters. Also sent for Kraft cheese knife and a measuring spoon. *[Coupons/ads were found in the Kraft cheese containers.]* I made cinnamon squares and some fudge. *[Hazel had quite a sweet tooth.]*

4/20—Sun.
Meyers Chuck to Snow Pass

Left at 10:20; arrived at 4:40. Fished till 6:40. Anchored next to *Nira* just North of Snow Pass Light. He had dinner with us. There is a fox farm over on beach. They barked all nite.

[High fur prices that followed WWI made raising foxes economically attractive. (A blue fox pelt was worth $100-$150 to brokers for Europeans in 1925.) Islands were in much demand for use as fox farms because the animals could run free. It was believed that wild animals produced better pelts than pen-raised. Nervous and shy, the foxes adapted well to the seclusion which islands offered. (Nine fox farms were started up near Ketchikan before World War II.) Nearby canneries provided cheap food in defective cans of salmon and scraps of fish. The animals also preyed on wild birds and their eggs. Fox farming did not require much capital.

A fox farmer could lease an island from the U.S. Forest Service for as little as twenty-five dollars a year. One or two pairs of foxes were enough to stock an island if the farmer could subsist for two or three years while the brood stock multiplied. Many fox farm operators built cabins on the islands and lived in them. Others visited the islands only to distribute food and skin their furs. ("Southeast Alaska—1911-1942 between Two Wars," http://www.akhistorycourse.org/articles/article.php?artID=79)]

4/22—Tues.
Kindergarten to Wrangell

Fished from 8:30 to 9:00. *Nira* didn't come out, so went back to see what was the trouble. His oil pump wouldn't work; said it would take 1½ or 2 hrs. So we went back and trolled till 11:00. He still was not out, so we went back again. Just as we got there, he started to come out. We decided not to troll, and go to Wrangell. Left Kindergarten at 11:10. Arrived in Wrangell at 3. Began to rain about noon and it rained all the way in. Lots of snow capped mountains close by. Went for walk with *Nira* when we got to Wrangell. He treated us to vanilla ice cream @ 15 cents! He insisted we eat dinner with him. Had roasted a chicken with dressing in a Dutch oven. Sure tasted good. He brot it over to our boat, as we had more room. Carl and I went for a walk. Stopped at the laundry. They only work on Mondays, but would put ours thru special—so we left it there.

4/23—Wed.
Wrangell

Sold our one lone fish—$1.80. We can't get on the ways today as other boat won't be off till late tonight. Carl put me overboard in skiff, and I took some pictures of the *Olympic*. We went for a long walk. Stopped and talked to an Indian working on a totem pole. Was very talkative and interesting. Walked thru main part of town. Came home and made a chocolate cake. *Nira* asked us to go up town and have dinner with him. Then we went to the show, at *Nira*'s expense, and saw *The Cisco Kid*. (Carl and I had already seen it.) Came back to boat and had cake and coffee.

4/24—Thurs.

Went on the ways at noon—another small boat was already on. He moved to the outside so we could get next to the wall. When the tide went out, he began to list to the starboard. He and Carl propped it up. At midnite he moved off. Carl scrubbed and copper painted about ½ of starboard side before high tide. Went for walk and bought a *Seattle P.I.* for 5 cents! *[The* Post Intelligencer *delivered its last print edition on May 17, 2009. It was the nation's largest daily newspaper to shift over to an online-only version.]*

4/25—Fri.

Finished copper painting and scraped about ½ of starboard side before high water. Moved off cradle at noon. Had pipes fixed at blacksmith shop. Bot groceries. Had dinner with *Nira*. Wrote letters to Mother and Zellah.

Postcard from Hazel's belongings.

4/26—Sat.

Fished from 6:00 to 3:00—only two fish. Very muddy. Only fished 7 fathoms *[forty-two feet]*. Started to get ruff around noon so came in. Rained.

4/29—Tues.

12 years ago Louis and I were married. *[Louis Bolme was Hazel's first husband—marriage lasted only a short time.]* Didn't fish today. Rained. Bot 1½ tons of ice and 2 cakes of bait, also more groceries. Carl bot a new pair of pants. *Nira* brot over his chicken and noodles.

5/3—Sat.—41 years old today
Sunny Bay to Vixen Harbor

Up at 4:20 a.m. Fished till about 2—no luck at
all. *Nira* said we had better go to Vixen, so
lifted leads and went. Got there about 3:30. Nice
day—rained some, and wind blew on way to Vixen.
Made myself a birthday cake with candles.

5/5—Mon.
Meyers Chuck

4:45 to 6:30. Was ruff and rolly. Carl wanted to
go to Ketchikan, but I thot it was too ruff. All
we got were fiddlers. It got ruffer and ruffer. As
we came in, I was very sick! Had to go to bed all
day. Used B.Y.'s Formula #18. Helped a little.
Carl borrowed a hot water bag from Mrs. West. This
business is sure the nertz. Carl worked on gear
all day. Bot some new stuff.

5/9—Fri.

Left Meyers Chuck at 4:20—went to Union Bay. While
Carl was eating breakfast, I steered too close to
Lemesurier Point, and all four lines got caught. We
had an awful time getting loose, lost one leader
and one plug *[a plug is a lure with one or more hooks attached]*, but
finally made it. Caught 7 salmon and one halibut.
Anchored at Vixen all alone. Very beautiful—full
moon on smooth water. Sunshine all day.

5/11—Sun.—Mother's Day

Didn't fish today. Burned all the old paint off of
hull, sandpapered, and repainted it green. Got
our mail from the packer—first since April 19. Got
sunburned helping Carl paint.

5/12—Mon.

Didn't fish. Finished painting on boat. Began to rain about 9, so had to quit. Later in p.m. the sun came out, so we got it all done. Ed Stringer gave us 21 cans of deer meat. I made him a cake in part payment. *[Bartering system is interesting.]*

5/14—Wed.
Ketchikan

Horrible day—rain and wind. Carl worked all day on letters for boat. I had a permanent—$4.00. Went up to see Eva. Had a bath.

5/15—Thurs.

Still raining. We put large OLYMPIC letters on boat. *[Commercial fishing boats are required to have letters on both sides of bow. Pleasure boats have letters on the stern.]* Carl worked on anchor.

Hull of boat is now dark green.

5/16—Fri.

Coast Guard came to look at our boat—$250.00 per month *[if used by Coast Guard as auxiliary vessel]*, but we had no room for 4 men. Everett Hudson came and stayed and stayed. Made banana bread. Had dinner at Pritchers', then to Townsend Dance. Made ice cream at Vernie's. She insisted on changing recipe, so it wasn't good.

5/17—Sat.

Bot 4 cans of milk, 8 lbs. coffee, sack of flour and sugar and more, which came to $22.00. Bot 2 pair of overalls for me, walrus tooth for Alan, greeting cards, and white moccasins for Arlene's birthday. *[I loved those moccasins! They were white fur with Indian beading on the tops.]* Run a "plug" fishhook in my finger. Hurt like H——! Had to go to hospital and have Dr. Ellis take it out—$5.00. Carl put up a boom.

5/18—Sun.

Mrs. *Sonsie* gave me some magazines from Yacht Club. Rained most all day. Tony from *Nada* came and stayed just about all day. Bot a pressure cooker from Burke but did not pay him—we owe $5.00 for it. Made meatloaf; cooked it in the cooker. Went to Pritchers' and played pinochle.

5/19—Mon.

Mars came in just as we were about to eat breakfast. We tried to get out as soon as we could, but he would not wait—smashed into us and the dock. Carl was so disgusted. We moved to "B" float. At 11 a.m. went to Union Oil for gas and water—then

to New England Fish Co. for ice and bait. Carl
got his birth certificate just before we left. Saw
Karl and Eva at New England. Left at 2 p.m. for
Meyers Chuck; arrived at 6:30. Pretty ruff in
spots. Wrote letters.

5/21—Wed.

Left Meyers Chuck at 5:40. Fished Lemesurier Side
till about 10—only 2 fish. Then went to Cannery
side. Caught one. About 11:30 got hung up on the
rocks near False Island—all four lines. Lost a
$5.00 lead, also cracked the R. bow pole. Carl
climbed up and repaired it while we were running.
Saw a whale. *Rayart* and us went to Vixen to tie
up. *Lollie Mae* and Stringer were already there.
After a short while *Nira* came too. I washed all
the windows inside and out. Carl cleaned out the
stovepipe. Everybody took naps. At 5 p.m. we all
went out again. We caught 2—11# and one 7# white.
Got in at 9:30—High Boat! *[Most profitable catch for the day,
as compared to all other boats in area.]*

5/22—Thurs.

Left Vixen at 7 a.m. Ed Stringer killed an eagle
before we were up. *[Alaska's Territorial government paid boun-
ties on eagles, seals, wolves, and the Dolly Varden trout. They gobbled
the fingerling salmon by the millions. Black bears were also considered
a threat to the salmon and were shot on sight by many—not Hazel. She
fed them! The concept of "balance of the ecosystem" and a concern for
the environment hadn't hit America, let alone Alaska, in 1941.]* Traveled to Sunny Bay—8:45. Fished there till 11:30.
Caught one 27# mild cure. At 11:30 left for Zimo-
via Strait. Stopped and trolled at Bold Island
for 45 min.—no luck. Went on to Wrangell—got there
at 6:30. Bad weather—wind and rain. Ed Stringer

and *Lollie Mae* were already there. *Nira* brot over chicken and noodles with carrots all cooked. Made a gingerbread cake.

5/24—Sat.

Up at 3:00, because all four of our boats had drifted out in the bay about ½ mile! (Someone didn't tie us up right). Fished "The Nose" for a while, then went across to Fritter's Cove. Caught two. Then followed *Nira* back again to Chickagof and Big Ben—no fish. About noon, tied up till 5—then went towards Quiet Harbor. No fish. Anchored next to a friend of *Nira's*.

[Hazel's entry notes that they followed another boat and both fished in the same area. For safety, the fisherfolk usually traveled and fished in groups. And when together, they always helped each other with repairs, shared boat parts, towed each other, etc. However, once they settled on area to fish, they became territorial and the attitude turned to "everyone out for himself."]

5/25—Sun.—Arlene's 4th birthday

Left at 4:00. *Nira* decided to wait and see what we could do before he would come out. We went down as far as the bigger island and back again, several times. Caught 5 fish. By 10:30 they had quit biting, so at 11:30 we went in. *Nira* was just coming out, so he turned and went back too. I made hot yeast rolls and cinnamon rolls, and *Nira's* friend came over for lunch. We went out again. Caught 4 more fish. *Nira* wanted to go back to Fritter's Cove, so at 8 p.m. we left for there. Had dinner ready by 8:30, but waited for *Nira*. He never arrived till 9:45, and he had already eaten. Anchored there all nite.

5/26—Mon.

Fished at Fritter's Cove, Roosevelt Bay, and Deep Harbor. Fished till 4 p.m. and caught 15 fish. Our best day so far—$21.00! Anchored in Deep Bay. South Easter came up, so we couldn't fish that nite. Both took baths. Had dinner on the *Nira*.

5/27—Tues.

Fished same place as Mon. till noon, then decided to go to Petersburg. Caught 4 fish. Went via "Over The Hill." Stopped twice to fish, but got none. Arrived at Petersburg at 6:45. Went past Le Connie Glacier and saw some icebergs. Sold our fish for $39.00. Then went to City Float and then home to bed.

5/29—Thurs.

Fished around Frederick Point and Ideal Cove till about noon—then decided to go over Dry Pass. First *Nira* got stuck in the mud, then *Rayart*, and then us! It was the nertz. Had to wait for high tide at 3 p.m. before we could get off. Fished all the way to Mud Bay. Anchored there. Saw a fox on the beach. Carl, Art, and Ray shot at bottles. The fox farmer came out next morning and asked us to not shoot, as it scared the foxes.

6/1—Sun.

Did some more painting—green, aluminum, and white. Wrote letter to Ella, also one to Arlene. One-armed Jack's wife came over to call. Carl sick—low stomach pain.

6/3—Tues.

Bot groceries and some more gear. Took Carl to see Dr. Benson—not appendicitis, but colitis. Gave him pills and a liquid to take after each meal. Took on 70 gals. gas and 1 ton of ice. Left Petersburg at 2:30. Fished part way to Portage Bay—no luck. Anchored there. Myrtle gave me some frozen deer meat. She made strawberry shortcake.

6/4—Wed.

Left Portage Bay at 3:30. Traveled till about noon, then began to fish at Security Cove. Caught 6. Quit at 5 p.m. Anchored at Security. Roasted the deer meat—sure tasted swell.

6/5—Thurs.
Security Bay

Our biggest day! 22 fish = 438#. Beat 2 other boats.

6/10—Tues.
Tyee

Storm-bound here. Bad South Easter. We broke loose from *Nira* at 2:00 a.m., and Carl and Lee had to get up and re-tie the boat. Then Lee made coffee for them. Ray and Art went "crabbing"—brot us several already cooked. Made a swell salad. Bot gas, but had to wait for low tide to get ice. By that time the….. *[This is the last—and incomplete—diary entry for 1941.]*

Hazel and Carl went home to Seattle for the Thanksgiving holiday as this picture shows. Taken on Thanksgiving Day at our home: Hazel with Arlene (me) at age four and Alan, my brother, at age six.

[The Japanese bombed Pearl Harbor on December 7, 1941. Congress voted to declare war the same day. The following day, hundreds of thousands of radio listeners heard President Roosevelt's six-and-a-half-minute speech, which included phrases that would become part of American folklore.

[He opened with, "Yesterday, December 7, 1941—a date which will live in infamy—the United States of America was suddenly and deliberately attacked by naval and air forces of the Empire of Japan," and ended his speech with, "With confidence in our armed forces, with the unbounding determination of our people, we will gain the inevitable triumph, so help us God!"]

Part III
1942

At War

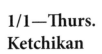

1/1—Thurs.
Ketchikan

Carl went to New England Fish Co. to go to work. Didn't need anyone today. Will call him when they do. Dinner on *Olympic* with Pritchers. Met Burke and friend at Stedman Cocktail Bar.

1/7—Wed.

Carl and I both have bad colds. Ice in bay. Spent $6.80. (5 sacks of coal—$5.75, 1 doz. eggs—$.55; 2 pkgs. cigarettes (Lucky's)—$.30; toothpicks—$.10 and *Newsweek*—$.10. *[Price comparison: one pack of cigarettes cost $.15 in 1942—over $5.00 in 2009. Also note that one dozen eggs cost $.55. When Hazel and Carl are out on the fishing grounds for weeks at a time, eggs sometimes cost them $1.00 a dozen as the packer must bring them out to the fishermen. It must have irked Carl to have to pay these prices, being an ex chicken rancher.]*

Hazel on the left and Carl smoking his Lucky.

1/14—Wed.

Very bad weather—heavy rains and 60-mile-per-hour winds. New linoleum for table—$1.75. Got brown wool yarn for men's sweater at Red Cross. Ordered C.O.D. from Sears: rubber boots and slippers for me, and rubber shoes and insoles for Carl. New red wool wrap-around—$1.00. Books from Library: *White Orchid*, *White Fang*, and *Klondike Kid*. Carl's cold is still with him.

1/23—Fri.

Package of wool thread from Mother. Spent $6.70. (21# Co-op Coffee @ $.30—$6.30, rubber heels—$.40).

[Hazel and Carl had free time and a relatively leisurely lifestyle for the first few months of each year because fishing season didn't usually start until about May. They sought employment during the off-season and were successful some years.]

1/26—Mon.

Sunshine finally! Washed my hair and washed clothes. Carl got his identification card from Coast Guard. Sent clothes to Laundry. Letter from Mother. Bot Bull Durham *[tobacco to roll own cigarettes]*—$.60.

2/4—Wed.

Carl started work on revamping kitchen. Made shelves on starboard door—took stove out. Ruth and Harvey left for Seattle. Wrote to *Chronicle [local newspaper]* in answer to their ad for office work. Spent $16.31 (blacksmith, bolts, rubber, swivels, saws filed, lead, beer, hair tonic, and Kotex.)

2/6—Fri.

Carl and MacDonald worked on rear door.

[After Japan bombed Pearl Harbor, the United States government initiated a highway-building project to connect the contiguous U.S. to Alaska through Canada in the name of civil defense. On February 6, 1942, the U.S. Army's chief of staff revealed a plan to construct a military supply route to Alaska. Five days later, on February 11, 1942, President Franklin D. Roosevelt authorized construction of the Alaskan Highway as a land transport route in the event that the Japanese seized shipping lines in the Pacific.]

2/20—Fri.

Beautiful day. Baked a cake—it didn't cook on the bottom due to the "soot door" being off. Rummage sale at American Legion Dugout. We bot bunch of junk for $7.60. Carl put window in front of the cabin, and also finished work on side door. I washed windows. Had venison sandwiches. Spent $10.10.

2/24—Tues.

Dull and very cold. Ice in the bay—fireboat came
in and broke it up. Carl went to see Whiton about
our gurdies—got real tuff, so the 2 of them went
down to see Hans on the *Gypsy*. After some dick-
ering between Whiton and Hans, Carl got the gurdies. Got 3 books from the Library. Spent $8.20
(bakery, beer, paint, gun shells, elastic, brown
ribbon, thread, birthday cards for Mother, Dad,
and Alan, *Alaska Sportsman [magazine]* for Mother
and Dad, *Chronicle*, and defense stamps *[also called
war stamps]* for Alan and Arlene.)

*[During the war, the government issued stamps for savings bonds to sup-
port the war effort. As a child in elementary school during the war years,
I remember bringing my dime to school each week to purchase a stamp to
put in my book. The teacher had our books and sold us the stamps. It took
$18.75 to fill the book, which would be redeemed for $25.00 about ten
years later. The book is replicated in the center of the picture below.]*

2/28—Sat.

Bad day—wind, rain and hail. Carl worked on gurdies—finally got them all installed. Mrs. Garlitts
Fortuna and sister stopped in while I was scrubbing floor. Carl had too much beer, and we had a
row—as usual. I walked out while cooking dinner
and stayed for 1½ hours. Came home. (I was so
cold, couldn't stay out any longer). Cooked dinner and went to Revilla *[theater]*. Carl went to bed
right after dinner. Spent $4.85.

3/5—Thurs.

Sun and some rain. Hadley Chamberlain came at 8:45
as I was getting breakfast—on his way to Kodiak.
He stayed till noon, then went back to the *Denali*.
We went shopping and met him at 2:00, and he came
back to our boat and stayed till the ship sailed
at 3:30. *[Hadley Chamberlain was my uncle—my father's brother.
Hadley was a carpenter and had been recruited from the Seattle area to go
to Kodiak to construct barracks for a base there.]* Spent $62.51.

3/8—Sun.

Rain—snow—hail. Carl painted lard cans (45#),
painted new kitchen chair, and installed new water
pump. It sure works swell; will get lot of good
out of it. Bot rubber bathtub from Montgomery
Ward—$6.19.

*[On March 8, 1942, construction of the Alaskan Highway officially began.
Trailblazing was primarily completed by the U.S. Army, while civilian
contractors followed them to widen and straighten the road.]*

3/12—Thurs.

Nice day—sun, but cold. Carl painted mast and fixed crack in deck. Also bot chain to tie the tires onto the boat. Ketchikan had first mock air raid attack at 11:30—5 sacks of flour were dropped at strategic places.

[Ketchikan's initial and slightly disorganized civil defense efforts in those first few months of the war had smoothed into routine by this time. Business owners had barrels of sand hauled to rooftops to fight fires caused by incendiary bombs. Air raid evacuation drills were common, and many people, including Hazel, took first aid classes. At the local school, evacuation drills ushered kids to a nearby gold mine tunnel. Air raid wardens patrolled the streets at night. It was also a time of blackout along the western shores of the U.S. from Alaska to San Diego. Blackout curtains were used after dark. (June Allen, The Forgotten War: June 3, 1942-August 1943)]

3/15—Sun.

Bad day—rain and hail. Carl put fasteners on all the shelves to keep things from falling out; also wired down gas tank for cook stove. Carl pretty sick. Has a cold and "toooo" much beer. I went to 7:00 p.m. show—*They Met in Bombay*—Clark Gable and Rosalind Russell. Letters to Mother, Zellah, and Orie. Spent $1.60.

3/17—Tues.

Fairly nice day. Washed clothes all day. Went to U.S.O. hut to see Alaska moving pictures. Then went to Stedman and danced. Harry Kimball came over and danced with me. Spent $6.35.

3/30—Mon.—Seward's Day

Nice day. Took bath before lunch. Big Ole came in with 1 pint of whiskey. I went to Red Cross nutrition class at 1:30 at Council Chambers. Carl brot home a black kitten. Spent $3.05.

[Seward's Day is a legal state holiday. It falls on the last Monday in March and commemorates the signing of the Alaska Purchase treaty on March 30, 1867. It is named for then-Secretary of State William H. Seward, who negotiated the purchase from Russia for the price of $7,200,000, which figured out to be about two cents per acre. Wonder what it's worth today.]

4/1—Wed.—April Fool's Day

Nice day. "Lonesome Pete" came down to boat from the Shamrock to get me to come up after Carl—who was drunk and fighting. When I got there—"April Fool!" (I didn't think it was so funny). Had my picture taken for my identification card. Carl and I walked down to McKay Ship Bldg. Co. to see about having the *Olympic* pulled up on their ways—$35.00. Too much money, so we came home.

4/3—Fri.

Nice day. Went to University Extension class on gardening at 2:30. *[Victory gardens, also called war gardens, were planted at private residences in the United States, United Kingdom, Canada, and Germany during World War I and World War II. They reduced the pressure on the public food supply brought on by the war effort.]* Carl went up to the Shamrock and stayed for hours, so I got mad and went to a show.

4/4—Sat.

Nice day. Exchanged library books. Went to Coast Guard office and got my identification card; also Carl's license to fish with the "Area A" corrected. Carl worked all day throwing rocks overboard and loading on a ton of coal. One ton of coal—$21.00.

4/5—Sun.—Easter Sunday

Beautiful day. Bright sunshine, but very cold. Went to U.S.O. Clubhouse for a program at 3:30—then to see *Barnacle Bill* at the Coliseum. Wrote letter to Mother. Blackie, the cat, jumped thru the window right on my stomach while I was in bed early this a.m.

4/11—Sat.

Beautiful day. Bought groceries from "Jimmie" the Jap. Went to St. John's Guild fashion show—$.50. Baked batch of overnight cookies. Carl worked all day putting in shelves in the bow of boat. Coast Guard sent me a letter to report on my identification card for new fingerprints. Letters from Mother, Orie, and Coast Guard.

4/13—Mon.

Beautiful day. Went up on the grid at 9:30 a.m. Had to wait till 1:30 for high tide. Went to the Red Cross tea for our instructor. When I came back, the boat was listed to the starboard. Had a hard time getting aboard. We were 2nd boat over. Carl fell into the bay, too. We sat up all night, watching the two boats. At 9:30 p.m., our boat righted itself and about ½ hour later, it listed to the port. The *Mermaid* listed also, and Carl broke a window trying to wake up the two boys on it.

[Fishing boats, especially in Alaska, need ongoing repairs. Leaks are a common problem that need repairing by going up on the grid. Maintenance is also required. Carl, who was handy with his hands (when he was sober), was continuously working to make the Olympic *more livable.]*

4/15—Wed.

Beautiful day. Got off the grid at 11:00 a.m. Both took baths. First time for Carl in the new tub. Then we went to bed for a couple hours. Went to Red Cross First Aid class. Carl on a beer binge and went to bed immediately after dinner. Had forced blackout—power went off for 30 minutes.

4/18—Sat.
Doolittle Raid

[On April 18, 1942, during World War II, eighty men embarked on an historic adventure that would strike fear into the hearts of the Japanese people and raise American morale at a time when it was at its lowest. It became known as the "Doolittle Raid" after its leader, Jimmie Doolittle. Their mission: to bomb key cities on the Japanese mainland in retaliation for the Pearl Harbor attack four months earlier. Some historians believe the bombing of Alaska by the Japanese was in retaliation for the Doolittle Raid. (Courtesy of Jack Strumpf, writer from Escondido, California)]

4/20—Mon.

Fair weather—some rain and sun. Got up late. Took a bath right after breakfast, then studied my Red Cross First Aid till 1 p.m. Went to Red Cross class. Got pictures developed at Schallerer's.

First meeting of Rifle Club at American Can Co. I didn't go. Carl stayed out till 1 a.m. He was soaking wet too—guess he fell off the dock again. I was mad! He's the nertz.

Hazel with friends from Seattle on Olympic.

4/26—Sun.

Rain. Intended to go on the grid, but too stormy. Will wait till high tide tonite (10:30). Bob came in; played pinochle. Went up on grid at 9 p.m. Stayed up all nite.

4/27—Mon.

Sunshine. Carl began to work on boat at 3 a.m. I tried to sleep, but there was too much noise. Gus on the *Essa* came at 5:30 to help Carl. I got breakfast for them at 7 a.m. Finished at

7 p.m. Had to wait till 9:15 to float off. Made coffee cake for First Aid class. Got crepe nightie from Zellah for my birthday.

5/2—Sat.

Horrible day—wind and rain. Went to Red Cross Canteen at 9 a.m. and worked till 4 p.m. Served about 300 people. Mrs. Pratt asked us to come to a party at the Yacht Club for Owen. He's getting married on Monday. Carl was so drunk we had to come home at 11 p.m.

5/3—Sun.

My birthday. Carl was pretty sick, but not too sick to demand some whiskey, which Ole had left with us some time ago. After his 3rd drink, I poured the rest down the sink. He got up at 2 p.m. and left the boat, and I never saw him again till I went for a walk at 6 p.m. He was in the Shamrock, almost too drunk to walk—had to hang on to me. I went to a show, but he wouldn't go with me. I got home at 9:30, and he was in bed. He wrote another check for $5.00, which makes a total of $20.00 so far for this drunken mess. I certainly had a nice, happy birthday! Behind the water bucket I found a pint of whiskey. I immediately hid it.

5/4—Mon.

Nice sunny day. Carl wouldn't eat any breakfast and left the boat at once. I took a bath and went to First Aid class at 1:30. From there I went to Owen's wedding at the Lutheran Church. I bot them a pyrex custard set with wire rack. Carl came in while I was eating but didn't stay. I went to

First Aid at 7 p.m. Home at 9:30. Carl came in for a few minutes and then left. Came home at 1:30 a.m.—so drunk he could hardly walk.

5/7—Thurs.

Wind and rain. Got up early. Had breakfast and baked scalloped potatoes for First Aid potluck lunch. Carl went with me. After lunch, Carl came back, and I practiced "drowning" rescue on him. (Guess I need to pay attention to this since he falls into the water a lot when he's drunk.) Mailed pkg. to Mother.

5/9—Sat.
Ketchikan to Meyers Chuck

Good day, so decided to leave for Meyers Chuck. Left Thomas Basin at 9:50 and arrived at Meyers Chuck 3:15. Good weather all the way. *Gypsy*, *Fortuna*, Ed Nygaard, and MacDonald all were there. Mailed letters to Orie and Arlene.

Fishing Season Starts

[Hazel and Carl fished by trolling. Joe Upton, author of Alaska Blues, has a good explanation of this method of catching salmon: "Trolling for salmon is a hook-and-line fishery—very different from net fishing. A boat will fish four stainless-steel lines that are reeled in and out on individual gurdies (winches). At the bottom of each line is a weight heavy enough to make the line lead straight down as it runs through the water. The actual fishing gear, the leaders and lures (or baits), is attached to the line at intervals and trails in the water.

[According to the Anacortes Museum in Anacortes, Washington, "Troll boats can be among the smaller commercial fishing craft and are recognized by their long outrigger poles. Trollers in the North Pacific usually fish for salmon; primarily Chinook, coho and pink."]

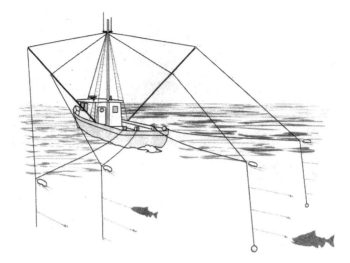

Troller. (Courtesy of Anacortes Museum, Anacortes, Washington.)

5/12—Tues.

First day of fishing. Left at 3:55 for Union Bay. Fished till 9:20 and only got one fiddler. Carl tried out all the new gear. Bob Burns came over in evening and played cards.

5/14—Thurs.

Too foggy to fish. Heavy fog till noon; then it was too high tide to fish. Carl dipped our anchor rope in tar. Then he helped me wash clothes. Took our guns and did some practice shooting on the beach. *Lydia H* tied up to us at 6 p.m.

5/16—Sat.
Meyers Chuck to Point Baker

Up at 4 a.m.—ready to go fishing. Cold and rainy, so we stayed in. Had breakfast, washed dishes, and did some mending. Went back to bed at 7 and slept till 8:30. Carl came in and said we would leave for Pt. Baker with Bob, so we left at 8:40. Carl thot we hit a submerged log going thru Snow Pass; we felt something bump. Arrived at Pt. Baker at 5:45. Stopped opposite Lincoln Rock and tied up to Bob—we vibrated too much, so we untied.

5/23—Sat.
Point Baker to Craig

Good day—sunshine. Left Pt. Baker at 5:10 a.m. with *Magnet* and Bert Stone. Arrived in Craig at 6:10 p.m.—13 hours for 75 miles. I got seasick just before we got to Dry Pass, but it didn't last long. Craig isn't much of a town. Saw Reichwein and Joe Otto. *Magnet* gave us some red snapper late in evening—put it on top of cooler. The next morning it was gone—seagulls.

5/24—Sun.
Craig to Kelly's Cove

Left Craig at 9:25 after filling gas tanks (67 gals.) at Union Oil. *Magnet* broke down at 11 a.m.—bum coil—so we towed them for a short distance, but then Carl gave Ralph an extra coil that we had. At 11:25 we started again for Kelly's Cove. We arrived at 12:55. None of the boats were out—no fish. Spent the day visiting. On way over here, Carl discovered a leaky gas pipe, so he fixed that. Made two lemon pies and bread pudding. *Coast*, *Slasser*, *Bowden*, and *Tonto II* are here. Spent $8.74.

5/25—Mon.—Arlene's birthday (5 years old)
Kelly's Cove

Beautiful day. Rained later. Got up at 4, had breakfast, and left at 5:20. At 6:10 Carl discovered another gas leak, so we came back and tied up at 7:00; Carl fixed it. I was sick most all day and stayed in bed. Spent $5.00.

5/27—Wed.

Nice sunny day. Left at 4:10, fished till 5:10. Broke tag line on starboard bow pole. Carl had to climb up the pole to fix it. We rolled so, I was afraid he would fall off. We soon broke the other bow pole. We caught 6 fish, but it got so ruff, we had to leave. Gave the packer our mail key. Highest Day for May! Sold fish for $17.10.

5/30—Sat.—Memorial Day

A year ago today we had a picnic lunch on *Nira* with *Rayart*. Wonder where we'll be next year. Got up at 4 a.m. to go out, but Carl had a bad scratch on his wrist and a red streak up his arm, so I made him stay in and soak it with Epsom Salts. *Coast* came back at 6:30 and wanted us to go to Little Bremerton on Lulu Island for clams and abalone. Arrived there at 7:15 a.m. Went ashore and did some practice shooting.

5/31—Sun.

Dull gray day—rained. Carl got up at 5:15, so I had to get up too. Washed windows. Mrs. Rensch gave us some abalone. Total earned for May—$26.70. Bot 50 gals. of gas—$6.00. *[That's 12 cents/gallon as compared to high of $2.74/gallon in Ketchikan 2009.]*

Bombing of Alaska

[In 1941, Brigadier General Simon Buckner, commander of the Alaskan Defense Command, proposed a covert construction project to build two Army Air Force bases on the islands of Cold Bay and Umnak—in the Aleutians. (Because the Navy dominated the Aleutians, it supposedly opposed Army involvement in the area.) Alaska was strategic territory. General Buckner realized that if the Japanese took these islands, they'd have an ideal staging location to attack the continental United States— starting with Seattle. Since this was before the Pearl Harbor attack, U.S. leadership wasn't convinced the Japanese posed an immediate threat, so General Buckner was not given permission to build the two airfields. Instead, he built them covertly. (This could have cost General Buckner a court martial. But, fortunately, his idea eventually was approved—just before the Pearl Harbor attack.)

[In March 1941, the 807th Army Engineers—in civilian clothes, so even the locals didn't suspect the buildup—started working on the airfields on Umnak Island and Cold Bay. To further protect the project, General Buckner made up a fictitious factory—the Blair Fish Packing Company. Supplies sent from other operating locations were marked to reflect the fake name.

[Since Umnak is mountainous and has no trees, it was doubtful a runway could be constructed. But the general solved that problem. He imported perforated steel matting, and within the first month, a three-thousand-foot-long, one-hundred-foot-wide portable runway was waiting for the first P-40 Warhawk fighter aircraft to land. The matting wasn't a perfect solution in the harsh Alaskan environment. Every once in a while the gusting wind rolled it up like a carpet.

[The Japanese attacked Dutch Harbor at Umnak in the Aleutian Islands on June 3, 1942. (Dutch Harbor is approximately nineteen hundred miles, as the crow flies, from Ketchikan.) Forty-three Americans died—thirty-three military and ten civilians—and eleven planes from Umnak were lost. Dutch Harbor was the only land in North America that was bombed by Japanese Naval forces during World War II. Few Americans knew any of

this because military officials restricted the media from covering operations in Alaska. Postwar commentators remarked that America would surely have panicked had it known that the enemy had attacked American soil. (Many people I query today are unaware that Alaska had been bombed. I also wonder if Hazel and Carl knew about the bombing. Remember that they had the best radio among the fishing fleet and listened regularly to the nine o'clock news, with friends joining them. Yet, Hazel never mentioned this important occurrence in her diary entries. Interesting.)

[Japanese troops occupied two Aleutian Islands—Kiska and Attu. The Alaska conflict was brief. It was a little-known segment of a larger war, with the weather proving to be the most powerful enemy. But some historians say it marked the turning point of the Pacific War.]

Japanese Attack on Dutch Harbor—bombing of oil tanks, June 3, 1942. (Photograph from National Archives.)

Bombing of Fort Mears at Dutch Harbor, June 1942.
(Photograph from National Archives.)

6/4—Thurs.
Hole-in-the-Wall to Kelly's Cove

Rained in night and on and off all day. Left at 5 a.m. for the Haystack. Fished till 8; too ruff, so we came in to Kelly's Cove. Got our mail—first time since we left K. Made a batch of wheatgerm cookies. Letters from Mother, Zellah, and Orie. Recipe book from Knox Gelatin, a Montgomery catalog, and peanuts from Lillian. Spent $.45.

6/8—Mon.—Carl's birthday
4:30 a.m.–7:15 p.m.

Rain and wind most all day. Water was fairly smooth till high tide (10 a.m.), then it got ruffer and ruffer. Lots of williwaws. I was sick most of the day and in bed. Carl set himself afire with a pocket full of matches. Broke the starboard bow pole tag line, and Carl had to climb up and fix it in all the rollers! Caught 10 fish—sold for $23.28. Buyer had no money to pay us.

6/9—Tues.
3:30 a.m.–5:45 p.m.

Rain and wind all day. Pretty ruff till high tide at 11 a.m., then it smoothed down till about 2 p.m. Then it got worse and worse, so we came in. Broke the starboard bow tag again, but Carl didn't have to do any climbing, thank goodness. A big salmon took one complete leader, and then Carl threw a spoon overboard. A sea lion took a fish off the line, leader and all. Total hours: 14. Sold our 14 fish for $31.08; still no money to pay us.

6/11—Thurs.

Dull gray day—some rain. Got up at 3:30—two boats on outside of us were still asleep. Carl had to pull them up to the end of the float and tie them up. Then he came back and couldn't get engine started. Worked on it till 5:45—had to change the timer. Only fished in the channel as the engine was missing. Fished till 8:30—then came in, and Carl worked on engine. I made a stew out of the tag end of the deer. Offered to help Mrs. Knaplund do some typing. *[Hazel's little typewriter often came in handy.]* Fish sold—$1.40. Got paid today. Spent $13.25.

6/12—Fri.

Dull gray day—some rain. Left at 3:45. Pretty ruff, and it got worse the longer we stayed out. Took some awful rolls—first time I've been scared this year. Main starboard pole broke all stays and dragged in the water—so we had to come back. I sure was glad. Carl bot new ropes for all 4 poles. I cleaned and polished all the hooks and spoons. Did some typing for Mr. Knaplund. Spent $12.58.

6/13—Sat.

Rolled and bounced all nite. Carl got up at 3:30, but wind was blowing so hard no one went out to fish. So we went back to bed and slept till 7:30. Carl hit his finger with a hammer yesterday, and it is all festered this morning. Made ginger-bread. One of the trollers gave me the molasses, so I gave him a hunk of my bread. Rained all day. Wrote 4 letters.

6/26—Fri.—Left Seattle 2 years ago today. Hole-in-the-Wall

Left Hole-in-the-Wall at 4:15—went to Snail Pt.—following Mac. It was awful ruff—huge rollers and chop on top of that. *Lavina* (native boat) was flagging for help, but before we got out there, a purse seiner towed him in. We fished till 7:30, but was too ruff, so we came in—no fish.

[I wonder what Hazel and Carl were pondering so early each morning as they headed for the fishing grounds. As birds were an important

factor in locating fish, they were probably scouring the bay for signs of sea birds feeding. Are there sea lions in the area? Where will the salmon be today? How deep or how shallow will they be? What will they bite on today—spoons or only bait? Will we be lucky enough to make expenses today? Or will our recent poor luck continue?]

6/27—Sat.—Left Ketchikan 7 weeks ago today.

Up at 4 a.m. Had breakfast before we left. Sure seemed good to be able to eat first. Left at 5 and fished till 7 p.m. Fair day, some rain and sunshine—not ruff, thank goodness. Cooked a good meal at noon—first one since we began to fish this year. Got 24 kings—sold for $30.00. Spent $1.20.

6/30—Tues.

Nice day. Up at 4:30, but Carl worked on gear till 5:45 a.m. Trolled to Steamboat Bay till 10 a.m., then went over to Cannery and got gas, water, coal, and groceries. Left there at 11:45 and came back to Hole-in-the-Wall. The wind came up shortly after noon, and a thick fog blew in. Crafts on the *Lindora* came in today. No fish. Started to knit a rug out of old pieces of wool. Spent $24.04. Total hours run for month—197 hours and 30 minutes. Total fish sold for month—$234.25.

7/1—Wed.

[During the month of July, aided by good working/weather conditions, the Army Corps of Engineers sped up construction and built more than four hundred miles of the Alaskan Highway.]

7/2—Thurs.

Beautiful day. Left at 5:15. Fished till 12:15. Not many fish—few and far between. A small Indian boy fell overboard, and a young Indian woman dove in after him. Both OK. Spilled a butterscotch pudding all over the floor, walls, table, and even on Carl's pants! Sold fish for $3.70. Letters to Mother, Zellah, Edith, and Orie.

7/3—Fri.
Hole-in-the-Wall to Kelly's Cove

Beautiful day. Left at 4:45 and fished till 8:30. Then decided to go to Kelly's Cove and wash clothes. Trolled across till 11:30—then picked up and ran in. Only 2 fish. Washed clothes all day. Did some typing for McCune. Fellow on the *Trosky* was sent to Ketchikan on the plane—rupture, I guess. Sold fish for $1.42.

7/9—Thurs.—Arrived in Ketchikan 2 years ago today.
Coronation

Left at 5:45 for Cora Point. Lots of birds and ducks, but no fish. Came back to Egg Harbor (8:30), ready to go in, but decided to try a round or so first. Began to catch cohoes right away. Such a swell day—not one bit ruff. Have never seen it so smooth at Coronation. Fished all day till 7:30 p.m. Broke two tag lines, both bow and main on starboard side. Sold fish for $19.48. A transport convoy ship went by Cape Decision about 3:00—much smoke and lots of gunshots. A plane flew over the convoy all the time. *[An old Navy man told me that he thought the gunshots would likely have been from the troops on board, as they*

needed to practice shooting their guns whenever they could.] Bought
33 gals. gas—$3.96.

7/11—Sat.—Nine weeks ago today we left Ketchikan.
Cora Point to Pt. McArthur

Carl got up at 3:00 and 4:30, but as no one else
left, we went back to bed. Finally we left at
5:30. Fished all the way from Cora Point to end
of Spanish Islands. The tag line on the starboard
bow broke at the very top. Carl had to unbolt the
pole from the deck to fix it. No bites. Picked up
and went to Cape Decision. Fished till 9:30—no
bites. Handle Bar Johnson came by and wanted to
go into Pt. McArthur, so we went in. Saw a bunch
of black fish just before we came in. We also saw
about 5 black bears on the beach during the day.
First bears we've seen.

*[Black bears are the most abundant of all the three species of North
American bears. In Alaska, they inhabit most of the forested areas of
the state. Smallest of the North American bears, black bears spend their
winter months in a state of hibernation. Upon emergence in the spring,
they feed mainly on green vegetation, but they will eat nearly anything
they encounter. As summer progresses, feeding shifts to salmon if they
are available. Berries, especially blueberries, are an important late sum-
mer-fall food item.]*

7/12—Sun.
Pt. McArthur to Cora Point

Left McArthur at 6:25. Almost decided to go to Egg
Harbor, but fished Cape Decision, and then picked
up and went to Cora Point. Johnson soon followed
us. Fished all day till 9 p.m. Good weather and
smooth water. After we sold, we discovered that
all the other boats made $30 to $40. Got all their

fish early this a.m. Always our luck—in the wrong place. Sold our fish for $17.64.

7/13—Mon.
Cora Point

What a time we had last nite! Anchored (9:00) at Cora Point in the bite *[a "bight" is a curve or recess in a coast-line, smaller than a cove]* where the buyer was and went to bed at 9:30. We were rolling pretty good before we went to bed, but it got worse and worse. Neither of us could sleep, so at 10 we got up, pulled up the anchor, and intended to go to Ratz Bay. *Chance* and *Ocean* left at the same time, so we followed them into a small bite between Cora Point and Ratz Bay. It was 10:40 before we got back to bed and slept hard all nite. Not many boats out early today—we were 2nd one and no more for an hour or so. At 11 a.m., *Coast* and 3 other boats came over from Cape Pole and asked all about what we doing—said that Noyes was dead. Carl didn't give him much encouragement about fishing here, so they went on to Sitka. Saw bunch of seals playing with a school of fish at Cora Point. Made some fudge. Gave packer letters to mail. Sold fish for $47.22.

7/14—Tues.—5:15–9:00 p.m.

Didn't sleep very good last nite. Anchored at Cora Point, and we rolled constantly. It was after 11 before I could get to sleep, and then I woke up often. Rainy and foggy when we started out, but around 8 it cleared up and was a nice day from then on. *Elizabeth D* came by at 3:30, and at 6 p.m. *Merker* and Slim Frinch came by, but none of them stayed. Made a sweet potato pie—not so hot. Lots of boats stayed in today—wonder why? Good weather and pretty good fishing. A Navy patrol boat hung around here all afternoon—didn't seem to be going anyplace. Finally went off towards Helm Pt. Sold fish for $32.64.

7/19—Sun.—8:00–11:00
Malmsbury to Gedney

Up at 6:30. Pretty foggy, so we stalled around waiting for it to lift. A bull shark swam right by the boat—all we could see was a black fin. Handle Bar Johnson came by from Egg Harbor, so we followed him to Gedney. I canned 5 cans of cohoes and 7 cans of white kings. My first attempt at canning fish. Saw a black bear on the beach. Spent $15.35.

7/20—Mon.—9:00–3:15
Gedney

Carl got up at 4, but such a bad day, we slept till 7:30. Finally at 9 a.m., we went out. Only 2 boats out ahead of us. Rain and cold wind. Soon as I started to get dinner, we began to catch fish on every line, so I had to go out and help. Weather got wetter and colder and ruffer, so at 3:15 we came in. After we tied up, a boat came in from Alexander and Malmsbury with over 2,000 lbs. of cohoes! Fish prices went up one cent today on kings ($.18 a pound) and cohoes ($.08). Sold fish for $32.75.

Hazel with large catch.

7/21—Tues.—4:00 a.m.–7:30 p.m.

Left at 4, before breakfast. Had coffee while we waited for the lines to come in. Began biting right away, and by 10 a.m., we had about 40 fish. Cold wind, but brite sun. Water was ruff and rolling early but calmed down about noon. Most boats went in around 11 except Ed. He stayed till 2, then he went in. We caught about 50 fish after he left. *Hi Yo Silver* came by and asked what we were getting for cohoes. Carl shot at a sea lion that was eating our fish. Fished till 7:30, and we were both pretty tired so came in. In the early a.m., we got on a reef and lost the starboard main line, complete with 25 fathoms of wire! Lost a pair of pliers too. *[Losing what sound like small items—150 feet of wire, a pair of pliers—seems trivial today, but in the 1940s, with a war on and living on a fishing boat off the coast of Alaska, replacing such items was much more difficult, and costly, than a quick drive to Home Depot would be today. Maintenance items such as sparkplugs for the engine, had to be special ordered and delivered via parcel post.]* Sold fish for $94.80.

7/22—Wed.—4:15–8:30

Left at 4:15. Nice sunny day. Water smooth except for big ground swells. Canned 7 cans of halibut. Some of the pieces had worms in them, but I threw those away and only used the good ones (I hope). First halibut I've canned so hope it turns out OK. Lots of fish today. I helped Carl most all day. Lost a gaff hook and had to make 3 turns to get it. Caught a huge king—43 lbs. dressed! Fished till 8:30 and then had to wait about 30 minutes before we could sell. No money—have to wait for packer. Lost another pair of pliers. Sold fish for $89.80.

7/24—Fri.—4:15–8:00

Carl's hands are pretty bad with fish poisoning.
I did a lot of the fishing, but he wouldn't let
me clean. Beautiful day—warm and sunny. A bunch
of sea lions played all around the boat, and one
came up under the boat and took a fish off the
line I was pulling in. It was a huge brown thing,
about 2 tons. Carl shot at them with the .30-06.
Then later we got a 43 lb. king, and Carl's hands
were too sore to play him, so he shot it with the
pistol. Caught 1,306 lbs. of cohoes, 44 lbs. of
kings, and 13 humpies. Best day so far for month
and year. Sold for $113.63. We had to get up twice
during the nite to soak Carl's hands—they were
so painful.

[After Hazel's retirement, an article in the Seattle Times was written about
her fishing years, including mention of the "fish poisoning" episode:

> There came a day when Carl's hands and arms turned
> red and swollen, and he was in pain. No radio, no doc-
> tor, so other fishermen diagnosed his complaint and its
> treatment: constant hot poultices and no fishing. "If you
> can run the boat, I'll do the fishing," Hazel told him. So
> for six weeks she lived an unvarying routine: putting out
> the lines, each with 10 hooks, pulling them in when the
> ringing of a bell signified a catch, flipping the fish off the
> hooks, putting the lines back in, cleaning the fish as they
> were caught—from 4 a.m. until she got through. And in
> between, the poultices to make and the meals to cook.]

7/25—Sat.

Carl's hands were too bad to fish, so we stayed in;
soaked them in Epsom salts every 30 minutes.

[There are several types of fish poisoning. The most commonly reported marine toxin in the world is ciguatera. It is associated with consumption of contaminated fish. (Note that on July 22, Hazel canned some halibut, and she was unsure of the quality.) It has also been suggested that ciguatera may be caused by occupational exposure to ciguatoxic fish organs during repetitive handling or processing of fish. Victims suffer for weeks to months with debilitating neurological symptoms, including profound weakness, sweats, pain and numbness in the extremities, and diarrhea. Prolonged itching is sometimes associated with ciguatera.]

7/26—Sun.

Carl's hands are still very bad. He wanted to go out this morning, but I said no. Hard to pass up $80.00 a day, but if his hands got worse, we'd be off a lot longer. Mrs. Chase on the *Ella C* stayed in today and came and stayed here all day—bothered me so, I couldn't do the washing till she left at 1:30. Carl is still drunk, and acts and talks awful. Spent $12.90—$10.00 on whiskey.

7/27—Mon.

Still we are laid up with Carl's hands, and he's still drunk. The cook from the *Oregonian* came over and had cake and coffee with Mrs. Chase and us, and Carl got mad and jealous and said things to me that I'm afraid I'll never forget! Mrs. Chase was here again from 5 to 2! She sure is a nuisance. Made a cake and took a bath. Carl got some water. Until Carl apologizes and promises not to talk to me the way he has, I'm not going to do one thing for him—cook, fish, or anything else. I intend to stay ashore tomorrow if he goes out—and I almost hope a bear gets me. I'm so blue and discouraged and just plain sick—to think Carl would ever talk to me in such language. Jack Brindley came over for a visit, and Carl was in bed. Finally he got up and went right over to *Lindora*, while Jack was still here! After Jack left, I took the skiff (9:00) and rowed up to the head of the bay and back (10:20). Would like to have stayed there all nite. Carl was in bed, snoring—never even missed me. Made a bed upstairs on the seat and bench but didn't do much sleeping. I can hardly cry anymore. I'm just numb to it all.

7/28—Tues.

Carl still drunk and still has fish poisoning. He got up at 3 a.m., and we had a beautiful fight! I went out and sat on the float till 4:00 when I saw Mrs. Chase coming over to the float again, so I went in and shut the door and pulled all the curtains and went back to bed till 9 a.m. when Carl let her in. She came downstairs to see what was the matter with me! I was very rude and would hardly talk. At 10:30 a.m. I washed clothes and went after water. Carl was very sick and very sorry! *[Really?]* 50 gals. gas—$6.00.

7/29—Wed.

Carl still has fish poisoning. We rolled so early this morning that we had to move at 4 a.m. Went back to the scow, but anchored out—so Mrs. Chase wouldn't pester me and so Carl couldn't get anything to drink. Washed clothes, and at last have them all washed up again. Saw a young deer on the beach early. Got water, and visited Mrs. Garleetz on the beach. *[Hazel was getting the water from a stream.]* Made some ice cream. Carl is very contrite. Changed oil in the engine. 5 qts. oil—$3.75.

7/30—Thurs.—5 a.m. to 12 noon

Pulled anchor and started out. Carl's hands are better but still not too good. Lost the skiff as we went out the harbor and had to make two turns to get it. Pretty ruff, and tides were very high. We rolled and rolled, and everything fell over on the floor. I did my first job of cleaning fish today. Took me about 1½ hours to clean 20 fish. Too ruff to do any cooking, so all we had was sandwiches. After 9 a.m. we got very few fish, so we came in at noon. Washed my hair. *Coast* came in tonite. Sold our fish for $12.95.

7/31—Fri.
Gedney to Tebenkoff (Pile Drivers' Cove)

Got up at 4, but a bad wind was blowing, so didn't go out. Lots of other boats stayed in too. Made 2 pies. Went over to see Gladys and Jack Brindley. They were going up to Tebenkoff in late afternoon, so we went too. Saw a mama bear and her cub on the beach. Also saw an eagle sitting on Davis Rock. Wrote letters to Mother and Zellah. Total for month—$707.31.

8/2—Sun.
Gedney to Tebenkoff and return

Left at 5. Didn't know where to go—Tebenkoff or Malmsbury. Finally decided on T. Beautiful day—smooth water. Broke a tag line on the port main pole. Carl got out in the rowboat to fix it. Fished all by ourselves all day. No bread on the scow, so I mixed up some cornbread at noon. When I went to lite the stove, it had a hole in one of the pipes. Carl was too busy to fix it in the afternoon. Finally he got a chance to put in a new burner. Had bread in the oven and our dinner on the stove again at 6 p.m. when we got so busy I had to go out and help. It got pretty ruff too, so at 7 we decided to quit—had fish on all the spoons too. It was 8:30 before we got to the scow. I cleaned all the fish today—126 cohoes and 10 humpies. *[This would have taken Hazel about ten hours according to her entry on 7/30 (1½ hours for twenty fish). It's easy to forget that in addition to the arduous work of catching the fish, they also had to clean them each day.]* Sold for $90.42. Bad leaks all over the cabin in the night.

Hazel cleaning the catch of the day.

8/5—Wed.
Gedney

Another bad day—rain and much fog. Didn't get
up till 9 a.m. No boats went out. Spent the
whole day fixing leaks and drying out wet bedding and clothes. Bad leaks over the canned
food and the bed.

1942 original diary entry

8/6—Thurs.—8:30–5:30 p.m.

Too foggy to go out early, so waited till the fog lifted a little. The fresh water system on the engine got too hot, and the steam gushed out of the tank. Ruff and roll-ey most all day. I got sick a couple of times and went to bed. I woke up, and smoke was coming from the engine compartment! I yelled for Carl—he flew downstairs and yelled at me to pull in the lines. I just got started when he said it was only the belt on the generator, and he fixed it right away. But it was a box of matches—fell off the top shelf! *Pat* gave us some venison tonite, and I gave him a piece of cake and some cookies. Had to come in early on account of fog. No bread at the scow again. I'm still cleaning all the fish. Sold for $22.87.

8/12—Wed.—4:30 a.m.–2:00 p.m.
Gedney to Tebenkoff and return

Left at 4:30 for Tebenkoff. Cold and rainy but lots of fish. Fog commenced to roll in. We thot it might roll away, but it got worse, so we picked up and started for Gedney. I got sick and vomitted all over the place and had to go to bed. We got lost in the fog on the way in—took us about 2 hours to get back to scow. I cleaned most of the fish, then went to bed for the rest of the day. Fish sold for $73.41.

8/13—Thurs.
Gedney

Carl got up at 4:00 but too foggy, so came back to bed till 6. Then he decided not to go out. I was still pretty sick from the day before. Slept till 9:30—got up and had a bath and got breakfast. At 10:30, Carl decided to go out—stayed till 11:45. Only caught one fish, so I canned it—made 8 cans. Fire under the gas dock while we were tied up to it! Jack B. was there too. Fish sold = zero; 50 gals. gas—$6.00.

8/15—Sat.—4:40–5:15
Gedney to Tebenkoff and return

Left Gedney at 4:40 and went to Tebenkoff. Good weather all day and smooth water. Big ground swell in late afternoon. Fished till 3:30—the swells got bigger, and we were both tired, so we quit and came in. Bill Reichwein came in just behind us, so we got paid tonite. I cleaned 150 fish *[eleven hours of work]* and got tired, so Carl cleaned the rest. Sold fish for $121.26. Best day for August!

8/16—Sun.—Storm-bound
Gedney

Got up at 4:30—too foggy, windy, and rainy. Went back to bed and got up again at 6. Wind was still blowing hard, so decided not to go out. Had breakfast and worked on gear. The boats that did go out soon came back. Rained hard all day. Caught enough rainwater to fill tank. Made gingerbread. About 7 p.m., the *Eddy* and *Albatross* came in, sold fish, and tied up to us. We were tied to the *QU*. A williwaw came along, and *QU* broke loose from the float, and we all started to drift. Carl started the engine, and I threw the ropes off. We got loose and went around to the oil-dock side—but the wind was getting worse, so we anchored out. Lit the lamp for the first time tonite.

8/19—Wed.—4:40–6:15
Gedney to Tebenkoff and return

Left at 4:40 for Tebenkoff—right behind the two
Danes. But we got ahead, and were the first ones
over there. The wind almost blew us off the deck,
and the fog settled down all over. We started for
Trollers Island but couldn't make it as the fog
settled too fast. So we turned and started for
Pile Drivers' Cove. But before we got there, the
fog all flew away. Put the lines in about 6:15.
The wind died down some, but it was cold all day.
The sun was bright, and the water smoothed out,
and we caught fish all day. Started for home at
5:20 and had to wait in line to sell to the *Silver
Horde*. May not be able to sell our fish tomorrow—
Reichwein's broke down and no packers available.
If a plane comes by tonite, we sell—otherwise,
no. *[Apparently float planes occasionally take the place of packers if
there's a problem.]* Carl's spark plugs came tonite. Sold
fish for $95.78.

8/20—Thurs.—4:30 a.m.–9:00 p.m.
Gedney to Tebenkoff—then to Malmsbury and back to
Gedney

Left Gedney at 4:30 and went to Tebenkoff. Nice
day—sunshine, but a cold breeze and smooth water.
Good fishing all day. A sea lion followed us for a
long time—took fish off the line and also spoons
and hooks. Carl shot at it but missed on account
of the boat rolling. Cleaned fish all day—too busy
to eat so had Dagwood sandwiches—onion, bologna,
cheese, and eggs. At 4 p.m. we picked up the gear
and started for Gedney—but before we got there,
5 boats came out. We knew the buyer wasn't taking
their fish, so we steered for Malmsbury. Had dinner

on the way. Got to scow (Karl Hansen) at 6:30. *[Karl Hansen was a fish buyer who had a reputation as a kind-hearted, honest guy who never refused credit or help to any fisherman in need.]* Sold, and went over to see Jack and Gladys, who fished at Malmsbury all day for $60. Left Malmsbury at 7 p.m. on our way back to Gedney. Arrived at the mouth of the harbor at 7:45 and at Gedney entrance at 8:45. Bright moon, but it really was too dark to travel. Was glad when we tied up at 9:00. *QU* gave us some venison he and *Pat* got this afternoon. Sold fish for $116.08.

8/22—Sat.—7:30 a.m.–8:30 a.m.
Trollers Island to Gedney

Carl got up at 4, but too foggy, so came back to bed. Got up again at 6:30—too foggy and rainy to fish. Had breakfast and left for Gedney. Lots of purse seiners. Reichwein hadn't arrived yet and still no word from him. Malmsbury has no ice, so they won't buy any more fish. No gas here, and no bread. Cooked the deer meat. Rained hard all day. Bot 4 fish from *Pat* to can.

8/24—Mon.
Gedney

Still sitting here waiting for a buyer! Cleaned and scrubbed the galley, washed floor and some clothes. *[Hazel did a lot of scrubbing of woodwork and floors. It was necessary due to soot from the oil stove, coal dust from the heater stove, and grease in the galley.]* Jack B., *Flo Ann*, and *Dibbles* all went to Malmsbury this morning. Ella Chase asked me how to make bread—also bot some of my Kotex. *Flo Ann* came back again at 8:30 p.m. to tell us there would be a buyer at Trollers Island tomorrow nite. They only made $5.00, and Jack made $7.00. Letters to Mother and Zellah.

8/26—Wed.—4:50–6:00
Trollers Island

Left Trollers Island at 4:50 and went to Ellis Point. *Slim* came by at 7:00 a.m. on his way to Icy Strait. Wanted us to come too, but we had ordered a drum of gas from the packer for tonite. *[This was the first diary entry that mentioned ordering drums of gas. Wonder if it had to do with the rationing of the gas due to the war?]* Fished till 5 p.m.—only had 21 cohoes. Fog, rain, and wind began to roll in, so we headed for the harbor. The *JR* wasn't there, but the *Antoinette* was. Mrs. *Ella C* was sitting on the beach under a tree in the pouring rain. Then she parked herself on the buyer. I made B.P. *[baking powder]* biscuits for dinner—buyer has no bread. Jack B., *Flo Ann*, *Dibbles*, and Franz all left for Security. Sold for $19.91. 50 gals. gas—$6.00.

8/27—Thurs.—5:20–10:30
Trollers Island to Security

Left Trollers Island at 5:20 and went towards Point Ellis. Started to fish at 6 a.m. Fished till 7 a.m. and only caught two cohoes. *June* went by with his poles up, headed toward Security, so we picked up and followed him. We had to go slow, as *June* doesn't go as fast as we can go. We yelled at him, and he said he was going to Point Baker via Rocky Pass; he had never been there before, but he had a large-scale chart. Got to Security at 10:30. Only 5 boats fishing there. We stopped and talked to Happy Jacobson. He had just come down from Sitka. *Pinkie* just came over from Tyee. *Flo Ann* said he was catching as many kings as cohoes, so we decided to go in and talk to Franz. He said Jack B. and *Dibbles* had left that morning for Wrangell. *Elsie* came in from Tebenkoff and said the *JR* would be here late tonite. *Cemae* came in, and Ferguson came over to see us. Just came out from Ketchikan with ice. Has already made $10,000 at Sitka. I made 4 loaves of bread and some cinnamon rolls. Ferguson is going to Pt. Baker via Rocky Pass at 10 a.m. Friday. Wants us to go too. Will see how many fish we have by 10 a.m. Saw a black bear on a rock when we first got into the harbor. Saw three more bears later, looking for humpies.

8/28—Fri.—5:15–2:45
Security

Left at 5:15—first ones out. Not many fish and very cold—North wind. At 6:45 a.m., the *JR* came by and asked us how to get into the harbor. We saved three humpies for the bear. This buyer will be here till Monday morning—then we won't know what to do. Got 2 buckets of water and looked for the bear—but he didn't come down tonight. *[Can't believe Hazel fed the bears—others shot them!]* Lots of new boats here tonite. Just heard there are no fish at Baker. Gave packer letters to mail, to Mother and Zellah. Spent $1.20. Sold fish for $29.93.

8/30—Sun.—5:30 a.m.–3:45 p.m.
Security

Had a good breakfast before we left. About 3 boats out ahead of us. A dull cold day—the wind was like ice. After we sold to the *JR* (Reichwein's scow wasn't there), we tied up to *Flo Ann* to *Ella C*'s wharf. After we had been there a while, we saw *Ella C* coming, so we went out and anchored. But just as they got to the buyers, their clutch broke. Had to anchor right there and skiff their fish to the buyer. *Ella C* had towed the scow, float, and *Lawrence P* to Security the day before and wore his clutch out. Wanted us to tow them to Petersburg! Told them we were on our way to Point Baker. Finally Reichwein came over and got the *Katherine* to tow him to Craig. *Pat* came and towed *Ella C* up to Reichwein's scow. Mrs. *Ella C* stayed with me while Carl tried to work on their engine, and did she rave and rant. *Flo Ann* came over and stayed till dark and told all about the experience. Mr. Franz is leaving for Point Baker in the morning via Rocky Pass, and we will go with him. Sold fish for $38.04.

8/31—Mon.—10:05–5:45
Security to Rocky Pass

Left Security at 10:05 following Mr. Franz thru Rocky Pass. Passed *Jerry* going the opposite way. Mr. Franz went so slow, we only got to the So. end of the pass by 5:45, where we anchored for the nite. Will go in to Point Baker early in the morning. Had Mr. Franz over for dinner. 380 humpies (about 1,900 lbs.), 17 kings (233 lbs.), 1,133 cohoes (9,379 lbs.). Total lbs. of fish caught: 11,512 lbs. Average = 19 days fished @ $58.87. Total hrs. run = 228. Total fish sold: $1,077.41.

9/1—Tues.—5:45–8:30
Rocky Pass to Point Baker to Salmon Bay

Left Rocky Pass at 5:45—had breakfast on the way. Left Mr. Franz because he was too slow. Arrived at Baker at 8:30. Got our mail—included telegram for Carl. His father died July 27th. *[So sad not to know that your father had died until several weeks after the fact! It's also maddening to me that Hazel made no comment regarding the death of her father-in-law.]* There were also three letters for Carl and his draft board questionnaire. I got 7 letters. Got $18 of groceries and $12.00 in gas. Got to Salmon Bay about 3 and started to fish. Saw Hank T. and asked him about fathoms, and he gave us a smart answer. Fished for about an hour, then went in. Tied up to *Lindora*—much beer drinking till late.

9/3—Thurs.—5:30–6:00
Coffman Cove to Snow Pass to Salmon Bay

Left Coffman Cove at 5:30 and followed *Pat* and *Lindora* to Snow Pass. Fished at Snow Pass all day. A whale came up so close to the boat I could throw a book at it. The buyer could not get any salmon cans for me, so guess I'll have to can our deer in glass jars. Went over to Salmon Bay to sell and anchor for the night.

9/5—Sat.—5:30–3:15
Salmon Bay

Left Salmon Bay at 5:30 and went over to McNamara Pt.—followed MacDonald. He was only fishing 7 fathoms *[a fathom equals six feet]*, but Carl passed Al Rhymes, and he was fishing 11 fathoms. So we went deeper too. Pretty good fishing up till noon. Lots of steamers going South—2 yesterday and 3 today. Either a lot of whales or an awful active one is playing around here. He nearly jumped out of the water once. Dull gray day and the wind began to blow, so we went in early—started to rain very hard. No buyer—we waited till dark, but he didn't show up. *Pat* (from Wrangell) tied up to us.

9/9—Wed.—5:50–3:30
Point Baker

Was lazy today and didn't get a very good start. Had breakfast before we left. No fog today, but a cold wind blowing. Not many fish and lots of boats. Both of us very tired, and fish were not biting, so came in early. Made apple pie and had little pigs for supper. Jack Monroe has no ice—can't buy tomorrow unless ice comes from Wrangell. Wanted us to take the fish to Ketchikan—60,000 lbs.! *[I tend to believe this figure is incorrect; however, I re-checked the original diary and that is what Hazel wrote. I'm thinking it should be 6,000 lbs.]* Sold our fish for $54.78. Mailed Sears, Roebuck order.

9/13—Sun.—5:40–7:00
Salmon Bay

Left harbor at 5:40—lots of fog, but not too bad. Went out to Calpoys Point, and the fog got worse and worse. Couldn't see the light, so picked up the lines and started in. The fog settled down all over everything. Followed the shoreline and kelp—got lost—and when we did come to Salmon Bay, didn't recognize it and couldn't see any of the boats till we were almost on top of them. Sure glad to get back. The fog didn't lift till after 1 p.m. *Knickerbocker* and Big Ole came over to see us. Rowed ashore and walked around. Carl tried out some of the old shells that Dad gave him. Buyer left for Wrangell at 7 p.m. Sent our $50.00 check in on the packer—to the bank. [The good old days when people were so trustworthy.]

9/15—Tues.—5:30–3:00

Carl got up at 4 a.m. and turned the radio on! So of course I had to get up too. Had coffee and toast and then left for Calpoys Pt. Sun came out and it was a beautiful day—smooth water. The 3 whales are still with us. Not many fish today. We didn't catch anything the last 2 hours, so at 3:00 we came in. Got 50 gals. gas. Carl dropped one fish overboard when he was pitching to the buyer—one that I had cleaned! Carl had a good time watching all the drunks—*Pat* on the buyer's boat and a hand troller on the beach. Spent $12.60. Sold fish for $26.07.

9/18—Fri.

Wind and rain all night. Got up at 5 and also at 6 but decided it was too stormy. So went back to bed and got up at 8. *[Weather is the most important element in the salmon trolling business. It can make or break a troller. It's a tricky business even with weather conditions at their best.]*

Hotcakes for breakfast. *Knickerbocker* came over to borrow some tools from Carl. Cleaned out the cook stove, and now the darn thing isn't working so good. Canned 3 pints of fishballs and one pint of meatballs. *Knickerbocker* came over for dinner, and I had to scrub the chair with Dutch cleanser after he left. *[This fellow fisherman must have been filthy.]* Made a fire in the Skippy stove, but before I lit it, Carl decided to clean the soot out of the chimney. Such a mess—nearly a bucket full of soot! Fishing is over for the season.

9/20—Sun.—12:10–5:35
Salmon Bay to Ratz Harbor

Very foggy, so didn't get up till 7 a.m. So thick we couldn't tell which was the mouth of the harbor and which was the head. Took a bath and washed my hair. *Knickerbocker* came over and brot us some magazines. Carl went after two pails of water. About noon the fog began to lift, and 4 boats pulled out for Ketchikan. *Lornty* started to leave too, so we decided to follow them. We soon passed the first 4 boats and got behind *Lornty* (but they didn't know the way as well as we did). Our fresh-water system in the engine went hay-wire—pumped hot saltwater out of the pipe in the floor. Had to slow down, and Carl rigged up a hose so it would run into the bucket. Decided to stop at Ratz H. instead of Meyers Chuck. Soon after we anchored, *Helen A* came in, then *Lornty*, and then *Knicker-bocker*. *Lornty* also had trouble with the water system, so came back to Ratz. Smiths came and tied to us, and we talked till 11:30, the latest we had been up for 5 months. One year ago today was our last day at Baker.

9/21—Mon.—12:30–3:00
Ratz Harbor to Meyers Chuck

Up at 7—but too foggy to travel. *Knickerbocker* left early, and *Lornty* left about 8 a.m., but it was still pretty foggy. Fog lifted some at noon, so we decided to leave. Went out at 12:15, but the water system was so bad Carl decided to go back and talk to Olson on the *Ocean*. He had gone hunting, so we left anyway. I kept the tank filled with seawater, and it didn't get any worse, so we kept going. North wind, and the tide in our favor. About ½ hr. before we got to M.C., Carl opened the engine up, and it began to make drinking water. *Helen A*, the *Vag*, and *Motion* were all there at M.C. Mrs. West's boy asked if he could go to K. with us tomorrow—curses! Spent $8.75.

9/22—Tues.—9:45–3:00
Meyers Chuck to Ketchikan

Got up at 7—left M.C. at 9:45 with *Helen A* and Mrs. West's boy. Pretty ruff and windy till we got to Camano Pt. at high tide; then it was smooth all the way to K. Had to pour water in the tank all the way. Got to Thomas Basin at 3:00. Went up town and got our mail—12 letters. Had dinner and then went for a walk.

9/23—Wed.
Ketchikan

Went up town at 9:30. Deposited $1,750 and the $50 check we sent in at Salmon Bay. Bot a new Zenith radio. Did some washing. Harvey I. came by at noon and said Ruth was working at New England, as is Vernie P. Letters from Orie and Lillian. We saw Mr. Hansen of Union Oil Co., and Carl asked him for a job. At 3:30 he came down to the boat and asked Carl to come to work tomorrow morning at 92½ cents per hour. Spent $80.35 (Radio was $75.95). *[This was a significant amount of money to spend on a new radio. In fact, it represented about 3 percent of their entire year's fishing income! However, the radio was the lifeline for Americans in the 1940s—especially residing in Alaska, I would think. It provided news, music, and entertainment, much like television today. Programming included soap operas, quiz shows, children's hours, mystery shows, and sports. Kate Smith and Arthur Godfrey were popular radio hosts. Like the movies, radio faded in popularity as television became prominent. Many of the popular radio shows continued on in television. Red Skelton, Abbott and Costello, Jack Benny, Bob Hope, and Truth or Consequences all had popular shows.]*

9/24—Thurs.

Carl's first day at Union Oil. Fixed him a lunch, and he left at 7:30. Made a batch of cookies and a lemon pudding. Took a bath and walked down to see Carl at noon. Came back and bot some new walking shoes and a bank draft for Lillian. Carl came home at 5:15, and after the dishes, we went for a walk. Stopped at drug store for ice cream, and then went over to Pritchers for a while. Spent $7.70.

9/25—Fri.

Carl's 2ⁿᵈ day at Union Oil Co. Did some more washing. Cleaned out cupboard under the stove and scrubbed the floor. Wrote a letter to Mother. Asked Mrs. Smith *Lornty* about the job at Forest Service on Gravina Island. They had just mailed a letter to *Eena*. If *Eena* doesn't take it, we might. The *Silver Horde* came in late last night bound for Seattle at midnight tonight. Vernie came over. Spent $5.80.

9/29—Tues.

Horrible day—wind—and it rained a regular downpour all day. Carl forgot all his papers for the Union Oil job and his rain cap, so I took them down at 10 (in the rain). Bot a new green umbrella. Went to First National Bank and applied for bookkeeping job and also put my application in at Federal Employment Office. Carl came home at 11:30—had to go to doctor's at 1:30 for Union Oil Co. examination. Made a tomato soup cake. Started to count our canned goods. Spent $3.45.

9/30—Wed.

Another horrible day—rain and wind. Didn't feel so good so didn't do much work. Tony came in at

12 and stayed till 1:45! Went up town between rain showers. Carl came home with a canvas coat that a former employee left—just fits too. Had baked beans, turnips in milk, cabbage salad, and tomato soup cake. Total fishing days = 69. Average $36.06 per day. Total for season: 25,398 pounds = $2,488.87. [*This was the most successful year, monetarily, of all their seven years of fishing.*]

10/2—Fri.

Carl's first day off. Many leaks over bed and around portholes. Rained hard all night. Carl fixed a canvas over the front window. Went to employment office—they sent me to Spruce Mills—talked to Helen Taylor Davis, but the man I was to see was out. Will go back tomorrow. Carl went to Customs Office to have "Ketchikan" changed from "Seattle" on our boat registry. Also bot him some new shoes. Spent $9.78.

10/3—Sat.

Permanent from 9:30 to 1:00. Washed my hair as soon as Carl left for work (7:30), and at 8 a.m. the employment office man came down to the boat to tell me that there was a vacancy at Sears, Roebuck. Went to Spruce Mills at 9. Mr. Daly was out, and the other man said nothing till the end of the month. Sent money order ($1.00) for Customs Office to change "Seattle" to "Ketchikan." Went to Sears office at 1:30 p.m. and saw Miss McDonald—filled out 4 application blanks. I got the job. Miss McDonald told me to come back at 4. Worked from 4 to 5. Mrs. Pratt came over and invited us to a clam chowder supper at Yacht Club at 7. Carl didn't get home till 5:45. Much drinking at the party—so we came home at 12 p.m. Spent $6.86.

10/5—Mon.

First full day working at Sears. About 9 boxes of merchandise came today, and all I did was check and sort packages. Came home for lunch. Carl was home at 5:30 and had a fire started when I got home at 5:45. He went to a defense meeting with Bill Funk at 7. I stayed home and washed some underwear and wrote letters to Mother and Zellah. Letter from Orie. Spent $3.58.

10/8—Thurs.

Miss McDonald from Sears gave me a key to the office. First pay day for me—$16.50 minus $.17 for Social Security = $16.33. First money (wages) I've earned since Game Dept. in June of 1940. Carl was home before I got there. As a special event (pay day), we had frozen fresh strawberries and cream for dinner. Spent $1.70.

10/9—Fri.

Rain and wind. Regular April weather—sun, then some more rain. Carl called me up and said a Union Oil Co. boat was leaving for Seattle and we could order some groceries to come up one month from now. So we ordered 4 cases—1 case Roth's spare ribs, 1 case Roth's Vienna sausages, 1 case Crisco or Snow Drift, and 1 case grapefruit. Bought a newspaper—$.05.

10/10—Sat.

One week ago today went to work at Sears. Ordered groceries and meat to be delivered this a.m. Miss McDonald took her ½ day off. After one week, still

I have not had a day off. Sent order to Sears for Zellah's slip—also Carl's shirts. Carl met me at the store, and we ate at the Model—then went to Coliseum to see *John Doe*. Bobbie Peterson came by at 9:30 p.m. and wanted to borrow a hammer and 2 chisels. Carl hated to loan them, but what can you do! Spent $9.82.

10/13—Tues.

Carl's cold is no better. A cold rainy day too. Only one chisel was returned. Was Carl mad! Cleaned Carl's Army pants in solvent. First blackout since we came back to Ketchikan. Just finished reading *In Alaskan Waters*. Carl went to his Home Guard meeting at 7:30—just before the blackout. Letter from Zellah. Mailed birthday card to Zellah. Carl got his first paycheck—$50.72.

10/17—Sat.

Another awful day. Did some shopping at noon. Carl got our laundry back tonight. Gus gave Carl a drink of gin, and that started things. He left the boat at 7:30 and at 11:45 hadn't come home yet, so I got mad and went to the midnight show at the Coliseum. He passed me on the bridge and didn't even know me. When I came home at 2 a.m., he was here with Lars, both drunk. Went to bed at 3. Spent $16.91 ($9.55 for beer and whiskey).

10/18—Sun.

Rain and more rain till about 9 p.m. when it cleared up for a while. Made a meatloaf and a gingerbread. Carl got up at 3:30 p.m.! Was sicker than a couple of horses. Had <u>another</u> leak over the bed—all the blankets were wet on that side, so I had to dry them all. He came home at 5:40, ate dinner and left—it was 11:50 before he came home again. Ruth and Harvey stopped in for a few minutes at 9:30, and the boat and I were in a mess, as usual.

10/19—Mon.—Alaska Day (Holiday was yesterday, but celebrated today.)

Got up at 6:30—raining, and it had been raining hard all nite. Carl was pretty sick from hangover. I went back to bed and slept till 9 a.m. The sun was shining when I got up, and it didn't rain all day. The paper stated that the lakes had risen 5¾ feet. [Wow!] Ate lunch at the Totem—bean soup, cocoanut cream pie, and coffee for $.55. Bot some woolies—also some cake pans with ring-arounds. Pretty cold today. Mrs. Sogaard came in to tell me that we (Red Cross Nutritions) were to have another luncheon on Saturday and wanted Vernie to come and help! Mrs. Burnette came over and invited us to a party at the Yacht Club this coming Sat. Jimmie Coffman came in to listen to our radio. I have CARL'S COLD! D—! Spent $2.55.

10/25—Sun.

Carl had to help with the scrap gathering from 10 a.m. to 2:30. [Citizens participated in scrap metal drives, usually sponsored by community groups and sometimes by schools, to support the war effort. Americans donated their nonessential goods, and the recycled steel and other materials were used to make ships, weapons, and other tools.] It rained about as hard as I ever saw it—just spilled out of the skies. Received a letter to change "Seattle" to "Ketchikan" on our boat. Carl had his dinner at the Model—so he was not interested in my beans and ham and chocolate cake.

11/4—Wed.

My ½ day off. The water tap was frozen, so Carl had to go way down to the other faucet for water. He filled the large tub so I could do some washing. Also made a 7-min. frosting for the banana cake. Got my watch out (that I dropped on the deck about 2 years ago), and it has run all right so far. Roasted the venison, but it wasn't done—so will have it tomorrow.

11/5—Thurs.

Cold! Cold! Cold!! Ice in the bay all around the boats. Alice had her ½ day off. Carl came home for lunch. We had hot soup and coffee—sure felt good on such a cold day. Got paid today.

11/10—Tues.

Horrible day—rain and wind all day. Carl went to his Guard meeting and came home with a coat, pants, hat, and gun—and he looks like heck in them.

Alaska Territorial Guard

[Alaska was still a territory in 1942. It became a state in 1959. The Alaska Territorial Guard (ATG) was a military reserve force component of the U.S. Army, organized in 1942 in response to attacks on American soil in Hawaii and Alaska by Japan during World War II. The ATG operated until 1947. Carl was a member. (Don't know if I would have wanted him to protect me, as he was usually enebriated!) It was comprised of 6,368 volunteers who served without pay. The ATG served at least two vital strategic purposes to the entire Allied effort during the war: (1) It safeguarded the only source of the strategic metal platinum—an important component of telecommunication equipment—in the Western Hemisphere; (2) it also secured the terrain around the vital Lend-Lease air route between the United States and Russia.]

Carl in his Territorial Guard uniform.

11/12—Thurs.

More and more rain! Fell down in the mud on my way back to Sears at noon today—such a mess! Hurt my shoulder. Carl went to his Lodge tonight with Bill Frink—the first time since we came up here. Pay day for me. We did not get paid for yesterday. *[Armistice Day holiday.]* Letters from Ada, Zellah, and Ella.

11/15—Sun.

Very cold and windy. Began to snow in afternoon, and it stayed on and then froze—awfully slippery. Didn't do much today. Turned Carl's trouser legs up and relined a cap. Then we stored a lot of our fishing clothes in the tin cans.

11/16—Mon.

Cold and snow on the ground. Carl had to help on the oil tanker today—and such a cold wind. Blackout at 7:30—right in the midst of doing the dishes. It lasted all nite. Had to get Tuesday breakfast in the dark. Carl got his check today—too much, so Tom said they will take it out of the next one.

11/19—Thurs.

Snowed in the nite—about 2 inches or so. Pretty ruff and slushy. Had to go down as far as Bon Marche to get across the street. Began to melt about noon, and we sure had a lake. Letters from: Orie, Meisnet (for $10 taxes on boat), and membership card to Bothell Lodge.

11/20—Fri.

Carl's day off. An awful day—just poured all day—and the wind blew a gale. I've lost my umbrella. Carl spent over $10.00 today—and got sort of drunkish. Pritcher sold the *Verle* today for $2,000 plus the *Alona* from Ray Gilner. Carl and I both have colds.

[The Alaskan Highway was officially opened to military traffic on November 20, 1942, when the first truck made the trek from Whitehorse to Fairbanks. The highway was not usable by general vehicles until 1943. It measured about fifteen hundred miles in length. It has been said that the building of the highway was the biggest and hardest undertaking since the building of the Panama Canal.]

11/26—Thurs.—Thanksgiving Day

A year ago we were at Zellah's in Olympia, and now they have moved to Kent. Mother and Dad have sold their place and live in West Seattle, and we are up here! Snowed and rained all day. Made two pumpkin pies, dressing for the chicken, and then began on the chicken. Didn't have a pan big enough—used a frying pan with a dishpan for the cover. Roasted it almost 3 hours, and it was pretty good.

11/28—Sat.

I was so sleepy that I went back to bed as soon as Carl left. Got up at 8:50, and in a few minutes Carl came home! Had slipped and fell on a barrel and was shook up pretty bad—so he came home and stayed till about 10, then went back. Was told that this was his last day at Union Oil! (Probably because of his boozing.) Bot some more Xmas cards at noon, also a magazine subscription for Alan and then ate at the Up and Up. Had to join the d— old Union today for $3.00. Sure was mad at the old gal that came in to "get" me. Carl and I went to see *Louisiana Purchase*—good.

12/3—Thurs.

Snow and very cold. Ran out of oil and nearly froze all day. Awful busy—wore my slacks again today. Didn't feel too good this morning, so didn't eat breakfast. Got paid and got overtime for the 3 hours I worked Tuesday nite. Carl nearly scared me stiff—told me he had lost $40.00—but he found it just before we went to bed.

12/4—Fri.

Didn't go to work till 1 p.m. today. Burned my hand on some hot steam. Blisters on all four fingers on my right hand.

12/6—Sun.

Still cold and snow. Saw about 500 sailors marching from the ship. Carl and I went for a walk and saw a steamer with the bow all stove in. One ship went South and one went North. Too cold, so we came home. The venison that Blackie gave us was tuff. Wrote to Mother.

12/9—Wed.

Rained and thawed all day—sure was a wet mess. Carl chewed some tobacco and swallowed some! Made him deathly sick all nite too. He helped Smith work on the "Army" restroom. Carl bot me some Indian moccasins. He is talking about going to Seattle.

12/12—Sat.

Slept till 10:30—rained all nite. About noon the sun came out, and it was very nice for the rest of the day. I called Sears at 10:30, and Alice wasn't busy, but she needed some change. So I went up and went to the bank for her—that was all I did. Went to Travel Bureau to see about permits to go South—lots of papers to sign, pictures to be taken, thumbprints, etc. Went to Hard Castle to see about reservations, and the 26th of Dec. is the first sailing we can get. Then we went to Coast Guard to see about taking the *Olympic* to Seattle. Blackie came over for dinner and stayed till 1:30. I left them at 7:30 and went to see *Skylark* at the Coliseum.

12/13—Sun.

We didn't get up till about 11:30. Made a batch of pinoche *[candy—similar to fudge, but made with brown sugar]*. Had another blackout from 5:45 to 6:15. Blackie came over and ate with us—in the dark. I took his Hansen's Book and typed the course from Seattle to Ketchikan. Blackie and Carl talked till 1:30—till I finished typing.

12/14—Mon.

Rain and cold. Washed all day. Carl had soup for me at noon. Made another batch of pinoche and packed a box of fudge and pinoche for Mother and Dad. Blackie is trying to talk us out of the idea of taking our boat to Seattle—says we should go on the steamer.

12/22—Tues.

More snow. Worked from 8 to 12, 12:30 to 6, and from 7 to 10. Much more freight today—so busy we had to get a girl to come in and answer the phone. Had Carl's chicken ranch picture framed for him for Xmas. Carl sure has been good about getting meals and washing dishes. Got 8 Xmas cards.

12/24—Thurs.

Still more snow and a cold wind. More freight this morning! Only ½ hour for lunch—worked till 6 p.m. Carl bot a pork roast for tomorrow. More Christmas cards and a package from Zellah with socks for Carl and me—rubber apron and my high school picture for Carl. Card and hankie from Ella. Beads from Maggie and Alice.

12/25—Fri.—Christmas Day

Very tired, so I slept till 11:30. Bad day—snowed, and in late afternoon a Southeaster began to blow, and it blew very hard all nite. Had our dinner about 5 o'clock—pork roast, mashed potatoes, gravy, cranberries, asparagus, and pumpkin pie. Carl was on one of his sprees again—gone all evening and then came home and slept all nite. I got mad and went to see *Dumbo* at the Revilla. *[That will certainly get even with him. Ha!]*

12/28—Mon.

Carl is still "in his cups." I don't know what to do—I'm so discouraged. This has been going on more or less for a month. More freight at the store again today. It snowed some more, too. Joe came to town, and Maggie was very happy! Blackout at 5:45 for 30 minutes.

12/29—Tues.

Still cold and snowing. The sidewalks are one sheet of ice and very difficult to walk on. Carl was in bed all day—too sick to get up. Letters from Clara and Hen. Also from Orie.

12/31—Thurs.

My ½ day off. Nice day—sunshine, but still cold. We got our radio back today from Service Electric Co. Carl is still "in his cups." New Year's Eve, and he is too sick to do anything—except go to bed!

Part IV
1943

Routine Winter

[*At the beginning of Hazel and Carl's third year in Alaska, Hazel was working part-time at the Sears mail-order store. Some historians say that the Sears, Roebuck catalog helped to build the American West. The mail-order catalog was a simple idea in one sense, but it was at the same time a major improvement over the rural general stores many Americans had relied on previously. Sears, Roebuck bought an extensive array of items in relatively large quatities. It then sold its goods at lower prices than local merchants could offer. An interesting note is that when ordering clothes from the catalog, they sent the clothes first and then you paid, just in case they didn't fit. They sure don't do that anymore.*

[*In historical terms, the concept of the Sears catalog was a key event in the evolution of American consumer culture. And it seems that Sears also played a role in the commerce of the last American frontier.*]

1/2—Sat.

No work at Sears today. Didn't do much all day. Slept late. Mailed packages to Mother and Zellah, also Xmas thank-you letters to everyone. Carl was very sick—didn't get up all day. Ed Nygaard gave us some fresh herring.

1/3—Sun.

Carl was a little better today, but still pretty sick. I cleaned up and then read to Carl most of the day. At 2:15 we went to the Revilla to see Lou Costello and Bud Abbott in *Ride 'Em Cowboy*. Good program on radio in evening. Bot the *Seattle Sunday Times* (Dec. 27). *[Note that newspaper delivery is several days late, but this was still a time when newspapers were a primary source of news—especially in-depth news.]*

1/6—Wed.

Worked at Sears today. Raining and very windy. Very high tide at noon—the ramp was straight out. *[A long ramp connected the floats (where the boats were docked) to the upper shore. It needed to be long due to the rising and falling of the tide. When the tide was high, the ramp would be straight out. When the tide was low, the ramp would be almost straight up, with many steps to climb. See picture of ramp, page 82.]* Carl had lunch all ready: chili, tomatoes, and little pig sausages. It was good, too. Went to Revilla to see Wallace Berry in *The Bugle Calls*—in the pouring rain. I crocheted on my hat. *[Hazel was adept at crocheting, tatting, and knitting. She participated in these pastimes in her latter years while watching television—never looked down at her work and never needed to read directions. I learned the basics of crocheting and knitting from her as a young girl. I still possess and treasure several pieces of her handiwork.]*

1/8—Fri.

Started out to be a fair day, but later it rained hard. Carl took a long walk in the rain. Went up to Thompson and Hattrick's at noon and bought me

a pair of rubber boots (men's) for $4.50. Wore
them home in the rain. They look awful, but they
keep my legs and feet dry. Extreme low tide at 9
p.m.—very hard to get down the ramp. It is still
pouring down. Pay day. My first Victory Tax was
deducted today—50 cents.

The Victory Tax

[The idea of taxing citizens to pay for war probably goes back to the Stone Age. In the United States, however, individual income taxes to pay for war did not begin until the U.S. Civil War. The first federal income tax in American history was initiated in August 1861. One of its purposes was to assure the financial community that the Federal (Northern States) government would have a reliable source of income to pay the interest on war bonds.

[Some form of income taxation continued after that, with various political factions supporting or opposing. But in 1916, federal income taxation—more or less in the form we now know it—became a part of the Constitution (the 16th Amendment).

[World War II brought about in the U.S. a sense of shared sacrifice among the citizenry, the likes of which have probably never existed before or since. The so-called "Greatest Generation" made sacrifices not only on foreign battlefields but also on the home front. Although more than sixteen million Americans wore uniforms of their country during WWII, they didn't fight alone. Housewives turned into industrial riveters; youngsters collected scrap metals; gasoline was rationed; families went without many food items.

[And almost everyone paid taxes—with those having the most wealth paying the most taxes (as much as 94 percent of income above two hundred thousand dollars per year). Even those with low incomes were expected to ante up. In 1942, Congress enacted a temporary, two-year Victory Tax. The rate was 5 percent of all income above $624 per year. (An interesting aspect of the tax was that people who paid these taxes were to have their monies refunded to them when the war ended.)

[In 1943, the Victory Tax rate was lowered from 5 percent to 3 percent, and the post-war rebate idea was repealed. (But allowances were made for offsetting deductions, in lieu of the rebate.)

[In 1944, true to its original intent, the Victory Tax was abolished. But that wasn't all good news because the general tax rate was increased. (Congress giveth, Congress taketh away.)]

1/10—Sun.

Got up early so we could put linoleum on down-stairs galley floor. Pancakes for breakfast. A beautiful day—the sun was nice and bright. Would liked to have gone for a walk, but the linoleum must be put on first! Went to the wanigan to lay it out flat for measuring and cutting. Ray Pratt and Mrs. Burnett were there—heard a lot of dirt *[gossip]* about the Yacht Club.

1/11—Mon.—Blackout

Rained some more. Alice had the whole day off. Not much business at the store. Carl bot a $17.50 Skippy stove that burns oil and a $6.00 tank for it from Harbor Hardware. Went for walk and watched the *New Zora* unload herring. Got a few of them for us to eat. A man was in the freezing room and became unconscious while we were there. Blackout from 7:00 to 8:00.

1/12—Tues.

The man that collapsed last nite was Ed Nygaard! He died before the doctor arrived. Haven't heard what was wrong with him. He was a good guy.

1/14—Thurs.

My morning off. Pancakes for breakfast. Made a peach pie and jam tarts; made some spaghetti and cheese *[Macaroni and cheese is better!]* tonite and a gelatin salad. Did some ironing. The iron Blackie sold us for $1.00 wouldn't heat up. Snow again (about 2") and very cold. Started to use ½ Nucoa *[first commercially available margarine]* and ½ butter today. Not bad at all. Expected it to taste much worse. Electric iron—$1.00. Harbor Hardware—$31.68.

1/16—Sat.

Carl took the oil stove back to Harbor Hardware and got our money back—it wouldn't burn. Then he went up to the Exchange and bot a pot-burner for $17.50. *[The Exchange was a combination second-hand shop and outboard motor shop.]* Then he bot an old rusty stove from Winnie from the *Emily R* for $2.75. It will take him a week to clean it up. I baked the cookies this morning and scrubbed all the floors. Had my hair washed and finger-waved. We went to the Red Men's Dance. Not so good—too many kids. I was the only one with a long dress till a Native girl arrived with a canary yellow net. *[Hazel loved those long dresses. Probably reminded her of her socialite days.]* Most of them were in slacks or sweaters and skirts and bare legs with half socks. Came home at 12:00 (Intermission). It was so cold; all the windows were iced. Didn't open a window when we went to bed—too cold. Fireboat broke up the ice around our boats today. *[The Red Men is a men's social club that is still active in Ketchikan. This fraternal organization traces its origins back to the Sons of Liberty at the Boston Tea Party.]*

1/17—Sun.

Got up very late—10 a.m. It was so cold I hated to get out of bed. Winnie was here while we ate our breakfast. Ice in the wash pan; ice all over the windows; icicles on the ceiling. *[I cannot imagine this!!]* They melt and drip on my neck while I'm cooking breakfast! Thick ice all over the bay. Carl had to break it all up around the boat. The fireboat came in and dragged the ice out into the bay. *[The winter of 1943 was reportedly one of the Territory's worst winters in a hundred years.]* Carl had much help in cleaning up the old stove.

Hazel and Carl stroll through an Alaskan downtown. She enjoyed dressing up. Wonder where these clothes were stored on the boat.

1/18—Mon.

Still cold and snow, altho not as cold as Saturday. No icicles on ceiling this morning. Carl was
writing to Orie in Bremerton *[Navy town in Washington
where his brother lived]* when I left for work. Stopped
at beauty shop and had my hair combed and curled
in the back. Very cold at the store. I wore my
slacks with Carl's underwear under them. Carl
bot some weather stripping for the doors to try
to keep some of the heat in. Carl is still working on the old rusty stove. Letter from Mother.
Got paid today —$20.19. And also had to join the
d— old Union for $11.50! $10.00 for initiation
and $1.50 per month, and for what?! Valentines
for Arlene and Alan—87 cents.

1/20—Wed.

5 degrees above *[zero]*. Colder than ever last nite—ice
on everything this morning. So cold it makes you
cry. Carl is still working on the stove. Spring
catalog from Sears today—also card from Montgomery
re: their new spring catalog. Worked on Carl's
gray wool shirt. Washed my tweed suit skirt. *[See
picture on previous page.]* Suppose I've ruined it.

1/21—Thurs.

Still colder—4 degrees above *[zero]* today. Sink
froze up again. Carl cemented the oil stove and
repainted it—also painted the cook stove. Winnie
was over while we ate. She was drunk.

1/22—Fri.

Still cold, although a wee bit warmer. People were
skating on ice between B and C float. Carl bot

some wool underwear, wool shirt, and wool pants. *[Seafaring men were partial to wearing wool, as it was the only material that would retain warmth when wet.]* Also bot 9 lbs. of powdered milk. Maggie's morning off. Also pay day. Trollers meeting at the Yacht Club tonite. *[The Yacht Club wanigan was connected to the floats at Thomas Basin—not far to walk. See picture, page 30.]*

1/23—Sat.

Still cold and icy. A bit warmer, but not much. Mrs. Burnett came over before I went to work and asked us to come over to a clam chowder dinner at the Yacht Club. Carl and I didn't want to go, but we couldn't get out of it very well. We played cards and talked till 12 p.m. Carl went home every half hour or so to keep the fire going. It snowed again in the nite.

1/26—Tues.

Took the day off. Still pretty cold. Carl started in at 9 o'clock to put the new stove in. Had to take out the Skippy, cut down the bench, fasten the stove down, rig up the stove pipe; tube for the oil gauge, etc. It was 5 p.m. before he was ready to lite it. It smoked for a while, but eventually it began to burn—got almost too hot. So Carl turned it down a bit, and then it began to smoke—and no matter what we did, it would not burn. Had all the doors and windows open and nearly froze to death. By 12:30 midnite, Carl gave up in disgust, and we went to bed. So cold we had to get up and put on socks. I did some washing while Carl was "stoving." Tried to bake some spuds, and the gas stove went out about 3 times. By 7 p.m. the spuds

were not cooked, but we ate them anyway. Carl put
in a new burner in the cook stove.

1/27—Wed.

Still cold and snow and ice. Went to work at 9:30 as
usual. As soon as I left this morning, Carl began
to tear the stove out; decided to turn it around,
but it was too hot. Bob was here to help him. Carl
found a wad of newspaper in the chimney—no wonder
it was smoking so. It burned much better. But Carl
is not satisfied with the stove pipe arrangement so
will tear it all out again tomorrow! Still working on my dim-out curtains. Making them for some
of the other boats as no one seems to have a sewing machine but me. It's a little different making
them to fit windows for boats.

1/30—Sat.

Snowed all day. Poor day at the store—about the
worst since I've been there. My salary is now 65
cents per hour with my raise. *[Federal minimum wage in
2009 is $6.75/hour; Alaska's minimum wage is $7.25/hour.]*. Carl put
linoleum all around the stove and on the floor in
our closet. Vernie Pritcher bot a fur coat today
from Sears.

1/3l—Sun.

Got up late. Rained all day. I worked all the day
on the forecastle *[raised deck at the bow of a boat]*—scrubbed
all the woodwork and windows. Took all the clothes
out of the tin cans and rearranged them all and
relabeled the cans. Cleaned everything off the
shelves and cleaned up all the soot that had accu-
mulated—such a mess. Scrubbed the floor, also the

cabin floor. Carl and I went for a short walk in the rain. Before I went to bed, I had a good hot bath in my rubber tub.

2/3—Wed.

My ½ day off. Made an appointment for 10:30 at Colonial for a finger wave. Got up early and washed my hair right after breakfast. When I got up there, with my hair still wet, she couldn't take me because her furnace was not going and no heat and no hot water. Went to "Eva's" and to "Center"—but they were both full. So went to Champion and bot a pair of black slippers. Then went home and made a chocolate cake; had lunch and went to work. After supper tonite, we went to the Coliseum to see *To Be or Not to Be* with Jack Benny and Carol Lombard. Snowed in the night, and everything was all covered again. Letters from Mother and Orie.

2/6—Sat.

Had morning off so had a finger wave at Colonial at 9 a.m. Snowed all day. Not much business at the store before the freight arrived at 3:30. Bot a new *[mechanical]* pencil from Sears—hope it arrives before I quit. Went to see *Riders of the Purple Sage* at the Coliseum. Much snow when we came home. Spent $13.31 today.

2/7—Sun.

12" of snow all over everything this morning. Carl had to shovel it all off before breakfast. Mrs. Wilson and Mrs. Gill came by for me at 1 p.m., and we all went to the stork party for Margaret McCombs on the bus. Had to wear my rubber boots and carry my new shoes in a bag. About 15 women there—only knew 6. I gave Margaret a knitted soaker I made. *[A soaker, or pilcher, is a 3-corned baby garment that is placed over a diaper.]* I won at Bingo—an address book to carry in my purse. Loads to eat—sandwiches, nut bread, salad, potato chips, chocolate cake, and white cake. Several of us came home in a taxi—too much rain. Spent $.55 today.

2/9—Tues.

Blizzard! Cold North Wind all day—and williwaws. Almost blinds a person to walk. Kids are sledding on the hill down from Revilla Apts. Carl went to his Guard meeting tonite. Stayed home and wrote letters to Mother and Dad, Zellah and Alan. Spent $1.40 today.

2/10—Wed.

Awful wet sloppy day. Had to wear rubber boots. Fairly busy at the store. Carl had lunch ready at noon. He used some fish cakes that I had canned but did not pressure cook. I wouldn't let him eat them, so he was very much peeved at me. Carl got some groceries at Ferry's—thru the blackout entry. *[During the blackout times, the late Ted Ferry told of building a blackout entrance to Ferry's Food Store on the curve of Water-Tongass Avenue so that customers could come into and out of the store after dark without leaking any light. (June Allen,* SitNews*)]*

2/11—Thurs.

Wet, rainy day. *Prince* boat did not come in—is due at 7 p.m. tonite. Brot home 4 wallpaper books from Sears. I might paper the lower cabin with it. *[Ever hear of anyone wallpapering a fishing boat? The finished product* *would be interesting to see—using books of <u>samples!</u>]* After dinner we went to see Bob Hope in *My Favorite Blonde*. Carl bot some groceries at Ferry's Food Store. Spent $15.11.

2/16—Tues.

Rained most all day. A bad thunder and lightning storm about 6:30 p.m. or so. Carl bot fuel oil for oil stove. Resigned from Sears today—to take effect on April 1ˢᵗ. *[Surprised Hazel is resigning this early as fishing season doesn't start for a few months. However, Carl is expecting a check from the sale of his chicken ranch soon, so perhaps she can afford to quit early.]* Bob came over about 7:45, and we played pinochle. Carl came up to the store and nailed some tin over the rat holes. Spent $10.68.

2/20—Sat.

Nice sunny day—and warm. Not much business at the store. Carl received a check from Bremerton for $400.00 (from sale of chicken ranch), also a letter. Mrs. Gill gave us a little black puppy. Guess we'll have to give him away—no place for a dog on a boat. Went to see *Twin Beds* at Coliseum. Had a blackout while at show. Spent $14.68.

2/21—Sun.

Another nice day. Cleaned and scrubbed. Did some ironing. Mr. Peterson came after the dog. Sure hated to let him go. He was so good—didn't cry at all last nite. Vernie gave Carl a hair cut. Spent $25.00.

2/24—Wed.

Another nice day—almost too good to be true. No business at the store. Maggie and Alice started to paper the back room. Sent a bottle of toilet water to Mother and shaving set (soap, talcum, and lotion) to Dad. Sent $1.00 in war stamps to Alan and some eagle feathers and $.25 stamp to Arlene. Spent $12.50.

2/25—Thurs.

Still nice weather. We are still getting up at the crack of dawn for Pratt—and he never comes. Not much business at Sears. Maggie and Alice are still papering the store—but not me! The new girl from the 10-cent store will begin about March 8. She will start for more money than I am getting now—after 6 months. It's the nertz! Spent $1.61.

2/26—Fri.

Still good weather, although some fog till about noon. Maggie and Alice are still papering. Not much business at the store. Bot a red sweater from a refused C.O.D. Pay day. We did not get paid for working on the 22nd—Washington's Birthday! *[Interesting that Hazel got no pay for a national holiday. Today one receives EXTRA for working on a national holiday.]* That's Sears for you. Spent $10.45. Total spending for Feb.—$210.41.

3/2—Tues.

Still good weather. Maggie's ½ day off. She is getting very cross. Most everything I do doesn't suit her. Will be glad when April 1st comes. Wilma H. (the new girl) came in to talk to Maggie today. I don't like her! Carl did more painting—anchor, chain, also roof of pilothouse. He went to Guard meeting tonite. Spent $5.40.

3/3—Wed.

Mother and Dad's birthday. *[Hazel's parents—my grandparents—were born on the same day, though my grandfather was one year older than my grandmother.]* Not much business at the store. Carl is working on the letters to spell "Ketchikan" to put on back of boat. Mr. Nunan of New England Fish Co. came to see how I was getting along with the Red Cross soliciting at the Basin. *[Thomas Basin, their homeport, was one of four docking ports in Ketchikan in the '40s.]* As evenings are "the only time I have," I suggested Mrs. Burnett take my place. She was glad to help, so I turned all material over to her. We went to see the Coast Guard Glee Club sing at Coliseum at 9:30. Not so good, but the show was better than I thot it would be. Spent $15.62.

3/4—Thurs.

Still good weather. Not much business at the store. Carl is still painting—roof, side lites, etc. Letters from Zellah, Katy, and Totem Mfg. Co. At 8:30 a U.S.O. show at the high school—we went and enjoyed it a lot. The best thing we've seen since we've come to Alaska.

[The United Service Organization (U.S.O.) is a civil group that provides morale and recreational services to U.S. troops throughout the world. It has been in continuous operation since 1941. U.S.O. centers opened around the world as a "Home Away from Home" for GIs. The local U.S.O. was a place to go for dances and social events, for movies and music, for a quiet place to talk or write a letter home, or for a free cup of coffee and treats. (I remember taking home-baked cookies to our local U.S.O. club with my mother.)]

[From 1941 to 1947, the U.S.O. presented more than four hundred thousand performances, featuring entertainers such as Bing Crosby, Judy Garland, Bette Davis, Frank Sinatra, Glenn Miller, and most famously, Bob Hope.]

3/6—Sat.—Alan's birthday (8 years old)

I hope Alan got his eagle feathers OK. Still good weather, although not as warm as it has been. 16 crates of freight came in this morning at 9:30. Our generator came. Pork steaks for dinner. Carl did some more painting on the boat. 4 weeks from today will be my last day at Sears, thank goodness. Spent $15.65.

3/9—Tues.

Not such a good day, some rain. Very cold at the office. Alice was informed today by Sears that she cannot work for 4 months after the baby arrives. So-o-o-o, if I was going to continue to work, I'd be assistant manager at $30.00 per week plus a bonus. Threw one of my good forks overboard with the dishwater. First time I've done such a stunt. Went to Coliseum to see *Sea Wolf*. Spent $6.70.

3/10—Wed.

Rain. My ½ day off. Got up late. Worked on income tax. Carl paid the tax with a P.O.M.O. *[Post Office Money Order]*. Maggie sure was mean today. Will be glad when I'm thru. Blackie came over at 10 and stayed till 11:30. We ate ½ of the cake I just made. Carl is drinking too much beer. Spent $182.95. (Income tax was $180.36.) *[Hazel and Carl's 1942 income from fishing was $2,488.87. They had other periodic small amounts of income.]*

3/13—Sat.

More snow and rain. Not so busy at the store. Carl's back is on the bum again. Guess he twisted it when working in the hold. He was not here when

I got home tonite. Waited and waited, and finally about 6:30, he came in—very drunk. And he went to bed immediately. I threw a bottle of beer and a bottle of whiskey in the bay. I was mad and left. Went to the Model and ate a $.90 dinner, then to Coliseum to see *Holiday Inn*. Carl was mad at me when I got home. Spent $23.65. (Bot a skiff from Blackie for $20.00).

Hazel and Carl in their skiff.

3/14—Sun.

Got up late. Snow, and then sunshine. Put a "for sale" sign on our skiff *[the small boat in which they're sitting, in the photo]*. Kelsey on the *June* came by and said he wanted it and would pay for it next week. Made an apple pie and some scalloped spuds. Carl and Blackie went for a ride in the new boat and broke the steering bar on the outboard motor. Put some heat on Carl's back, but it didn't seem to help much. Wrote 3 letters.

3/16—Tues.

Still cold—but no rain. Ice in the Basin again this morning. Carl's back is a little better. He worked all day on the new skiff—painting and repairing. My cookbook from Sears came. Sent 2 old wallpaper catalogs to Arlene. *[I used them for art projects.]* Spent $4.18.

3/18—Thurs.

Nice day, but cold. Carl painted the inside of the skiff. Went for a walk after supper—saw the 11 new crash boats at Float D.

[Ketchikan was a base for a squadron of Coast Guard crash boats. They were basically rescue boats that provided assistance to mountain climbers, seriously ill tugboat crewmembers who needed transportation to shore hospitals, emergency calls to weather and radar stations, and aircraft emergency ditching calls. Sometimes aircraft would run out of fuel and need a tow. Some of the boats had to go out to sea just to provide a radio signal to be used as an approach beacon so aircraft could get down to sea level to find their way onto a field. The crash boats also spent their nights patrolling offshore on the lookout for Japanese submarines and their days hauling passengers and mail between Annette Island and Ketchikan.]

3/23—Tues.

Snowed off and on all day. Ran out of heating oil again at noon and nearly froze before some more arrived. My Montgomery Wards catalog arrived today. Carl had too much beer again. He went to his Guard meeting, and then he and Mr. Morf of the First National Bank went on a drinking bout afterwards and didn't get home till 11:30. I went to the Coliseum to see *Road to Zanzibar* with Bob Hope and Bing Crosby. Spent $16.48.

3/24—Wed.

And it still snows. Carl put up the windshield swipe—and drank too much beer. He received a letter from Bothell Bank and a check for $3,273.11. *[The check was Carl's share from the sale of the family chicken ranch. It certainly was a sizeable amount—close to twice as much as their last year's fishing income.]* He should have been pretty excited about that much money, but in his condition it didn't even register.

3/26—Fri.

Still more snow—and a strong wind blowing. Maggie's ½ day off. Carl and his pals are still at it. I wanted to go to the U.S.O. show tonite, but Carl was in no condition to go any place. I'm getting awfully fed up with such doings. Pay day. Only one more left. Spent $3.83.

3/27—Sat.

Wilma's ½ day off. Cold and windy—snowed some. Took some time off in late afternoon to do some shopping. Rube McCombs came in and ordered a highchair for their 5-day old baby girl! Carl sold some old rope for $5.00. Vern Hale came over from Annette with the bodies from the plane crash today. *[These bodies from Annette Island were from a well-known crash that occurred on January 5, 1943. A book,* Hearts of Courage *by John Tippets, recounts the fascinating story of the survivors' thirty-three-day grueling ordeal—during one of the Territory's worst winters in a hundred years.]*

4/1—Thurs

Rained most all day—cold. Maggie didn't show up till 12:45. The new girl, "Tempa Swan," came at 12:15. I was alone and didn't know anything about it. Maggie sure was mean today—jumped all over me—especially so when the new girl would ask me anything. Tomorrow is my ½ day and my last! My knobby knitter came today. Carl went to dentist for his repaired upper plate. The guy was drunk and didn't show up for work, so no teeth till tomorrow. Spent $2.25.

4/2—Fri.

Last day at Sears—thank goodness! Rained hard all nite—several leaks and wet bedding. Maggie never said a word about me leaving—good or bad. Alice Hale had a baby boy at 5 this a.m. (6 lbs. 6 oz.). Spent $27.01 including $3.50 for whiskey.

4/3—Sat.

Carl got up about 7 and went for a walk, then over to Blackie's and drank tea till I got up (9 a.m.). After breakfast, Carl went to the dentist to get his uppers back. I scrubbed and washed dishes, tried to fix the pillows, did some mending, sprinkled clothes. At 2:30, Carl and I started out for a walk and ended up on a spending spree. Carl was very sick after dinner so I gave him a bath, and he went straight to bed. Tried my new frying grill—it works fine. Spent $48.14. (Carl's tooth—$7.50.)

4/6—Tues.

Very rainy and blowy—blew the oil heating stoves out a couple of times. Had pancakes for breakfast on my new griddle. Went to hospital to see Alice Hale and Margaret McCombs and their new babies. Carl bot some wood to make a silverware drawer to go under the table. Gus gave us a big hunk of halibut, and I gave him a piece of rhubarb pie. Letter from War Board—Priority for boat.

[The National War Labor Board was created by President Roosevelt, by executive order on January 12, 1942. The Board was established to determine procedures for settling disputes that might affect war production. The Board had the options of offering mediation, voluntary arbitration, and compulsory arbitration to try to resolve controversies but had no power to enforce its decisions. It was also authorized to approve all wage increases, where the total annual remuneration was below five thousand dollars.]

4/7—Wed.

Coast Guard Laundry caught on fire at 4 a.m. The whole building and furniture store next to it burned completely. The flames shot 50 to 75 feet in the air, even in the rain! *[I recently spoke with an elderly acquaintance from my hometown in Escondido, California, regarding this Coast Guard Laundry fire in Ketchikan. She related to me that her first husband died in this fire. Following is a copy of the letter from his commanding officer, explaining the fire and his death.]* Carl bot me an Easter present—an Alaskan pillow top. More of a peace offering, I think.

[Following is a copy.]

ADDRESS REPLY TO:
DISTRICT COAST GUARD OFFICER
ALASKA SECTOR, THIRTEENTH NAVAL DISTRICT
KETCHIKAN, ALASKA. AND REFER TO FILE No. ___73___

OFFICE OF
DISTRICT COAST GUARD OFFICER
ALASKA SECTOR
THIRTEENTH NAVAL DISTRICT

UNITED STATES COAST GUARD

Ketchikan, Alaska
12 April 1943

Mrs. Hanna Lea Olsson
1700 Pacific Avenue
Manhattan Beach, California

Dear Mrs. Olsson,

It is difficult for me to inform you of the tragedy that overtook this command that took the lives of three of our finest young men, among whom was your husband, Leonard, on Thursday, 8 April, 1943. He had turned in at midnight after coming off watch. When the fire was discovered at 3:50 o'clock that morning, he was called by the watchman. He was trapped while aiding in calling the other men who were asleep. The smoke had become very dense, preventing him from finding his way to safety. However, those he had awakened did get out. He died in the service of his country while performing this duty. The officers and men of this command have keenly felt this loss and salute him.

At two o'clock this afternoon we all paid final tribute to your husband by the military section of the Ketchikan Cemetery. It is very hard to express the feelings of myself and his comrades in this letter, but I wish to say that there was no finer, more gentler or manlier man in my command. In this, your great hour of trial please accept our condolence.

Most sincerely yours,

E. A. ZEUSIER, Captain, USCG
District Coast Guard Officer,
Ketchikan, 13th Naval District.

4/8—Thurs.

Nice day. Did some washing. Mrs. Gill gave us
some clams and some parsnips. Mert gave us some
salmon. Went up to look at the fire—a horrible
tragedy. Bot some aluminum ware from Mrs. Burnett
for $5.00—a whole apple box full. Letter from
Zellah. Spent $9.50.

4/9—Fri.

$5.00 more of aluminum ware from Mrs. Burnett. An
electric iron and an electric waffle iron—besides a
lot more. Asked them over tonite for clam chowder.
They can't eat anything in aluminum, so I borrowed
her cooking dishes. Crazy Dutchman's boat sank in
the harbor today! Don't know why yet, but lots
of speculation around here. Letter from Lillian.
Spent $8.05.

4/11—Sun.

Tried to have waffles on Mrs. Burnett's iron. Not
hot enough, so had hotcakes instead. Carl asked
Bill Fredericks to have dinner with us, but after
I got everything ready, he wouldn't come. We
had baked salmon, cheese sauce, baked potatoes,
rhutebeggers, [rutabagas are root vegetables] and cookies.
About 9:30 p.m., Judd Cheaver arrived—from his
Standard Oil barge—so drunk! We had to go up to
the Shamrock and then to his boat. Spent $10.00
($5.00 for beer, etc.).

4/13—Tues.

Carl is still on a bender—worse today. Didn't eat
any breakfast and left as soon as he got up. Came

back about 11, and we went for a ride in the out-board. Got out in the middle of the Channel, and it stopped. I had to row all the way back. Carl worked on the outboard for a while—then left and went up town. I got dinner ready, but he didn't come home. I went to the Library and stayed till 6:30. Went to the Revilla. Carl was horsing around all that time.

4/19—Mon.

Carl kept me awake most of the night. After he got up (5:30) I went back to sleep and didn't get up till 9:30. Did some washing. Rainy, cold, windy day. Bot 6 yards of black satin for window shades. Had our dinner at 6—then went for a walk. I went to Revilla to see Spencer Tracy in *Tortilla Flats*. When I got home at 9:15, Carl was gone. Door was padlocked—and I had no key. Had to sit on hatch and wait till Carl got home at 10 p.m. Very cold and windy, and I was freezing cold. Letter to Zellah. Spent $6.60 ($5.00 for beer).

4/20—Tues.

Carl kept me awake till 3:45—then got up at 7. I stayed in bed till 10:00. Dick Hogden from Marine Hardware asked Carl to come up and put seals on his liquor stock, so I went up to help him. We ate breakfast at the U and I, then worked till 12:30 when we ran out of stickers. Carl went to bed and slept for 3 hrs. I did some more washing. Mrs. Burnett came over for a while. Cold with rain and wind. Spent $22.95.

4/21—Wed.

Rain, rain. All night and all day. Wrote letters to Mother and Zellah. Took Ella's needlepoint to cleaners to be steamed for framing. Mrs. Burnett came over at 6 p.m. and wanted me to go to the show with her. She paid my way—$.60 beginning today. *[Movie prices in 2009—ten dollars.]* She came home and had coffee and doughnuts with us. I took her home, and she showed me her new hat, dress, and slack suit. Charlie hasn't got his pay yet, and she needs about $100.00. I offered to loan her that amount. She said she'd come over in the morning and see Carl. Check for $9.90 from Sears for 1st prize in vitamin contest. *[Wonder how this contest was conducted.]*

4/23—Good Friday

Nice day, but cold. Did some painting in galley. Went to Library and read *Cosmopolitan* all afternoon. Bot a corsage for my coat. When I came home at 5 p.m., Carl was here with a Canadian Air Force man—both drinking. Pauley came in tonite and told us that his wife was getting a divorce. Blackout tonite from 9 to 9:30. When I was in the Bon Marche today, Mr. Pool gave me my withdrawal slip from the Union. Spent $1.50.

4/25—Easter Sunday

Got up at 8:30—another beautiful day. Got all dressed up in my new Easter hat and gloves. Carl and I went to Methodist Church, but Carl wouldn't stay. Went outside and waited till I came out. Carl's Canadian soldier boy came down and waited till Carl came home. After dinner we went for another walk.

4/26—Mon.

Beautiful day again. Got up at 11:30. Did some more painting. Cleaned and straightened up the forecastle. After supper we went for a walk—stopped at the Stedman and had a few drinks and danced a waltz. Got home at 10 p.m. Afterward, Carl went to Shamrock and got home at 11:30, and was I mad! Bill Fredericks and *Pat* came in from Meyers Chuck with 1,100 and 900 lbs. Letter from Zellah. Spent $14.00 ($4.00 for drinks).

5/5—Wed.

Rained and sun shone on and off all day. Lee Harbrough came by and left us a can of moose meat—very good. So we asked him over for supper. Made some bread from Macca yeast that was a year old. Mr. and Mrs. Jim McDonald came over and spent the evening. Two boys on an Everett boat came and tied up next to us. They had a fire yesterday and were cleaning up the mess, and it sure is a mess too. Mr. Faires, the deaf man, came over and gave us a candy bar. Mert came by—pretty well oiled—and offered to loan us $20.00 if we were broke!

5/6—Thurs.

Nice day. Carl worked on tiller chain. Went to OPA office *[Office of Price Administration]* to see about sending some of my canned salmon to Mother and Zellah. Also to Express Office to see about rates—would be about $2.00. After our dinner we went over to see Mr. and Mrs. Smith on the *Lornty*. He broke his ankle this morning and will have to have it in a cast for 2 months. He tripped over some rope on the dock. Received birthday cards from Mother,

Zellah, and Ella. A prospector wanted to buy our boat today. He was serious.

[The OPA oversaw the rationing of products—certain foods, rubber, gasoline, etc.—during the war years.]

5/9—Sun.—Mother's Day

Felt much better today. Nice day, so we tried out the outboard again. It was pretty ruff. Two steamers were going and coming, so we came back. Went to the ballgame, and Carl "muffed" a homerun. Felt kind of sorry for him since he was such a good player when he was in his prime and sober! *[In his younger days, Carl played for the Seattle Indians, a Triple A farm team.]*

Ketchikan's baseball team competed against players from other parts of Alaska and Canada. The town of Ketchikan was originally built on pilings, and there was no flat area for a ballpark. Their baseball field, in the early 1900s, was part of the tide-flat. When the tide returned, homeplate was under twelve feet of water. Note the spectators, dressed in suits and standing. In 1931, the U.S. Corps of Engineers dredged this site to create Thomas Basin. This was the homeport of Hazel and Carl's Olympic. (Photograph from Ketchikan Museums.)

Stopped at Ruth's—had coffee and doughnuts. Came home with arm loads of magazines. Had fresh salmon for our dinner—that *Jerry* gave us.

5/12—Wed.

Got up at 8:30 and as soon as we had breakfast we went over to Whiskey Cove. Visited with Wilsons, Gills, and Johnsons—had 2 meals. Came home at 4:30 with daffodils, carrots, and rhubarb. After our lunch, I went to the Health Center to a fish demonstration—smoked fish, canned fish, etc. We are thinking very seriously of buying the place next door to the Gills on Pennock. A one-room shack and a strip of land—all cleared—for $300.00.

5/15—Sat.

Another beautiful day. After breakfast, Carl decided we should do some painting. Painted green from the rail down to the guard—black on rail and guard and gray on inside of guard. Went for a ride in the kicker, but too ruff to go out in the channel. Bot some groceries and meat. Took our baths and went to bed but not to sleep—ate candy bars in bed at 2 a.m. Spent $5.60.

5/17—Mon.

Still good weather but not as nice as yesterday. All ready to leave for Whiskey Cove to go on the cradle when Tom Barnaby came over. He told us the *Josephine* just about wrecked everything going off the cradle last nite, and we would have to wait till midnight. Then later Mrs. Wilson came over and said we couldn't go on till noon Tuesday. So Carl got in the skiff and painted the green on the boat above the water line. Mrs. Wilson took our skiff across with her as her gas boat wasn't working too good. Packed up all our good clothes and extra things in suitcases and cartons. Will leave them at Wilsons' for the summer. Letter from Mother.

[I find my aunt's diaries at once fascinating and frustrating. They provide, in one sense, a detailed glimpse of day-to-day life in the commercial fishing community in Southern Alaska in the 1940s. They also merely hint at so much of an adventurous segment of my aunt's life, and in that sense, they fail to deliver the goods. Her factual entries are like a skeleton that never fleshes out. I want to read, in her own terms, Hazel's joys and triumphs and agitations and provcations—in short, her soul translated into written words.

[But what I'd like is not there—at least not directly. I find echoes of my aunt's emotions, but so much is left unsaid. So I suggest that as you read these pages of diary entries, you do as I did—read between the lines.

[Here is an example of what bothers me, this entry on May 18, when a fellow fisherman's boat is destroyed. Boating disasters—ships sinking in storms or catching on fire—are part of life at sea, especially in Alaska. But I'd love to know what was going on in my aunt's head when she wrote this entry.]

5/18—Tuesday
Ketchikan to Whiskey Cove

Raining! It would be, when we are all ready to go on the cradle. The *Brownie* fell over on the grid last nite, tore off his keel, and everything was wrecked! So he sold the whole works to Pritcher for $100.00! We bought the groceries @ $.10 per can—½ gal. of Wesson oil, 1 can molasses, 6 small cans of milk, and the rest (65 cans in all) were corn, string beans, and peas. We left Ketchikan at 12 and went rite on the cradle. Carl and I scrubbed

the bottom (still in the rain). Then Carl worked
on the rudder. And so—home to bed at 10 p.m. Had
to turn our bed around, as our heads were lower
than our heels. *[They're spending the night while on the grid.]*
Letters to Zellah and Mrs. McDonald.

[Here was a literal shipwreck but one in which rainwater, not a turbulent ocean, caused the calamity. The loss of the Brownie *almost certainly meant a turning point in the man's life—perhaps the end of his career as a fisherman. And yet my aunt—a kind and caring woman—accounted for the incident in terms of the benefit for her and Carl—a windfall of food, "(65 cans in all) were corn, string beans, and peas," at a great price. And then she finished off the entry as just another day—closing with a comment about going to bed after having written letters to her sister and a friend.*

[The Brownie *and its former owner were now gone—from the diaries and, apparently, from Hazel and Carl's life. She never mentioned him again. This is maddening to me. Where did he go? How did he cope? Did Hazel and Carl ever hear from him—or at least of him—again? He dissipated as if he were smoke in a high wind.*

[About the only time Hazel's diaries show genuine emotion is when she expresses anger about Carl's drunkenness and attendant bad behavior. And even then, the entries give sparse mention of what she truly must have felt. This meagerness seems so much in contrast to Hazel's statement to me that she "bared her soul in those books."

[I don't think that Hazel was lying; I think that, instead, she used her journals as a sort of personal shorthand—not a full-fledged description of events she wished to share with someone else but, rather, memory's aids, notes that triggered personal emotion, thoughts, recollections—good and bad, happy and sad. There has to be so much more to Hazel's story. Details. Sentiments. Sensations. Curiosity. Wonder. But like the wrecked Brownie, *all of that and more are irrecoverably lost.*

[In a way, Hazel's staccato style is symbolic of the shallowness with which we often perceive others. I knew and loved my aunt, and yet I find so little of her warmth, her charm, her character in her diaries. I know that

there was much more to my aunt than she captured in her writing. Fascinating in a historical sense, her factual entries, for the most part, lack in perception. Her journals show the shell but not the substance of the person. And because she died without adding more and delving deeper into the intellectual and emotional aspects of those incredible years, a goodly portion of my aunt is lost forever. I must assume this is as she intended it, and perhaps her holding back represents a kind of metaphor for the transcience of life itself.]

5/20—Thurs.
Whiskey Cove back to Ketchikan

Still raining. I painted the main poles while Carl painted, and when I finished the poles, I helped copper paint. *[Copper painting of the hull was usually the last chore the fisherman performed before going to sea. An interesting aside is that the copper paint was toxic and they probably were wary of breathing it for fear of getting sick.]* Mrs. Gill gave us some potatoes and some currant jelly. Mrs. Wilson gave us some kippered salmon *[dried or smoked]*. We went off the cradle about 1:30 and came back to Ketchikan. Carl got too much beer, as usual. Letter from Orie. Letter to Lillian and package to Arlene.

5/21—Fri.
Ketchikan

Still raining. A bad storm last nite and not much better today. *[This rain business must have gotten very old—it has rained steadily for several days.]* Carl is still at it! Had a nice dinner all ready at 7 p.m., and he didn't come home till 7:30. So I went to a show and left him on the bed! *[As if he cares.]* Saw *Rise and Shine*. When I came home, he was gone—and had not eaten his dinner! Was I mad! Bot 5 lbs. of powdered milk for $3.55 at the Olympic Bakery on my way home from the show. Spent $3.95.

5/22—Sat.

Some rain and some sunshine. Washed my hair. Went to town and did some shopping. Oil cloth $.45, note book $.15, gingham $.30, hair bow $.50, rickrack $.25, candles $.20, dinner mats $.30, magazines $.35, scrub brush $.10, cheese $1.00, chili con carne powder $.15, napkins $.25, marshmallows $.28, cauliflower $.25, green pepper $.10, and frozen string beans $.35 cents. Carl is still at it—came home very polluted.

5/23—Sun.

Rain and sunshine—also windy. Carl is still at it. Left this morning at 7:30 and never came home till after I left at 12:45. I went for a long walk. Had coffee and pie at Stedman and then went to the Revilla. Home at 5 p.m. Carl was in a drunken stooper *[sic]*. We had dinner, and he went back to bed. At 10:15, he got up and went back to the Shamrock—so he said. It was 12:30 before he came home again—very drunk. He sure is a mess, and I'm getting more and more disgusted each day. Wish there was something I could do about it besides just crying, but what can I do when he will stay home only long enough to sleep.

5/24—Mon.

Still raining and blowing. Carl left early before breakfast—never came home till 12:30. Slept a while and then left again. Said he would be back in half an hour. I went up town, mailed some letters, bot some things. By 3:30 when Carl did not come home I got good and mad—went up to bring him home. He was eating at U and I with Jerry, Gus, and Louis. I dragged him out and back to the boat—put him to bed and hid all his trousers so he couldn't leave the boat. Then I went for a walk and mailed some more letters. When I got home, here was Carl all dressed up in my slacks! Of course he couldn't fasten them around the waist. I made him take them off and he went back to bed—and I kept him there all nite. Wrote 5 letters. Letter from Orie.

5/25—Tues.—Arlene's birthday (6 years old)

Carl is still in his cups. Had to go up to the Shamrock and drag him home. Received a letter from Zellah (with one from Aunt Flora); also a deed from Henry Stone for Carl to sign. Did some typing for A. A. Woodward. Carl and I went for a walk and visited all the beer parlors on our way home.

5/26—Wed.
Ketchikan—Whiskey Cove—Meyers Chuck 1:00–5:20

Raining. Got up at 4, had breakfast, and went right over to Wilson's. Tied up at their dock. Carl went ashore and rowed out with the bow poles. Mrs. Wilson came down to see us. It was raining all the time. After we got the poles up, we went into Mrs. Wilson's for coffee. Also paid her the $5.00 for the grid work and the $300.00 for the house and lot. Then we went over to Union Oil—gas, fuel oil, grease, and water. Went back to Thomas Basin about 8:30. Carl took the deed from Henry and had it notarized. The girl came down to the boat about 10—said she had forgotten to put her seal on the deed. As soon as Carl came back, I took it up to her—but the signature was wrong. It should have been Carl Albert Stone, and he had signed Carl A. Stone—so I had to go back to the boat and get Carl, and we both went back—then we mailed it to Orie—airmail. I went and bought some groceries, and when I got back Carl was in a drunken sleep. I found the bottle and threw it overboard. At 1 p.m. we left for Meyers Chuck. Carl was so sick I had to do all the steering—and was he mad at me for throwing that bottle away! Arrived at M.C. at 5:20. Talked to Wests, *Vag*, and Mrs. Persons. Is Carl ever sick! $305.00 to Mrs. Wilson for shack.

5/27—Thurs.

Carl had a miserable nite, and so did I. I made a bed on the floor and tried to sleep there, but Carl called me all the time, so I didn't get much sleep. He did a lot of walking. Took all the tubes out of the new radio and put new ones in, and still it won't work.

5/28—Fri.

Carl is feeling a little better—only had to get up about 3 times in the nite. He took the main poles down and painted them. Also put a new aerial on one and connected it with the new radio, but it still won't work. Connected the old aerial with the small radio and it works swell.

5/31—Mon.—Memorial Day
Meyers Chuck

Got up early, and as it was a nice bright day with a wind, I did all the washing. Such a mess—didn't get thru till 3:30. Poor Carl nearly pulled his arms out of joint, packing the water in 2 five-gallon cans. One of the "old boys" here chopped off the index finger on his left hand—just below the 3rd

joint nearest his hand. Carl came running for me
to come and do something! The man's daughter was
there, but was so nervous and excited. I sure was
glad for my first aid training. I tied it up and
put on a splint. Totals for May: Amt. earned—0;
No. of lbs.—0; Running time—5 hrs. 20 min.; No.
of fishing days—0; Average per fishing day—0.

6/1—Tues.

Still windy. If weather is OK tomorrow, we will
follow *Vag* to Point Baker. Made a batch of snow-
balls. The *Kay* went to town at 4 a.m. with some
fish. They also took the man with the chopped finger.
Gus Olin came back from Ketchikan this morning
about 11 a.m. Olin has been in the hospital for 3
days, knocked down by a bus. He started for Meyers Chuck yesterday morning—got as far as Guard
Island and broke down. The Coast Guard had to tow
him back. Then he started again this morning and
had some more trouble—drifted for a while till
a cannery tender came along and towed him in to
the trap.

*[Southeast Alaska had numerous salmon traps in the 1940s. They were
huge contraptions bolted into solid rock on shore and covered with chicken
wire. About 80 percent of the canned salmon at that time were caught by
traps. The fishing fleet supplied the rest. (No wonder Hazel and Carl had
a difficult time making a living when competing with the traps.) Many
of the traps were maintained by individual canneries. Salmon pirating
of the traps was a huge problem for the business. A lot of money was
made by the robbers. The bars on Creek Street benefited greatly from
this enterprise. (Now I understand how beer could bring 25 cents a glass.
It's called "supply and demand" plus money in the pockets. Carl and his
fishermen buddies had to compete with these prices too.) This salmon
trap industry had political problems, however, and was declared illegal
in 1959 when Alaska gained statehood.]*

6/2—Wed.

One week today since we left Ketchikan. The *Kay* came back this morning with the news of Wilsons' *Mischief* boat explosion. What a shame. It was a swell boat too. *[Wow! Once again a boating disaster (explosion!) and the next "item of interest" is Hazel making a pie. Hard to believe that an event of that type would be* <u>trivial</u> *in this fishing community, and yet ... once again, I'd love to know more, but that's all there is.]* Made a rhubarb pie, ironed, and washed the windows—both inside and out. Carl cleaned the smoke stack and stove of all of the soot (at 6:00 this a.m.). Weather was too foggy for traveling. Letter to Orie.

Official Fishing Season Starts

6/4—Fri.— (6:00–9:10)

Our first day of fishing for 1943. Got up at 5, had coffee and toast, left at 6. Dull gray day—cold. No fish till 7:45—a 9# red. We fished till 9:10—when it commenced to get ruff—so we came in. The sun came out late in the afternoon. We ate our fish. Carl helped Mrs. West fix her chicken coop, and I worked on a jigsaw puzzle.

6/8—Tues.— (10:15–2:30)

Carl's birthday. Up early, ready to leave at 10 a.m.—but too windy—so we went out to fish a while. Didn't catch anything but a big old blue shark, about 150 lbs. and 6 ft. long. Had to shoot it 7 times. Then we had an awful time—had to tow it behind till it was good and dead, then we both about killed ourselves getting it aboard.

[Captain Larry Hendricks of the Sea Star *on* Deadliest Catch *TV series said that in the '40s all that fishermen kept of sharks was the liver—in five-gallon cans. Shark was considered a scrap fish in those days and was not thought to be edible. Larry's father was a sardine and shark fisherman during the war, the same years Hazel and Carl fished. He said Vitamin A and an array of other drugs were made from the livers for use of the troops. The shark fishermen were exempt from the draft, as this was considered a "vital industry."*

[According to the Baja California Information Page on the Internet, superstition held that throwing the remains of the shark back into the sea would chase the other sharks from the area. So, after extracting the livers that they packed in one or two of those five-gallon cans, the fishermen piled the remains of the sharks on land, there to attract legions of flies and other insects.

[Today, we put almost the entire shark to use. Tourists buy the jaws, modern drugs use the cartilage, and we eat the meat as well as the liver. (http://math.ucr.edu/ftm/bajaPages/Tales//Donjuancho.html)]

We caught several little ones—too small to sell—and one large one, but Carl lost it. Tried to go back and get it, nearly ran into *Vag*. So we came in—very much disgusted.

6/11—Fri.—(3:50–1:10)
Meyers Chuck to Point Baker

A big seiner came in at 12 midnite and tied up to the float. Woke me up. Carl got up at 1:15 and went over and talked to Jack Gooding, but the wind was blowing—so we all went back to sleep. At 3:30 Jack called us, and as the weather was good, we decided to leave. It was 10 to 4 when we left, and as soon as we got out in the open, we began to roll. I tried to make some coffee—had to hang on with one hand and keep the coffee pot on the stove with the other hand. Not much wind and no sun. The closer we got to Prince of Wales Island the smoother it was, till at Ratz Harbor it was smooth. 4 hrs. to Lincoln Light. We passed Ole and *Fortuna* at Ratz, and at Koffman's Cove, Mercedes and Stella. 7 hrs. to Salmon Bay. 7½ hrs. to Calpoys. Carl took a nap—and then the heat indicator wouldn't work. Arrived at Point Baker at 1:10. Tied up to Jack Monroe's float. Went to bed early, as we intend to fish in the morning—although we are the only powerboats here. Jack Monroe gave Carl a carton of cigarettes.

6/12—Sat.—(6:00–8:25)
Point Baker

Up at 4:30—Jack Gooding had to wake us up. Dull gray day and cold, wind was just like ice. We left at 6 a.m. and trolled till 8:35—not a nibble. Hit bottom with both bow poles—took a hook off of one spoon. Came back to float and had breakfast. Made a rice pudding and a devil's food cake. Jack Monroe expected the *ARB 3* [*A.R.B., a cannery out of Seattle, had company-owned, boat-numbered packers*] from Wrangell with some fresh meat, so we waited for it so we could have some for our dinner. But we waited and waited, and it didn't come—so we ate. It's a good thing we didn't wait, as it was 6:30 before it got here. Carl and I helped Jack M. put all the groceries on the shelves. The barge started to fill the gas tank at 10:30, and it ran for about 2 hrs. and made an awful noise. We will get gas tomorrow, and if the weather is OK, we will go on to Cape Pole. When Carl went to bed at 10 p.m., the bilge was ½ full of clear water—so we've got a leak some place. Carl will have to work on that tomorrow.

6/13—Sun.

Rainy, wet day. Up at 8. Carl worked on the "leak." Took on 55 gals. of gas and bot some ham, steaks, corn flakes and cheese. It all came to $10.00 including the gas. Had rib steaks for dinner. At 2:15 p.m., Stanley Housmer and his partner came in from Meyers Chuck, towing Mrs. Persons (Carl's Glamour Girl). She left her bedding on our boat while she put up her tent—in the rain. *[Carl apparently wasn't very chivalrous toward his "glamour girl."]* Weather permitting, we leave at 4 in the morning for Cape Pole.

6/14—Mon.—(6:20–10:45)
Point Baker to Cape Pole

Up at 5:15. Jack woke us up. Very wet and raining hard. Moved Stanley (who was tied up to us) so we could get out. Had some coffee and butterhorns and left at 6:20 a.m. Rained most of the way, but not bad—some mist and haze, but we kept pretty close to shore. We rolled some across the mouth of Shipley Bay, and I commenced to get sick. Went to bed for about 30 min. and then I was all right. Arrived at Barrier Island Lite at 8:15 and at Pole Anchorage at 10:45. 2 or 3 boats in the harbor, but no one we know. The *ARB 3* is here, putting logs under the scow. Went up to see George and Mary Smith and to see if he could fix our new radio. He only worked on it a few minutes and said there was a short in the antenna wire. He soldered it and checked it all over and only asked $2.00, but Carl gave him $2.50. Mary is a very good housekeeper; her place was as neat as a pin, and such a nice garden. The little dog that Chris tried to give us last year came in; he sure is cute. Mrs. Smith came down to see our boat.

Ocean and Bob came in; then *Knickerbocker*, *Eena*, *Jerry*, *Mumps*, and Jim Coffman. *Knickerbocker* came over for a visit, and so did Bob.

6/15—Tues—(5:00–10:15)
Cape Pole

Up at 4. Had coffee and went out at 5. Beautiful day—smooth water and sunshine. Caught 2 kings by 6 o'clock. By 9 the wind was blowing a gale so decided to come in. Smith Bros. are buying—have no ice—the fish are piled on the floor. Some are 4 days old! Don't know how much or when we will get our money. No gas and no bread. We caught 4 fish—3 mild cure and one white. Made ice cream. Rained all afternoon. Salmon prices in Ketchikan today are: 26-18-14 cents. *[Refers to size or types: large, small, or white. Whites bring a lower price.]*

6/16–6/20—Wed. thru Sun.

No fishing—too stormy and very foggy.

6/21—Mon.

No fishing today—buyer can't buy any more fish—no more ice. Besides, it is so foggy you can hardly see out of the harbor. Slept late and had pancakes for breakfast. Made an apricot pie. Mrs. Travis on the *Alice E* came over for a while. Bot some groceries at both stores. About 8 p.m. the buyer came back from Craig, and now we can get our money and also sell our fish. Smith Bros. and Einstoss are having a price war, and for all our fish before today, we get $.20, and after today, $.30. *[Sounds like the "price war" is between two buyers. Retroactive payment of 20 cents a pound for fish previously sold, with new catches fetching 30 cents a pound.]*

6/22—Tues.

First day of summer, also longest day. Up at 4, but so foggy we went back to bed and got up again at 6. Still very foggy, so stayed in. It was pretty foggy all day. *Alice E* got lost and could not find the harbor; *Betty K* ran around till one o'clock before they knew where they were. We went out in the skiff and tried to hand troll, but no luck. After supper, walked out to the point, past Shakey Jack's. Lots of columbine, buttercups, Indian paint brush, and wood-hyacinth. Bob Burns came over, and we played pinochle till 9:45.

6/23—Wed.—(6:15–1:30)

Up at 3, made coffee and all ready to go at 3:45, and then the fog came! It was pretty thick, so we waited a while. Had breakfast, and still it was soupy out. No one else seemed to be in a hurry to leave, so we waited and waited; finally went back to bed at 5:30. Got up at 6:15 and went out. Good weather and smooth water. Fished on this side of Warren Island and then out in front. Only caught 3 fish. Talked about going out again tonight, but most of the other boats were skunked or only got one, so we stayed in. Got paid for all our fish—$25.00.

6/24—Thurs.—(5:00–1:45)

Quit Game Department 3 years ago today. Up at 4, coffee and then ready to leave at 5:00. Good fishing day, smooth water. Caught 8 fish—$30.88. Joe (the Filipino) came in from Malmsbury with 15 kings. They were only paying $.21, so he came over here to sell. He says there are no fish at Alexander or at Sitka. *Donna* and *Coast* are at Sitka. We want to wait for our mail before we leave; it should come early Sat. morning. Letters to Dad and Mother, Orie, and ordered embroidery catalog. *[Compared to that $.21/lb., in a Washington State grocery store, summer of 2008, king salmon was selling for $15.95/lb. Of course, the comparison is not quite fair since one price is for the wholesaler and the other is for the end consumer, but even putting the middleman's share in the equation makes for a tremendous difference.]*

6/27—Sun.

Another wet rainy day. Too bad to go out. Bob Burns and *Vag* were the only ones to go out. *Jerry* left for Malmsbury. We caught all the rainwater we could (2 pails and the small tub), and I washed some dirty clothes. A Coast Guard boat came in late in the afternoon. It will be stationed there to check up on all fishermen, coming and going. 6 young boys on board—they asked us over to inspect the boat; it sure is nice. Bot 2 lbs. Sanka coffee.

6/29—Tues.

Got up at 4. Rain and foggy and then the wind began to blow. At low tide we were on bottom so had to pull up the anchor. We went out to mouth of harbor, but it was so ruff we came back. Rowed over to see *Red*. Carl went to the creek for some water while I got dinner. *Red* came over and ate with us. No boats came in all day. Sure is a lonesome place. Two hand trollers—the buyer and us—are the only ones here in this big bay.

6/30—Wed.
Egg Harbor

Carl got up early, but I didn't. Still stormy and foggy and rain. Caught some more rain water. Made a pie. *ARB 2* came in—no fish any place. Didn't do much but read all day. *[Hazel enjoyed reading throughout her lifetime. During her fishing years she frequented the library. She read many of Jack London's books and others about Alaska. And of course, she enjoyed the many magazines shared by fellow fishermen.]* Carl took a bath and washed his hair. In the late afternoon a plane flew in, low, right over our heads—then went up and over Alikula Bay. Totals for June: Amt. earned = $61.21. No. of pounds = 299 lbs. Running time = 65 hrs. No. of fishing days = 6. Average per fishing day = $10.22.

7/3—Sat.—(5:10–10:50 and 4:50–7:50)

Up at 4, coffee-ed, and then ready to go. Much fog. Was pretty thick around Aats and Alikula but not too bad in Egg. Water smooth. About 9 a.m., it cleared up, but still a cold and dull gray day. Fished till 10:50—no bites, so we came in. 3 kings and 4 cohoes $20.86. As Carl had one of his famous "dreams" last nite, I had to do some washing today. Washed out the "spots" on the blankets and his pajamas. Had our dinner and then took a nap. Ready to go out again at 4:50.

7/4—Sun.—(5:00–9:20)

Another holiday. Up at 4, coffee-ed, left at 5:00 a.m. Wet, cold, and rainy. A regular winter day, not a bit like summer. Caught a whopper, but it got caught on the rear line and tore loose, taking a complete leader with it. Caught a couple more, but lost them too. Fished till 9:20—and only got one, so we came in. And such rain! We caught enough to fill the tank. I washed my hair. Made some ice cream, and asked *Red* and Charlie Coe, the buyer, to come over and have some. Bot some cheese (2 boxes), brown sugar, and shoestring spuds. Some celebration for the 4th! No money—the buyer is broke. *[Wonder if this was a result of the fish-price war mentioned earlier.]*

7/7—Wed.

Our first summer day! Sunshine so bright it hurt my eyes. Wore dark glasses until 3 p.m. when it started to rain—and it was rainy and cloudy the rest of the day. We left at 5:10. Only had 2 cohoes, 1 white and 1 small red. So we picked up and went to Cora Point. Charlie Coe was ahead of us. He stopped and talked to another troller, and then kept on going toward Cape Pole. We put our lines in and caught 2 cohoes right away. Fished for an hour and didn't catch another fish so went back to Egg Harbor. We put our line in and right away we caught 2 large reds. Fished till 5:45. Had supper after we tied up. Poor *Red* didn't catch any today, either. Still no money. Sold at $28.19.

7/8—Thurs.—(6:25–11:15)

Had to get up in the middle of the night—Carl had another "accident." Had to change all the bed clothes. We didn't get up till after 5—rain and wind, as usual. Left here at 6:25 and fished till 11:25. Lost a gaff hook, tried go back and pick it up, but couldn't find it. Came in and had hotcakes. No *ARB* again today—so no money and no bread. Had to make some bran muffins. 2 Scott boats came in from Helm Point with over 400 lbs. each, but they said it was very ruff. Also *Mumps* came back from Cape Pole. Had 3 large reds and 1 white—$31.92. Still *Red* didn't get any fish. Carl dragged the bedding in the salt water all morning—to get rid of the odor!

[Cannot fathom having to deal with diarrhea in the bedding on a boat! Wonder how they dried the bedding. Yuck!)

7/9—Fri.—(5:25–3:40)

Arrived in Ketchikan, 1940, 3 years ago.

Got up early, as usual, and went out at 5:25. It was a fairly decent day—no rain and smooth water. Fished till 3:40—only had 6 fish = $18.08. About 5:30—a government boat, the *P6*, came in and anchored. *[A PT (Propeller Torpedo) boat was a small, fast, unarmored, and lightly armed torpedo boat used by the United States Navy during World War II to attack larger surface ships.]*

7/10—Sat.—(5:10–3:20)
Egg Harbor to Cora Point

Left Egg H. at 5:10 on our way to Cora Point. Pretty ruff and windy. *Mumps* followed us over. Got there at 6:25, started to fish and we really began to catch them. Kings and cohoes—although the cohoes were small. The wind got worse and worse. Never felt such strong winds before! For a while they were just once in a while but they soon began to blow steady. It blew the fish blood up and on front of the cabin windows! It was sickening! *[Yuck!]* At 3:20, we had to quit as it was getting too much for us. Charlie was already anchored. After supper, we had to re-anchor as we were dragging. We didn't count our fish, but Carl thinks we have about $100.00.

7/11—Sun.—(5:00–10:00 and 4:00–8:15)

Up at 3. Still blowing, but not as bad as yesterday. As we were pulling the anchor up, Carl caught his foot in the rope, and away it went out! Knocked him down, and he hung on to the guard—or he would have been knocked in the bay. *[Sounds like a movie scene: Man gets caught in rope, dragged overboard, maybe drowns or is eaten by sharks. Apparently in real life this sort of incident—as with many others—is not as dramatic as movies.]* We left at 5 and fished till 6—caught one king. The *ARB* came over from Cape Pole, so we went in to sell. He was not buying but would take our fish to Egg Harbor. He put them in 1½ fish boxes—no count, no weight—no nothing. Not so good, but better than having to run to Egg or Pole tonite, in case of bad weather. After we "sold," went right out again and fished till 10 a.m. Had 3 large reds. Anchored up in bay, and I made a gingerbread while Carl took a nap. Then we had dinner, and I took a nap. By this time, the wind had gone down a lot, and the sun was out, too. So we decided to go out and fish some more. Caught 7 kings—one was a 42 lb. white. Ate our supper while fishing and then came in at 8:15 p.m. The *ARB* came back again tonite but did not take any fish. *Knickerbocker* came over to see what we did today—he only had 2 cohoes. And he said we would not get $.30 for large reds—for several days back! That $108.00 that we have coming will only be about $50.00 I guess. *[Guess the fish-price war is over.]*

7/12—Mon.—(5:00–9:10)

Much fog and rain. *Knickerbocker* said a South-easter was blowing up so we had better run to Egg H. Left at 5:00. It was very foggy; had to follow close to the shoreline. Took some dirty rolls before we got thru the pass. At 6:30 we got to Egg H. *Knickerbocker* was fishing, so we decided to try it too. Caught one 35 lb. white. Fished till 8:30 when fog and rain got much worse, so came

in. We did not get our $.30 per lb. on fish we had
caught, but today and yesterday's were no prices
on slips. *ARB* takes 24 hrs. to go to Ketch. from
here—if he gets to Ketch. before ceiling prices go
into effect, we'll get $.30—otherwise the ceiling
price. *[Sounds like the government has stepped in, due to war and
rationing. Also, since the government purchased the majority of canned
salmon for the troops, ceiling prices would be advantageous.]* Anchored
at Cora Point.

[Hazel's entries on average are much longer than usual. Wonder why.]

7/13—Tues.—(4:20–9:00)
Cora Point to Cape Pole

Ceiling prices on fish—effective today:

	Seattle	Ketchikan
Hal.	$.17 ½	.16
Salmon: Large	.22	.20 ½
Small	.18 ¼	.16 ¾
White	.14	.12 ½
Coho	.16 ½	.15

We rolled so all nite, didn't get much sleep. At
3 a.m., we bumped *Knickerbocker*, so Carl had to
get up and pull in the anchor rope. Then we rolled
more than ever, so we got up and went fishing. It
seemed smoother fishing than it did where we were
anchored. All we caught were small kings, and it
was getting windy-er, so at 6:30, we picked up and
went to Cape Pole. About ½ way over, we met *Ocean*
going to Cora Point. Arrived at 9—sold our fish to
Smith Bros. (but no money), and Tex said it was
more fish than he had seen all week, no fish there
at all. Tied up to the scow and washed clothes all
day. Used a lot of their rainwater. Had our T-bone

steak dinner and then got some gas. Went for a walk and picked enough salmon berries and blueberries for a pie. Blackie is leaving for Gedney in the morning, and I guess we'll go with him.

7/14—Wed.—(8:00–3:00)
Cape Pole to Gedney

Up at 4 a.m. all ready to leave, but Blackie wasn't up, and as a breeze was blowing, went back to bed and got up at 7. Finally at 8:30, Blackie came over and said he was going to leave. *Betty K* decided to go with us, so we had 3 boats. It was a good trip till we got to Cape Decision at 10:30. We got into the most gosh-awful sea-rips and rolls and ground swells. We rolled from side to side and took some awful poundings. The tea-kettle rolled off the oil stove and 2" of water was all over the floor. Blackie kept straight on going—towards Pt. Alexander. Finally when we were more than half way to Alexander, Carl got as close to Blackie as we could and asked where the heck he was going. His compass was off and he thot he was going to Gedney. *[Not very sophisticated navigational system compared to fishing boats of today.]* So we turned and went up the channel, which was much better for us, and finally the water got much smoother. Arrived in Gedney at 3 p.m. About 20 boats were anchored in there—but no scow. We tied up to *Lois D*—Jack and Gladys Brindley came over, and Mrs. Mc and I made ice cream for all. After everyone went home (9:30), Carl and I had a lunch. Saw 2 baby deer on the beach—very close, but didn't seem to be a bit afraid.

7/15—Thurs.
Gedney

Woke up at 4—but no one was going fishing so we went back to sleep till 9. Seemed good to sleep in. Made a pie of the blueberries, but it wasn't very good. Guess the berries were too green. Carl spent most of the day visiting all the boats. In the afternoon, Mrs. Mc and Gladys Brindley and I went for a row and walked up the creek as far as we could. McDonalds came over in evening to listen to the news. Radio doesn't work so good here. *[Today one would probably get a satellite-radio subscription and be frustrated not by lack of signals but by having too much potential listening material.]*

7/16—Fri.—(11:25–1:00 and 8:20–8:45)
Gedney to Tebenkoff

Didn't get up till after 7. Rain and more rain. Carl put out the buckets, and we caught more rainwater. Did some washing and scrubbed floors. Also did a lot of mending. At 11:25, McDonalds asked us if we would like to go to a fox farm up in Tebenkoff where he had a lot of strawberries. Foggy and still raining. Got to the fox farm at 1:00 p.m., and no one was home. Tied up to his float. Went ashore and looked the place over. Nice garden. We saw 10 little foxes and 2 mothers on the beach. About 5 p.m., Mr. Mc saw the *Sydney* coming, so I made a shortcake, and Mrs. Mc made some ice cream. All 4 men went ashore and picked strawberries. We ate the shortcake in dinner plates, and was it good. We went up and picked a roaster full of strawberries, got some rhubarb and lettuce. Left at 8:20 for Trollers Island. Blackie and *Alice E* were there. *Lois D* didn't come in tonite; hope they are all right. The packer *Chief Seegay* came into Gedney this a.m. to pick up fish, but no one had been fishing. Saw the fox farmer's sourdough jar. Radio works very good here.

[Sourdough is a leaven of dough in which fermentation is active, used as a starter mix for making bread and pancakes. It was known as "Alaska's Other Gold." It became so entwined with the identity of Alaskan old-timers that they were called "Alaskan Sourdoughs." Prospectors would often keep a bit of starter in an open can pinned to the wall near the stove in the winter, and if they had to leave the cabin for any length of time, they'd carry it in a pouch around their neck.]

7/18—Sun.—(5:10–12:30)
Gedney

4.4 foot minus tide this morning at 8—lowest for the year. Left at 5:10 and fished Gedney all day. Rain, fog, and swells. While I was cleaning fish, I inhaled some exhaust from the engine and got sick. Had to go to bed for a while. At 11:30 got up and cooked some bacon and eggs for Carl. By noon the situation got worse and worse. The wind and rain came down our necks, so we quit and came in. We had 42 cohoes and one small king—$43.49. John told us we were high boat. *Crystal* and *Nira* came in behind us. Came over to see *Lois D* (where we were anchored) and hardly spoke to us—guess they were too mad because we had more fish than they did. It's so childish. Made a strawberry pie. McDonalds don't seem to be able to catch many fish, so Carl looked his gear over and helped him with spoons, etc. Hope they get more fish now. Wrote letters to Mother and Zellah.

7/19—Mon.—(5:25–2:15)

Got up late. Left right away; made coffee after
we had our lines in. Miserable day. Rain, fog, and
wind. I got sick, and lost my breakfast. Had to
go to bed. Carl was in a dark mood all day. Gills
came by just as we were pulling in our lines. It
was so ruff, and the wind and rain were so bad,
we came in at 2:15. Tied up to Gills. They are on
their way to Noyes from Sitka—have cleared $1,000
already! She gave us a piece of blueberry pie,
and I gave her some strawberries. We visited with
them for a while. Carl had to work on the stuffin
box, as it has developed a leak. *[A stuffing box, or packing gland, is used around a propeller shaft at the point it exits a boat's
hull under water. It is the most common method for preventing water
from entering the hull while still allowing the propeller shaft to turn.]*
McDonald had $32.00 today—he sure was tickled.
We had $23.00.

7/20—Tues.— (6:15–10:30)
Gedney

Up at 4—but such a wild day; no one seemed to be
going out. Ate our breakfast and left at 6:15. It
was pretty ruff, and we rolled and tossed. Foggy
and raining, and soon it began to blow. The wind
got so bad we couldn't troll, so we had to come
in at 10:30. We anchored, and I went to bed and
slept for an hour. Carl was reading when I got
up, and we had drifted almost out to the scow. We
pulled up the anchor, and Mrs. Gill motioned for
us to tie to them, so we did. About 7 p.m. the
wind began to blow pretty hard, and we drifted
back and bumped *Lindora*. So we untied from Gills
and anchored by ourselves. *Lois D* didn't come in
tonite. 10 cohoes—$11.05. Sent our key in to get

our mail. *[Mail was sent and retrieved in a variety of ways. The steamships usually brought mail in from the states to the local post office. The post office sent mail out to the fishing fleet (when they were out for several weeks/months at a time) with the packers/buyers. Then when individual fishermen were going into town (Ketchikan) for one reason or another, keys to individual post office boxes were collected. Trustworthiness seemed to be a virtue!]*

7/22—Thurs.— (4:45–1:15)

Cold, wet, clammy day. Up early, had coffee and doughnuts, and left at 4:45. *[Think Hazel made the doughnuts. Couldn't go to the market!]* Rolled some, and I got sick and went to bed for a while. Fished till 1:15—so cold and rainy and no fish. Wanted to get some stove oil, but John was too busy, so we went over to *Lois D* and hung on for a while. Got a very cool reception. We soon left. While we were getting our oil, they went out of the harbor about 90 mph.

7/23—Fri.—(4:15–6:45)

Up at 3:00. Made coffee in thermos bottles the nite before. Made more coffee while Carl drank from the thermos. Left at 4:15 and headed for Pt. Ellis. Put our lines in near Trollers Island and began to get fish at once. By 7 a.m. we had a bin full. Didn't get a chance to eat breakfast till 7:30. A beautiful day—sunshine so bright it hurt my eyes—and smooth water. Fished all day till 6:15 p.m. Caught 120 cohoes, 3 kings and 6 humpies—over 900 pounds = $119.34. I've had a stiff neck all day. Dave Harris came here from Coronation, and he told Carl that cohoes would be cut to $.11½—always someone to take the joy out of life! *[Even though the price was low, seemed to be best-of-season fishing day.]*

7/30—Fri.—(4:40–5:15)
Gedney

Alarm went off as usual, but no boats seemed to be going out, so Carl went back to bed. We finally left at 4:40—some fog but not as bad as yesterday. Soon had the lines in and waiting for fish, when bang, bang—we hit with all four poles! The port bow pole broke a tag line, and the starboard main pole broke a tag line and lost a 15 lb. lead. We got out of there in a hurry! Trolled till about 8:30, when the fog came in. So we picked up and ran to Gedney (1 hr.) and put our lines in out there. The fog lifted after a time. We trolled back to Ellis Pt., but not very good luck today. Only made $34.74.

7/31—Sat.—(4:25–2:30 and 2:45–4:30)
Gedney to Malmsbury

L. N. B.'s birthday—56 or 57. *[This is a reference to Hazel's first husband, Louis Bolme.]*

Nasty, cold day and fog. Began fishing at Gedney, and fished to Malmsbury and back. The day got better as it grew later, but by 2:10 it was blank—no fish, so we picked up and came in. Sold, and left for Malmsbury (307 lbs. = $40.06). Got there at 4:30—anchored, and in about one hour, *Ruby S* came in. About 7 p.m., *Jerry* and *Chance* came in. We caught some more rainwater. Saw a huge bear on the opposite shore. Totals for July: Amt. earned = $874.02. No. of pounds = 5,806. Running time: 220 hrs. 40 min., No. of fishing days = 23. Average per fishing day: $38.00.

8/6—Fri.—(4:20–8:15)

Foggy—but we went out anyway. Started toward Malmsbury—2 boats ahead of us—but it was too ruff, so
we turned and trolled to Ellis Pt. Fog began to
settle down, and as we only had 5 fish, we came in.
John (the buyer) could not take any more fish—43,000
lbs.—no ice and no packer. He finally did take our
5. Tied up to *Motion* for a while. I washed clothes
all day. Carl and I made one trip for water, then
Carl made one alone. Shortly after we came in,
all the other boats came in too—no fish. At 5:40
p.m., Carl and Bill Fredericks decided to go to
Malmsbury for the nite, to be there for the early
morning fishing. We followed *Jerry*, but it was
too ruff—we pounded so! The water came up over
our bow—onto the windows, couldn't see out—thru
the side door and onto the floor. So we came back
and anchored in the small harbor on the right of
Gedney. Tied up to *Jerry*, and he and Carl drank
and talked (on Jerry's boat) till 12:30. Started
letter to Zellah.

8/9—Mon.—(5:00–12:15)
Gedney to Alexander

Smooth water. Trolled toward Malmsbury. Had breakfast in the bay. Fished till 10:25. Picked up and
started for Alexander. *Lornty* thot it would be
too ruff, so he didn't come. Sort of misty and
rain by the time we got there. Had a hard time
finding the light from the lighthouse. Sold our 20
cohoes and 1 king to Karl Hansen. Ate our dinner in
the café @ $1.00 per. Roast beef, browned spuds,
gravy, string beans, bread and butter, 2 cups of
coffee, and a small piece of banana cream pie.
[Gives a sense of the dollar's worth back then.] It poured down
rain all afternoon. Went up to store and talked
to the "gang" for a while. We saw *Tom & Jerry* and

their "nickel and candy bar" stunt. About 70 or 80 boats here. More still coming in. Still raining. Spent $28.98.

8/10—Tues.— (5:20–6:30)
Alexander

Got up at 5. About 99 boats were tied up to us last nite, but most of them left early. Foggy and rainy, but we went out anyway. Couldn't see Wooden Island, and after we left Breakfast Rock, we could not see the entrance to Alexander, so we came back. Met *Jackson* going out, but he turned around when he saw us come in. Had hotcakes and then took a nap. Rained all day. In afternoon we walked up to grid where Jack and Gladys were. Frank and Lela Wrench came over in the evening. After they left, we went up to Art's place. No one there we knew, so we came home—read a while and to bed.

8/13—Fri.— (6:30–9:15 and 10:00–6:15)
Alexander to Gedney

Up early, nice bright sun-shiny day. Decided to go back to Gedney. Had to leave before we had breakfast as *Laug* wanted to get out. We left at 6:30—nice for a while but soon began to get lumpy. It got worse and worse, and by time we got to Harris Bay, it was ruff. Didn't see any trollers at Malmsbury and only 4 at Gedney. Pretty ruff all day till about 4. Had a pukish feeling and went to bed for a while. Only had 22 cohoes = $27.50.

8/15—Sun.

Still blowing this morning, so we did not go out.
A few boats went out, but they came back soon. I
cleaned and scrubbed and did some washing. Went
over to see Eleanor's pups and took the black one
(Funnyface) home with us. Will keep him and give
him to Mrs. Gill when we get back. We got our
mail today: 2 from Zellah and 1 from Mother and
Orie. A purse seiner, the *Rainier*, came in late
this afternoon. Big Ole was on it. He isn't fishing his own boat this year. He came over and brot
his skipper. Lars Larsen and Kenneth and his dad
came over too. We all listened to the radio and
played with the puppy.

Hazel with black puppy, Funnyface.

8/16—Mon.

It rained hard all day. Too stormy to fish. Funnyface was pretty good all nite—didn't cry at all. Had a nice box with wool rags, and he seemed to like it. After breakfast we went over and tied up to *Lornty* for the day. Made a lemon pie for Carl.

8/17—Tues.

Up early—but still raining and blowing so did not go out. *Lornty* brot the white pup over, and he and Funnyface had a good romp. Made 2 loaves of bread. Wrote 3 letters.

8/18—Wed.—(6:25–1:30)

We left *Lornty* at 6:25—fished in front and then towards Pt. Ellis. Rain, cold, and wind. Decided to call Funnyface "Skupper." He was right at home fishing; the more the boat rolled, the better he seemed to like it. Got too ruff, so we came in with only 12 cohoes. Carl let a leader go thru the block and lost it—and nearly lost a 40 lb. lead. Not a good day. One hour later, *Lornty* tied to us, but the wind was so strong they decided to anchor out. It was pretty windy till after 10—then it died down a bit. Made a coffee-cream pie.

8/19—Thurs.

Up early, but such weather! Fog, rain, and ruff. So we stayed in, as well as everyone else. Made bread and cinnamon rolls. At high tide (3 p.m.), we did a lot of rolling. Wrote letters to Mother and Zellah. Skupper sure was wild today—just raced around inside and on deck too. He had 2 cohoe hearts—raw, also some raw carrot.

8/21—Sat.—(5:35–11:45)
Gedney to Cape Pole

Up at 5. *Eena* was running his engine and getting ready to leave to Cape Pole, so Carl asked if we could go with him. He said yes. Left at 5:35—made coffee and toast on the way. Pretty ruff, and wind was blowing. By the time we got to Table Bay, it calmed down and was as smooth as glass all the rest of the way. Sun came out, and it was a beautiful day. By this time we could see 8 boats coming out of Gedney on their way to Cape Decision. A fog bank came in at Decision, and we had to slow down for a bit, but it wasn't bad. Arrived at Cape Pole at 11:45. I took Skupper ashore and went to see Mary Smith. Bot a pie from Mary. We got gas, then went over and tied up to Gills. She invited us to lunch. Skupper fell off their boat, and Carl had to grab him (between the 2 boats). Then Mr. Gill took Skupper ashore, and he fell off the scow. Poor little guy—he sure was shivery when he brot him back. The Gills kept Skupper all nite, so I guess we won't have him any more.

8/22—Sun.—(5:50–5:45)
Cape Pole

Cold and foggy, but the water was smooth. Fished around "The Rock" all morning, many birds. Gills went in at 11 p.m., but we stayed out. We had about 10 fish when Gills left. Made hotcakes for breakfast. Tied up to Gills, and played with Skupper. He doesn't seem to be a bit lonesome—stays with them as easily as with us. The buyer is short of help, so we have to sell before 7:30. Got $51.28. The store doesn't open till 10 in the morning. Bot 74 gals. gas @ $.13 = $9.62.

8/24—Tues.—(5:30–5:30)

Nice day. Sort of a Westerly wind—but not bad. Not many fish, very scattered. Lost many; couldn't seem to hold them. Skupper is wilder and wilder. Tied up to Gills. Carl and Melvin went ashore (to get their money), took Skupper along, and he fell overboard again (3ʳᵈ time); Carl rescued him once more. Carl worked on engine again tonite.

8/27—Fri.— (8:05–2:00)
Cape Pole

Got up at 5, but didn't go out because weather bad. Had breakfast, and I darned stockings. At 6 a.m. Gills decided to go out. We had to move because we were tied to them. Went over and tied to *Lornty* for a while and talked to them. Finally at 8 a.m., we went out. Saw a large whale. Miserable day—fog, rain and wind—and few fish. 9 cohoes and 4 humps by 2 p.m. so we came in. Most boats were already in. We tied up to float next to *Lucky*. Mary Smith came over for a while. Later Mrs. Stone was over, and as usual she stayed and stayed and stayed! Rained hard all day; caught some more rainwater. Washed my hair and took a bath. *[Sounds like baths are an event of sorts since Hazel mentions them specifically. Also, they seem to depend, at least in part, upon availability of fresh water—rainwater in this instance.]*

8/30—Mon.

Blew and rained all nite long. Too stormy to go out, so Carl took the skiff and went over to Brueger float before breakfast. I had to ring the bell for him to come home. I made hotcakes for breakfast and then made a rhubarb pie. Scrubbed woodwork and floors. Carl spent most of the day at Brueger float. Several boats left for Ketchikan. *Silver Horde* is buying there but paying only $.12 for cohoes and $.17 for kings. Ordered a chicken (fryer) from Chapman. *[Interesting that Hazel had to "order" a chicken. No going down to the corner meat market.]* Saw the Northern Lights just before we went to bed. They were spectacular! Most beautiful we've seen.

8/31—Tues.— (6:00–3:15)

Up early, but couldn't decide if we should go out. Finally at 6:00 we left. Cold day, the wind was like ice. Not any powerboats, all hand trollers. Most powerboats went to Salmon Bay. *Knickerbocker* came today from Cape Pole. We had 27 cohoes = $30.55. I cleaned, scraped, and fixed 4 humpies for salting down but didn't save other humpies because season is over. But when we came in tonite, they told us they still want humpies. Darn! Totals for August: Amt. earned = $545.46. No. of pounds = 4,470. Running time = 180 hrs. 10". No. of fishing days = 20. Average per fishing day = $27.27.

9/1—Wed.— (6:00–2:45)

One year ago today we came here from Rocky Pass. Nice day today, sunshine but windy. No fish after noon, so came in at 2:45. Got gas and a chicken from Mrs. Chapman. We had 29 cohoes and 18 humpies = $37.20. Cash on hand = $1,300.00. 45 gal. gas @ $.13 = $5.85.

9/4—Sat.—(6:15–2:15)

Up at 5—Carl had his coffee, then we left. Fog and mist till late in the morning—then it cleared

up a little. Not many fish. Gills came by on their
way to Ketchikan, then *Eena* and *Lucky*. Fished till
2:15—had 20 cohoes and 5 humpies. About 6 p.m. *Betty
K* came in from Cape Pole, got gas, and expect to
leave for Ketchikan tomorrow morning. They have
not fished for the last 2 days, but before that
they had 2 good days—$170.00 and $180.00!

9/6—Monday (Labor Day)—(5:50–6:20)

Beautiful day. Sunshine and smooth as a lake.
Fished all day—lost many fish. Did not have time
to can the halibut. Whales were thick; could see
them everywhere. Fun to watch them. All the boats
were out today. Bob Burns hung up on a rock. The
crash tore his rigging down, broke, and it hit
him on the head a bad blow. *Wanderlust* tied up to
us, and we tied to *Cheechauker*.

9/8—Wed.—(5:20–6:25)

Carl got up ½ hr. earlier. We had coffee and then
left. So dark I could hardly see to steer out of
the harbor. We didn't catch any fish all morning.
Carl would get them up to the boat, and then some-
how they would get off the hook. Another beautiful
day. I aired out all the bedding; then I made some
biscuits and cinnamon rolls. At 2 p.m. we only had
6 cohoes and 1 hump. Then about 3 or so, we hit
some at the reef in Protection Bay. We quit at 6:25
and had 34 cohoes and 2 hump. Carl discouraged and
in a vile temper most of the day. $38.18

9/12—Sun.

Last nite was a horrible one. About 2:30 I woke
up and heard the wind blowing hard in gusts. I was

debating about waking Carl (he was sleeping hard) when I heard the *Eena* yelling. We both jumped out of bed, and sure enough, our stern line had broken, and we all four swung around and were "bow in" to the float. Of course it was pouring down rain and blowing a gale. I held the flashlight while Carl and *Eena* re-tied. After much-to-do we finally got tied to Zieski, our bow to their stern. *Eena* stayed tied to the outside of other 2 boats, and they all 3 tied to the float. By this time it was nearly 4 a.m. Carl had put on pants and coat over his pajamas, and he was soaked. The *Burnett* came in when we were re-tieing with a scow in tow with a wrecked seaplane on it. Had tried to land in Edna Bay and struck a log. It was too ruff to continue to Ketchikan so they came in here for the nite. No fishing—too windy. Made a fire and warmed up a bit. Too awake to sleep, so I read till nearly 5:30.

9/16—Thurs.—(7:45–6:25)
Point Baker to Hadley

Didn't get up till 7:00. No one fishing, so Bob said we had better head for Ketchikan. A good day—warm and sunshine and very little wind. Had a good trip and tied up to some piles in Hadley at 6:25. At 8:00 p.m., the cannery boat came in, and we had to move and anchor out. The wind began to blow in gusts. Had Bob over for supper (meatballs) from the round steak.

9/17—Fri.—(6:35–10:20)
Hadley to Ketchikan

Didn't get up as early as we should. Had coffee and doughnuts and then left. Beautiful day, but faced the sun all the way in—hard on the eyes. Got to TOWER at 10:20. Had breakfast, then went up to town. Letters from Mother, Zellah, Katy, Ella, Grace, and Orie. Dad is in the hospital with a broken hip. Wish I was there. Deposited $1,500 in bank. Got my bean pots, refrigerator dishes, glass shelves, sox, and slacks from Sears. After supper, we went to Coliseum to see *The Man Who Came to Dinner*—very funny. Mrs. Wilson and Mrs. Gill came by—they want to go over to Pennock *[Island]* tomorrow to look at our "Mansion." Spent $3.25. Last day of fishing season.

Total for year: 13,525 lbs. = $1,839.23. *[This year was not as good as 1942 ($2,488.87) but considerably better than the following year ($1,054.76).]*

[Alaska did not always have healthy salmon stocks. Prior to statehood (1959), the federal government was responsible for salmon management in Alaska. Overfishing was a major factor in the declines of the Alaska salmon fishery that occurred between 1940 and 1959. The federal government failed to provide sound management practices needed to sustain Alaskan salmon fisheries. (The government allowed the fish traps, which continued to ravage the stock.) By 1953, salmon stocks and the fishing industry were in such bad shape that President Eisenhower declared Alaska a federal disaster. This action was unique in that this disaster was attributed to an act of man rather than an act of nature. (Alaska Fishery Research Bulletin, *Vol. 1 No. 1, 1994)]*

Moving to Shack at Whiskey Cove

9/18—Sat.
Ketchikan

Had breakfast, left for Whiskey Cove at 8 a.m.
Low tide, so had to anchor out. All the neighbors
were there to greet us. We hauled about 7 rowboat
loads. Had to pack things into boxes, load in
skiff, row ashore, then haul them up to the shack.
We were both just about worn out. Mrs. Gill asked
us in for our noon dinner plus coffee and cake at
4 p.m. We made our last trip at 5:30. We were too
tired to eat dinner, so went to bed on the *Olympic*
before 8. It rained hard all nite, and we caught
enough water to fill the tanks by morning.

9/19—Sun.

After breakfast we went to Whiskey Cove—rain and
wind. Had to load and haul in rain all day. Ate
all our meals in our new home and slept in our bed
there. Our bed is a double one, but oh so hard!

Gills came over to hear the news at 9. Then I took a hot bath in the rubber tub. We were pretty tired, so we went to bed right after.

Hazel and Carl's shack was located at Whiskey Cove on Pennock Island. It was across the channel from Ketchikan and within rowing distance. The shack looked over at what is now the cruise-ship dock.

9/20—Mon.

I did not sleep well, but we did have a lot more room. Carl got up at 7 and made a fire. I got up about 8. We had breakfast and then to work! Carl cleaned up the shed and also took stove and chimney all apart. Sure was a mess—soot and ashes all over. Oven still won't keep shut. I made an apple pie and burned the top. Carl fixed the loose shingles on the roof. We went with Mrs. Gill to get some drinking water. Went out to boat and brot in more junk! Promised Mrs. Gill to care for the pup while they go hunting.

9/21—Tues.

Rained on and off all day. Skupper paid me a visit at 6 a.m. while I was still in bed—thanks to Carl. Carl made a trip to the *Olympic* before breakfast. Then he worked on the outboard motor most of the day. I washed some clothes. We also cleaned out the "Johnny." Mrs. Wilson came over with a quart of currant juice (our own currants). Carl made second trip to the *Olympic*.

9/22—Wed.

What a day! After breakfast, we decided to go to town, so Carl started the outboard, and it worked fine. Then he took it down to the skiff and cranked from 8:45 to 9:30, and it would not go. So he got the oars, and we rowed across, and it began to rain before we got there. Many big boats going by made a lot of waves! We arrived in K. about 11:30. Saw Harvey and the Pritchers—he doesn't want to go South now, and is she re-gusted! I got weighed—155 lbs.! We started home at 4:30—rain and wind and Carl intoxicated. My umbrella was too much of a sail, so had to close it. It got worse and worse as we went. We were both soaking wet. We finally got across to the other shore and were struggling along when Chris Hansen came out and insisted on us coming in. Mrs. H. had some stew, and she gave us each a bowl full—sure tasted good. At 6 p.m. we started off again—still raining! All my groceries, as well as everything else, floating around in the skiff. Flour wet, bread wet, powdered soap all over the onions, 5 broken eggs, toilet paper wet, Kleenex a soggy mess! Got home at 6:30. It took all nite to dry out! Spent $46.88.

Shack was located at Whiskey Cove on Pennock Island across the Tongass Narrows from downtown Ketchikan. Hazel and Carl routinely traveled back and forth in their skiff to town and to the Olympic in Thomas Basin, shown below. Location is next to cruise-ship dock today.

Whiskey Cove →

Thomas Basin, home of the Olympic—circa 1950. (Photograph from Ketchikan Museums.)

9/23—Thurs.

Carl started working on the oil stove soon as he got up. Made a trip to the boat. Started to install the burner at 12:00, and by 3:30, it was all ready to light. It started to smoke after burning for a while—Carl discovered several air leaks around the top. Used a whole can of stove cement but that seemed to do the trick. At 9 p.m., the Gills and the Bocks came over for news.

9/24—Fri.

Came to K. one week ago today. We went over to Wilsons early morning to get the things we had stored there all summer. She was making oatmeal cookies, so we all had coffee and cookies. Carl fixed the planks on our back yard and cut down all the weeds around the house. Then he made a wash bench on the porch. I washed all the windows and woodwork. Carl moved the porch door (it had a window) and put it in the kitchen. The people from Alexandra (Bocks) moved into the shed today. Mrs. Gill came over for news.

9/25—Sat.

Rain, Rain, Rain! Didn't feel so good today—so didn't do much. Carl worked on the path, carried gravel up from beach and widened the path.

9/27—Mon.

Started to do some more work on the ditch, but it rained so hard we had to quit. I washed clothes while Carl put some shakes on the east side of the house. Then he put a roof over the back porch and shed. Mrs. Gill made a short cake with red huckleberries and gave us two large helpings. Wrote 6 letters.

9/28—Tues.

Horrible nite, rained and blew very hard. We turned our heads around and slept with our feet next to the wall—too breezy. Went to town with Mrs. Wilson and Mrs. Gill. Pritchers came over at hi tide and put their boat on Wilsons' grid. Carl and I finished the ditch and piled all the brush in a huge pile in the middle of the front yard. Letters from Mother, Orie, and Florence. Spent $22.40.

9/29—Wed.

Beautiful morning, so Carl decided to go to town to see about getting the double windows. I washed clothes all day and made a red huckleberry pie. Carl came home about 4:30—inebriated! After dinner we went over to Clara [Gill]'s. She gave us some raspberry mousse. Spent $23.00.

9/30—Thurs.

Horrible night, blew very hard and rained and rained and rained! Rained so hard we could not work outside, so Carl worked on the outboard while I started painting the ceiling. Carl got the motor running and decided to go to town (in all the rain) to test the motor. He cranked half way across the channel, and still it wouldn't work—so he rowed across and never came back till 7:15—drunk again. I finished the ceiling and part of the walls—will finish tomorrow.

10/1—Fri.

A beautiful bright sunshiny day. Fishing season ended 2 weeks today. Decided to go to town.

Pretty stiff wind, and a bad rip at Thomas Basin.
Soon after we got to town, it began to rain—and
it rained all day and all nite. The wind blew a
gale, and it didn't just rain; it fell out of
the sky. Stopped to see *Lornty* and did some shopping. It was too stormy to row home, so Carl got
a room at Rosie's for $2.00, and we stayed there
all nite. Carl went out with his pals to the tune
of $40.00! I went to Coliseum. Ate dinner first at
Model—$1.00. When I got back to the room, Carl
was in bed, dead to the world. We had a fight—as
usual when he drinks too much. I didn't get much
sleep—cried most of night.

10/2—Sat.

Woke up at 6—too early, so went back to sleep and
got up at 9. It had stopped raining. Ate breakfast at DeLuxe—where Mrs. Burnett works. As we
came out, it began to rain again. We went down
to *Lornty*, and he and Carl and Stan consumed a
pint. Then they took us home. They were going for
oil anyway. We rowed ashore, and I fell on the
float—flat on my stomach—knocked all the wind out
of me. Carl went to bed immediately. I finished
painting the walls.

10/3—Sun.

Didn't get up till about 9—a beautiful day, sun
out all day and it never rained a drop. Went out
to the *Olympic* and worked there all day. Carl
couldn't get the oil stove to work; had a hole
in the stove pipe, and it was too drafty. He had
to come back to the shack and get some pipe and
fix it. Our mattress on the boat was wet on one
end, and our big quilt was damp. I cleaned up

all the dishes and such, then went back home and got dinner. Over to Pritchers' in evening, and I took my cake. On the way there, Carl fell. He was carrying the cake, and it flopped on its face on the beach!

10/4—Mon.

We went with Mrs. Wilson to town about 1:30. Second day that it did not rain. Bot our window from McGilvrays, also some thread for tatting a collar—which Mrs. Wilson will show me how to make.

10/7—Thurs.

Didn't get up very early. Too much paint smell last nite, so we did not sleep so good. Carl cleaned out the oil stove before breakfast was ready. It rained hard all day. We painted the dark woodwork white, and I finished the wallpaper border. Also papered the clothes closet door. Carl began to work on digging out the currant bushes.

10/9—Sat.

A nice day—no sunshine, but no rain and smooth water. We left for town about 10 a.m. The outboard worked swell till about half way across. Blew a head gasket. We had to row the rest of the way. Did my shopping and saw Clara Gill and Ina Wilson. We bought a new lamp table, inlaid linoleum for both tables; plastic for the edges, white enamel for inside, enamel for sink, outside house paint, pipes for sink, and window drapes. Ina towed our skiff home. Painted till 10 o'clock and got it all done.

10/13—Wed.

Carl burned the trash pile and also dug out all the berry bushes across the front, so now we have a clear view of the whole beach. Then he dug out the stump in the back yard and leveled it.

10/15—Fri.

Rained hard all nite and blew so hard the house shook. Washed clothes all day. By noon, it cleared up and the sun came out, so I hung all the clothes out and by 6 had some of them ironed. At 2 p.m. had an 18.1 tide. Carl worked on the eaves, gutter, and water barrel—and washed and scraped all the windows, both inside and out. Clara came over and spent the evening. Weather permitting, we will go to town in the morning. Used the new sink for the first time.

10/16—Sat.

Went to town! As the tide was so low, Carl had to drag the skiff a long way out to the water. We left about 9:15—good weather and the outboard motor worked perfect—both ways. Stopped in to see *Lornty;* they and Stan are going mud-shark fishing tomorrow down at Thorn Arm. Got back home about noon, and Carl and Clara began wrecking the boat shed. *[I have no idea why Clara helped Carl do this. Why not Hazel? Future entries give no clue.]* We made reservations on *Prince George* for Oct. 28. Mailed a birthday card to Zellah, but we didn't have any mail. It's been such horrible weather all week, so we cancelled tomorrow's visit with Ruth and Harvey. Thot they might get storm-bound over here! Groceries—$6.00.

10/17—Sun.

A beautiful day. Sunshine, and water was smooth as glass. Too bad we cancelled our date with Ifferts. Carl and Clara started again tearing down the old boat shed. They worked like horses all morning. Carl wrecked, and Clara lugged it up to the bank and piled it all on our place. They worked till 11:30, and then we got ready and went to Hansen's for 1:00 dinner. We had a nice time, and we left at 6:00. The outboard worked swell both ways. The radio sure was good tonite, could get almost any station. Waved at *Lornty* as they went by at 8 this morning. Ruby came over soon after we got home; had a big bag-full of shrimps. I was getting ready to take a bath this morning about 10—when Sophie came up and she stayed and stayed. I poured the water, got out clean underwear and towels and soap and she still stayed. The water was almost too cold by the time she left.

10/18—Mon.—Alaska Day

Carl and Clara began working on a new platform between the houses. They had to rip up all the old planks—so rotten they were just in pieces. Then they dug out all the mud and fixed drains here and there, and then lugged up planks from the pile on the bulkhead and put new sills in. It was an awful hard job, and they both worked so hard. I got dinner for them, did some wash, then made a pie and ironed. Mrs. Blodt spent most of the afternoon up here. I was taking a nap, and she walked rite in and stayed all afternoon. Ruby came over with some needles for me, and Mr. and Mrs. Wilson came over for a few minutes, too. We had just finished supper (7:30) when Mr. and Mrs. Blodt came! They stayed till 11 p.m.! And Carl was so tired! I didn't even make coffee for them, I was so disgusted.

10/19—Tues.

Carl and Clara worked on the rockery. It sure looks swell, and so much better than it did. We went over to Wilsons and bought a tiers for $5.00. I started painting the outside of the house. No rain since Friday!

10/21—Thurs.

Very cold, night especially. Sun shone all day. Carl made platform for tiers and put 2nd coat of paint on outside. I worked on our Travel Permits *[probably required due to wartime]* and wrote to Zellah and Insurance Co. Sophie came up and bothered me all afternoon. We will go to town early in morning and get our picture taken for the travel permits $1.50. *[Going from Alaska to Seattle for Thanksgiving holiday.]*

10/23—Sat.—Zellah's birthday

Came to town about 9:30. A beautiful day—sorry to spend 5 hrs. in a beauty shop. Took our permits to the Travel Bureau, but they were not notorized, so had to have that done—$1.00. Then went back to Travel Bureau and had our fingerprints taken, etc. The permits will be ready on Tuesday. We asked Jimmie Coffman to look after our boat while we are in Seattle.

10/24—Sun.

Another nice day—so I did some washing. Carl had to carry water from the creek—and he didn't feel

good today. Too much drinking yesterday in town
with the boys. I ironed, pressed, and mended the
clothes we will take with us to Seattle and packed
the suitcases.

10/25—Mon.

Another beautiful day, but very cold. Carl finished
painting the west side of the house and finished
the water system, so it will be all ready to use
when we get back. I finished pressing and cleaning
our clothes and got our suitcases packed.

10/26—Tues.
Whiskey Cove to Ketchikan

Up early. Today is the day we take the gas boat
to Ketchikan. Of course it had to rain, hard, all
day. Carl painted (varnished) both table tops
just before we left. Clara came over with us. The
engine didn't start for a long time, and then it
didn't work very good—too damp I guess. Ann Grant
came over and wanted to sleep on the boat while
we were gone. She is going to work at the DeLuxe
Café, and Wayne is leaving for Edna Bay. She can't
find a place in town to stay. Carl was mad because
I told her she could stay. But Jimmie would not
take care of the boat while she is here, so that
takes care of her. The boat is pretty damp. Had a
fire all day and dried it out pretty good. Got our
permits to go south. Also had the *Fishing News*
sent to Mother.

Seattle for Holidays

This is the Prince George, *the ship Hazel and Carl took for their holiday trip. This fire happened two years later when a fuel tank exploded while the boat was at the dock in Ketchikan. It had to be towed away from the town—which was built on pilings—so the town wouldn't burn. The ship was left to burn in the channel and ended up just a gutted shell. (Photograph from Ketchikan Museums.)*

10/28—Thursday
On *Prince George*

Left Ketchikan—on *Prince George*. Woke up at 2:30 and just couldn't go back to sleep again because Carl was snoring so loud. It poured down all night and all day too. We got up at 6, ready to leave by 9. Jimmie came over, and I gave him some bacon, butter, onions, and lemons. Jimmie and Clara helped us carry our luggage to the boat—in the rain and wind. We left the luggage with Carl, and Clara and I had a cup of coffee at the Federal Drug. Carl got a porter to take our luggage aboard, so we all went to the Stedman for a Tom Collins. At 10:45 finally got aboard. Ship's lunch was at 12:30, and we sailed about 1 p.m., so we could not wave to the "gang." It was so wet and foggy; doubt if they could have seen us anyway. While we were eating, the chief steward came to our table and said we had not checked in at Purser's Office. The ship could not sail till we did! Were our faces red! Then the cabin boy only brot one suitcase—said the other two were in some other stateroom. Carl talked to the cabin boy, purser, and chief steward—but by 12:30 we still did not have the suitcases. So Carl got mad and went to town with some of the officers. In about 15 min. we had the bags. A Mrs. Walter King is at our table, also a couple of stuck-up men! We got to Prince Rupert *[British Columbia]* at 7:45—raining as usual. We walked up town and tried to get into a beer parlor—too full. So we went in thru the Ladies Entrance. *[Canada's liquor laws at that time required that women have a separate entrance. The purpose was to prevent catcalls and general harassment from the men.]* Had to sit with a bunch of drunks and a black mama. Went to another beer parlor and sat with 2 other women and a soldier. We ordered 10 beers and they ordered 15! The waiter was pretty drunk, too. We sat there till after 10. Our boat was scheduled to sail at 11:15, but it was 1 p.m. before we left. I didn't sleep so well. Too much noise, I guess.

10/29—Fri.
On *Prince George*

Breakfast at 7:30. A beautiful day—sunshine and very cold. Smooth water too. Nothing exciting on boat; we both took naps right after breakfast. Arrived at Ocean Falls at 2 p.m. Sailed at 4 p.m. Walked around the town and sent a card to Clara. Went with Carl to a beer parlor. Started to get ruff after dinner about 7:30, so we went to bed. We did some rolling in the night, but I slept better than last nite.

10/30—Sat.
On *Prince George*

Another beautiful day. Sunshine and cold. Arrived in Powell River [a town] at 8:15, and the ship unloaded the paper it loaded at Ocean Falls. Sailed at 9:30. Beautiful weather all the way. After lunch, Carl and I went out on deck and stayed till we arrived in Vancouver at 2 p.m. Took bus to train depot. Left luggage and took a taxi back to town—$1.00. Went to a couple of beer parlors and walked back to the train. It departed at 5:15 and stopped at every village, town, and city for hours. 12:30 we arrived in Seattle. Tried and tried to get Mother—line was busy. Finally called Operator—line was out of order. Went up to Don's for clam chowder, then back to depot for our luggage. Everything was all locked up at Mother's. Arrived at 2 p.m.

*This is my grandparents' home in West Seattle
where Hazel and Carl stayed.*

*[Hazel and Carl stayed in Seattle from 10/31 to 12/12. While there, they
visited with our family and their many friends. They purchased an inboard
motor, an anchor hoist, and other important items needed for fishing that
weren't available in Ketchikan. They also purchased pieces of furniture
for their "shack" they had recently purchased. They had fifteen items to
be crated and shipped back to Alaska. Crating was fifty dollars and the
freight charge was a hundred dollars. They also had eye examinations
and dental work done—probably difficult to find in Alaska in the '40s.
Carl continued his drunken escapades while there, embarrassing Hazel
with her upper-class friends.]*

11/27—Sat.
Kent, WA—Staying at Zellah's

Muggy day. Tied two quilts. Carl went to Renton
and got his new teeth. Tried to get Carl to go to
a dance with Zellah and Rexford, but no luck. So
he played poker with the kids all evening. *[I was
six and Alan was eight. My mother was so mad at Carl when she found*

out he had taught her six-year-old daughter to play poker! I was good, too. As a young girl I recall that my Uncle Carl smelled "funny." Now that I know about his extensive drinking, I understand the smell.]

12/10—Fri.
Back in Seattle

Got up at 9:30—still no word from Carl. *[He was gone all the previous day and night.]* Called the Emergency Hospital. Dad went out to Henry's, then to City Jail, and to the Morgue. Still no word. Finally at 11 a.m. he called! Had been at Henry's all night, said he would be right out. I waited till 11:30, then walked down to bus and waited for 4 buses (12:20), and still he didn't show up. At 12:30 he called again and said a friend was driving him home. At 1 p.m., here they came—drunk as goats. We fed them, and after this guy left, I put Carl to bed. He had purchased a bilge pump for $20.00. He got up for supper and then went back to bed. Couldn't go to Thais', as Carl was in no condition to go. Mother and Dad went.

12/12—Sun.

Carl was sick all day. Stayed home on the davenport while Mother, Dad, and I went to Zellah's. Alan was selling Christmas trees on the highway in front of their house. The biggest and prettiest trees sold for 75 cents. He had sold several. We came home right after we ate. Carl had nite sweats all nite long. Had to change his nightshirt 3 times. We both felt rotten—my cold is so much worse.

12/13—Mon.
Seattle back to Ketchikan

Up at 5—cold and foggy. Left Mother and Dad's at 6 a.m.—2 large suitcases full of dishes, one sailfish, one over-nite bag and one gladstone bag. *[Hazel and Carl took a Canadian line to Vancouver, British Columbia.]* Boat left at 7:20. Very foggy. Had coffee and doughnuts in coffee room. No staterooms! Everything is so crowded—not even comfortable chairs to sit in. Arrived in Victoria at 12:20—left again at 1:30. We never went off the boat. About 900 soldiers came aboard with all their equipment, and 900 more passengers. Carl and I had to take turns sitting in our chair. If we both left, we wouldn't have a seat left when we came back. Very foggy all the way to Vancouver. Carl didn't eat hardly anything all day—even if it was all paid for. Got to Vancouver about 6:40. Took bus to *Prince Rupert* and went aboard to our stateroom. Sailed at 9 p.m.—so foggy, couldn't see a thing. The fog whistles blew every 30 seconds all nite long. Carl got hungry and ate some of his "stinky" cheese. He bribed a steward to bring us sandwiches and coffee at 10 p.m.

[Hazel and Carl returned to Ketchikan on the Prince Rupert. *The* Prince George *and the* Prince Rupert *were sister ships. They both arrived on the west coast in 1909. The* Prince *ships were considered among the finest short seas (inland and coastal waters) vessels in the world.]*

Prince Rupert. *(Photograph from Ketchikan Museums.)*

12/14—Tues.
Aboard *Prince Rupert*

Still cold and gray weather. Awful noisy people
on each side of us; slammed and banged doors all
nite and "A Pistol Packing Mama" song in front
of our stateroom. Got to Powell River at 3 a.m.,
and most of the noisy ones got off. My cold was
so much worse that I stayed in bed till noon. A
lifeboat drill at 11—but I was in bed. Four Coast
Guard boys from Ketchikan at our table. Arrived
at Ocean Falls at 10:30 p.m. Went ashore and got
coffee and a sandwich. Sailed again at 12:30. By
3:30 we were rolling, so I couldn't sleep. Not
so ruff, but we were taking it on the beam. Carl
got up and ate some more cheese!

12/15—Wed.
Aboard *Prince Rupert*

Got up early and had breakfast. Carl and I were
the only ones at our table—all the Coast Guard
boys slept in. Arrived in Prince Rupert at 3 p.m.
and didn't leave till 12:30 p.m. (or later) and
it was raining. After dinner we walked up town
intending to go to the show, but such a line up
we didn't wait. A cold wind blowing, so came back
to the boat. Carl's pal "Old Dad" made us two huge
sandwiches and a pot of coffee at 10 p.m. Rolled
some coming across Dixon Entrance.

12/16—Thurs.
Ketchikan

Arrived at 7:30, but it was 8:40 before we could
get off—so much red tape about immigration, etc.
Raining—of course! Jimmie came over after we were
home for a while. Carl paid him about $8.00. Went
up town and paid light bill ($1.00), had a hot
rum ($1.20), got my undershirt from Sears mail.
Cooked supper for Carl, Jimmie, and me. Had our
trunks and suitcases brot down by Cordell ($3.75).
Many callers: Jimmie about 5 times, Pritcher, Gene
Johnson, Big John (watchman), Blodt, Blackie and
Stanley. Horrible night—poured down and blew a
regular hurricane.

12/18—Sat.
Whiskey Cove

Good weather, but cold and frosty. Did some shopping. Sent *Alaska Sportsman Magazine* subscriptions
to Orie, Ma & Pa, Zellah, and Rex. Carl tried to
get the outboard going—but no luck—so between 12

and 1 p.m., we rowed home. Nice smooth water, so it wasn't too bad. Our shack was in good condition, but it took a long time to warm it up. Champ sure was glad to see us—slept here all nite; also the cat.

12/19—Sun.

Didn't sleep well—my cold doesn't seem to be much better. Carl left at 11 a.m. for K. and didn't come home till after 7 p.m. (pitch dark)—and he fell in at the Basin (again), all wet when he came home. Beautiful cold frosty day. Mrs. Wilson brot over a "note" stating that this property belonged to us.

12/20—Mon.

Another cold, frosty day. Carl went to town again today—why, I can't understand. *[She can't? After all this time?]* I felt worse today and had to go to bed. Had a fever too, I guess. Carl got home about 4 and wet to his knees. Pulled the skiff up and waded thru the water. Mrs. Wilson finally gave us our deed. Carl got some more lights for the tree.

12/21—Tues.

Cold day and windy, but not so much frost as the night before. Carl had to go to town once more. Three days in a row! Finished trimming the tree. Began to rain about 6 p.m., and we soon had water in our sink—for the first time! *[Interesting way to get water supply—rainwater directly into sink.]*

12/22—Wed.

Another wet, cold day. Carl stayed home from K. (first time since we came back from Seattle). Mrs. Wilson came over and invited us over for Christmas dinner, but we refused. I wanted to have our own dinner here in the cabin. We will go over to her place in the evening, and the Hansens will be there. Made candy all day—3 batches of fudge and 2 batches of pinoche. Packed a box of candy for Zellah and family and one for Mother and Dad. *[I remember that Hazel made candy often. She had quite a sweet tooth. My brother and I always enjoyed the fruits of her labor.]* Also sent them some canned salmon and some stick cinnamon.

12/23—Thurs.

Went to town with Ina at 9:30 and Sophie, too! Rained all day. Bought Carl a pair of brown felt slippers. Mailed Mother's suitcase, with candy and salmon in it for Zellah, too. Cost $2.02. Got ourselves a pork roast for Christmas dinner. When we got home, I gave Carl his slippers. Carl went over to see Griffin and took him a fruitcake and a glass of jelly. He has a cold, too, and was spitting on the stove!

12/24—Fri.

Cold, gray day—misty. Carl left for K. at 9:45, and not too smooth. He might have to stay in town overnight. Gene came over and invited us over for the evening. Sewed on my curtains most of the day. Very smooth all day, just like a lake, but no Carl. Was expecting him all day, but he never came. Went over to Ruby's at 7 p.m. Blodts were there, also Danny. They gave us a hankie each. She had a nice lunch, and we came home at 11 p.m.

and still no Carl. Was worried to death about him,
too. Champ and I went to bed, but not to sleep.
Was up at 1 and 2 and 3, so cold I had to get the
electric pad. By 3 a.m. it was very foggy so I
went to sleep, as I was sure Carl would not be
able to get over in the fog.

First Christmas
Our New Home – The Shack

12/25—Sat.

Carl came home at 7:30 a.m. Had a rose chenille
robe for me and a box of hankies. Blackie gave
me a box of hankies and a tie for Carl. Mr. and
Mrs. Chris Hansen came by at noon (on their way
to Wilsons') and gave me a glass baking dish and
a small bon-bon dish. Mrs. Wilson gave me an oval
glass baking dish. A beautiful day, sunshine and
smooth water, but by dark it began to blow. We
went over to Wilsons' about 6 p.m., played Chinese
Checkers and had a lunch. So stormy by 11 p.m.
that Hansens had to walk home. Our Christmas dinner was pork roast, roasted potatoes and carrots,
cabbage cooked in milk, celery, and rolls.

12/30—Thurs.

Carl was sick all nite. Rained and snowed a little.
Did some washing, and Vernie's washer burned out
a motor or something—anyway, it blew out a fuse,

and I had to finish washing by hand. Mopped the floor. Sophie and her old man went to town in the little skiff. At 6:30 she came up and invited us down for coffee.

12/31—Fri.
New Year's Eve

Chris Hansen's for dinner—4 p.m. Cold, clear day. Made a lemon pie. Danny came over for coffee. Wilsons, Blodts, and us left at 3:15 for Hansens'. Carl and Blodt did the rowing. Hansens served wine before dinner. Dinner was at 4—and this is what she had: fried chicken, oyster dressing, boiled potatoes, gravy, noodles, peas, carrots, pickled beets, celery, jelly, cranberries, bread, hot rolls, coffee, cheese, and mince pie. I washed dishes, Ina wiped, and Sophie half-heartedly helped. She sure acted like a fool! Then we played Chinese checkers and rummy. Mert looked at *Nat'l. Geographics*. At 11 p.m. we had a lunch—potato salad, spam, cheese, white bread, rye bread, pickled beets, strawberry shortcake with whip cream, and mince pie. We listened to the whistles from K., then we played more checkers and more rummy—till 5:15 a.m. In the meantime, it had snowed a little and then froze, so when we went home it was a crunchy crust. Stars were all out—the water was as smooth as a lake. Got home at 6 a.m. Champ was so glad to see us. We went to bed immediately and wanted Champ to stay in, too, but he had to go out and didn't bother us till we got up at 10:30.

And so endeth our 4th New Year's Eve in Alaska.

Photo of Hazel with two thirty-pound kings overlays their 1943 fishing record. This is a sample of the records Hazel kept for each year.

Part V
1944

Year of the Itch

Winter in Shack at Whiskey Cove, Pennock Island

1/1—Sat.—New Year's Day

Snow and very cold. While we were eating breakfast, we saw Gene catch a halibut out in front of his house. Later he came over with 2 huge slices of halibut and told us that our furniture had arrived. At hi-tide Carl rowed over to Union Oil and got 30 gals. of stove oil. Bill Frick was peeved because it was a holiday. *[Probably because liquor was not available.]* Very uneventful New Year's Day.

1/2—Sun.

Made a chocolate cake. Snowed most of day. All the trees and shrubs are covered, just like a lot of cotton. Very beautiful. Bright moonlight on the snow. Did some washing. Had Gene's halibut for dinner.

1/3—Mon.

Beautiful day. Cold, but smooth and still. We
went to K. in our skiff about 10 a.m. Took four
5 gal. cans to Union Oil. I got out and walked
to Thomas Basin while Carl rowed the 20 gals. of
fuel oil to the *Olympic*. I waited for Carl—had
coffee—then went up town. Stopped at Dick Harris'
and wrapped Arlene's skates and took them to the
post office—$.48 *[cost of a half-ounce letter now]*. Got our
mail and Ina's mail and packages. Got some more
Blue Willow dishes from Sears. *[These dishes are in antique
stores today.]* Went to bank to see about our balance
($1,400.00). Carl went over to see Louis Johnson
about bringing our furniture over. Weather permitting, he'll bring it over Wed. on hi-tide. Ruby
gave us some magazines.

1/5—Wed.

Lots of snow last nite but beautiful day, sunshine
and smooth water. Carl went with Louis Johnson
on his boat to get our furniture. At 10:15 they
were here. Jack Ickles and Blodt helped unload.
Everything arrived in good condition. A leg on
the dressing table got broken off, and the already
broken leg on the cedar chest came off. One of my
rose-color salt and peppers was all broken—but it
was badly cracked before I packed it. We worked
till 9 p.m. putting things away—hanging pictures,
putting things in drawers, etc. Sort of crowded
for such a small place, but it looks very cozy.
A cold wind is blowing tonight; suppose it will
freeze again. Saw a queer lite in the sky—looked
like a blimp.

*[The United States was the only power to use airships (blimps) during
World War II, and the airships played a small but important role. The
Navy used them for minesweeping, search and rescue, photographic*

reconnaissance, scouting, escorting convoys, and antisubmarine patrols.
Airships accompanied many oceangoing ships, both military and civilian.
Of the eighty-nine thousand ships escorted by airships during the war,
not one was lost to enemy action.

[As a child living in San Diego during the war, my husband recalls seeing
blimps tethered over Balboa Park. These small blimps, called barrage balloons,
were used to suspend aerial cables in the sky and foul enemy bombers.]

1/11—Tues.

A horrible day. It blew a gale all nite and all
day. Our oil stove blew out several times, so Carl
went up on the roof and turned the shield on the
smoke stack.

1/12—Wed.
Pennock to Ketchikan

Came to town about noon today. Beautiful day—sunshine. Still no mail from Mother or Zellah. Did
some scrubbing and cleaning. Cooked the salted
fish, but it wasn't very good. Went to the Coliseum to see Geo. McCohan—sure was a good show.
Half expected to get poison pains from the fish all
during the show, but we didn't. Bot some doughnuts and came home and ate them. Hope Sophie is
good to Champ.

1/15—Sat.

Some cat or animal ate all the "little pigs" that
I put in the cooler last night. Did some shopping.
Looked at Chrysler instrument boards. Started for
home about 1 p.m.—pretty ruff and a stiff wind.
Only rowed a short ways more when it got so bad
we (Carl) couldn't make any headway. White caps

all over the bay, so we had to turn back and go to Hansens'. Mrs. Wilson came by towing Jack Ickler and Anderson, so we rowed out and got a tow too. Got home at 4:30—just beginning to rain. Champ was glad to see us.

1/25—Tues.
Blackout from 7:15–7:30

Bad day, but Blodt wanted to go to K., so Carl and Sophie went with him in the big skiff. It was blowing pretty hard, so they put up a sail, but it didn't work so good—they took it down before they got around the Point. A small powerboat came along side and tried to tow them, but they got out of sight so I couldn't see. Began to snow and blow a gale about 2:30—so I guess Carl will not be home tonight. Waited till 5 p.m.—no Carl—so cooked my piece of fish and had some pudding. The wind blew the fire out—had to sit in the cold for about one hour. Then the top of the chimney blew off, and I could have a fire. Crocheted and listened to radio till 12—then read in bed till after one. Kinda lonesome, all alone. Sophie showed me her new coat before she went to K.—awful cheap looking. Gave her 2 letters to mail—one to Ruth and one for a Hug-Me-Tight pattern.

1/26—Wed.

Champ woke me up at 8:10. Another awful day—rain and wind. Hope Carl gets back today. Didn't do much as I was too busy watching for Carl. Went down to Blodts' to feed their cat, but it was locked up inside. Went over to Wilsons'. She made coffee and cake and hot bread and strawberries. Left at 4:30 and went to Ruby's. No Carl, so I stayed with

Ruby for supper. Had fried salmon. Played pinochle till 8 p.m., and Gene came home with me to see if he could get Blodts' cat out. Took a window out and pried a door loose—but still another door! So Gene said to wait till morning, and he would break a door down. Wild night! Champ was ill in the night and heaved all over the floor—even on the rug!

1/27—Thurs.

Carl came home at 9 this morning. Too ruff, and Blodt wouldn't come home. Carl put up a new chimney and painted it aluminum and then painted it all black on the inside. Filled the stove oil tank, too. Ina gave me her key to get their mail.

2/2—Wed.

A beautiful day. Sunshine. So I washed clothes and hung them outside. Left them out all night, and they froze. Carl worked at Blodts' all day. Had dinner at 5—Gene, Danny, and us. Playing Chinese checkers when Sophie came bursting in—and told everyone how to play! So we all quit. She stayed for me to help her with some crocheting. Had a woodstove fire in Clara's house all day.

2/7—Mon.

Sunshine! Cold and clear. Carl went to K. to work on hoist. I stayed home and worked on income tax. Clara kept Sophie away so she would not bother me. Carl came home about 5 p.m. Gills came over for news.

[Hazel and Carl seemed to have the best radio as friends always came over for the news. During the war, President Roosevelt mastered the use of mass

media by communicating with the public in his famous "fireside radio chats," in which he established a personal relationship with the American public unlike any previous president. As a child, I remember having to be very quiet while my parents listened to Roosevelt's radio chats.]

2/8—Tues.

Sunshine! Got up early (7 a.m.) and left for K. at 9:15. Beautiful day, cold and clear. Water smooth as a lake. Carl worked on anchor hoist all day. Went up town and sent some valentines to Alan and Arlene. Outboard worked swell on my way over, but half way back we hit a submerged stick and it sheared off a pin. *[The pin is a safety mechanism which fastens the prop to the drive shaft. If the prop hits something hard, the pin breaks instead of the prop. But the prop no longer works until the pin is replaced.]* So-o-o we had to row the rest of the way. Carl worked on the beach till dark. He fixed the outboard, so it works OK now. Gills came over for news at 9 p.m.

2/9—Wed.

Sunshine! Carl worked on the beach till the tide came in and floated the skiff, then he went to K. I stayed home and washed clothes. About 1 p.m. the wind began to blow, and it started to rain. Carl came home at 3—in a lot of slop. Couldn't remember if he turned off the oil stove. So he ate his dinner at 4 p.m. and went back to K. As it was so stormy, he didn't expect to come home. But at 5 p.m. here he came—wet and cold. The oil stove was off. Now he can't remember what he did with his suitcase! Outboard worked fine on <u>all three trips</u>. Gills came for 9 o'clock news. Champ wanted to stay all night with us—afraid Melvin would give him a bath.

2/17—Thurs.
Ketchikan

Nice day till about 3:30 when it rained and hailed. Carl worked all day on hoist. I helped him some, crocheted in the meantime. Went up town about 2:30. Saw Janet Smith *Lornty* and Lulubell Johnston. Bot 3 pork steaks—$.35; 3# new spuds—$.29; 5 bars Fels Naptha soap—$.35; pkg. Ivory Flakes—$.33; small head cauliflower—$.48; ½ doz. doughnuts, ½ doz. sweet rolls, small pie, loaf of bread—$.33. Total $2.13. Carl spent $2.25 for bolts, pipe, machine work. Stayed home and listened to the radio. No mail. Went over to see *Sonsie*—she said she would pay us when Charlie got his check—March 1st!

2/20—Sun.
Ketchikan to Pennock—to K.

A beautiful day. Sunshine all day. After dinner we went home (3:15) to get more tools for Carl. Saw a drunk Indian woman on the bridge. Police car came and took her. Saw Ruth and Harvey in Post Office. Went home with them, had coffee and cookies. Stayed till 11:30. Came home with 2 armloads of magazines. *[Magazines were a big form of entertainment in the 1940s when TV did not exist and radio shows were limited and usually broadcast in the evenings.]*

2/21—Mon.
Ketchikan

Cold day. Sun came out about noon. Carl painted gurdy and winch aluminum. I painted fore-peak with Kem-Tone. Gene came in about 4:30—had a bottle of whiskey but only stayed a few minutes. After supper we read the *Seattle Times* and to

bed early—both tired. Drunk guy (white) fell in-
between the next two boats from here. (Carl has
done that before—jumping from boat to boat when
drunk.) Spent $1.55.

2/26—Sat.

Rained on and off all day. Went to town right after
breakfast. Carl bot some alcohol for his *itch*.
Mailed card with $1.15 (for gum) to Dad for his
birthday—also one to Mother and a package with the
pink fastener, and a birthday card to Alan with
$1.00 in war stamps and a $.25 one for Arlene. Got
a new catalog from Sears. Bot some oilcloth—not
what I wanted, but no other choice. Asked Mother
to send me a cheap bedspread.

2/27—Sun.

Rain! Blew and rained most of the night. Carl didn't
work outside—too wet. We got ready to go over to
Hansons' about 3:30. Carl cranked and cranked on
the outboard but nothing happened. So-o-o, at long
last I had to row all the way across to Hansons'
while Carl continued to try to get it started.
When he would draw back on the rope, he would hit
my hand and the oar! We finally got to Hansons' at
4:35. Gills, Blodts, and Wilsons were all there,
came in Blodts' big skiff. Had dinner at 5 p.m.
Played checkers most of the time. Sophie was the
nertz; I sure get fed up with her. Had a lunch of
fried salt pork, fresh banty eggs *[banties, or bantams,
are miniature chickens]*, bread, smoked herring, cheese,
cake, and strawberries. Couldn't go home till the
tide floated our skiff—which was after 1 a.m. Of
course we couldn't get the outboard started, and a
cold north wind was blowing. At last Carl took off
the case, and it went. We got home the same time

as the "rowers" did. Made a fire and went over to Gills' till our place got warm. Went to bed at 3 a.m. and our bed was like ice—didn't sleep much.

2/29—Tues.

Another good bright day, so we got up at 6:30, and I started washing. Carl went to K. and worked on the hoist. He tried the outboard, but it didn't work; he is so discouraged after all the work and expense. I washed till nearly 3 when I ran out of water. Had turtle meat for supper—not bad. Started knitting some stork pants *[diaper covers for babies—also called soakers or pilchers]* for Rosemary Brott.

3/5—Sun.

Nice day. Got up late. I darned and patched all morning. At one o'clock, Clara, Melvin, Carl, Peck, and me walked across Pennock Island—and Champ too. It was a good walk, cold but not too bad. Lots of little lakes—all frozen—saw many deer signs, but never saw a deer.

3/6—Monday—Alan's birthday (9 years old)

Bad day—wind and rain. We left home about 9:30 and stopped at Union Oil for cable grease. Carl worked in the *Olympic*'s ice-hold all day. I worked on our income tax—it sure is a mess *[possibly due to Carl's inheritance money]*. Went up town and bot groceries. After our supper, we went to Coliseum—*Night Plane to Chung King*.

3/10—Fri.

Nice day. Sunshine. Made a package gingerbread. Clara Gill came in for a while. At 1:30 we left with the *Olympic* for Whiskey Cove. I steered while Carl dumped rocks. *[Evidently they had too many rocks for ballast.]* Tied up in the pond. Came home about 4. Had dinner. Carl went to bed early while I took a bath.

3/11 –Sat.

Sunshine and snow. Carl got up at 1:30 a.m. Called Melvin, and they went out and got the *Olympic* and put it on the beach. Bright moonlight. Carl came home at 4 a.m., and I cooked bacon, eggs, and toast for him, and at 5 a.m. he went back to the boat. At 6 a.m. he came home—slept till 7 and then went back. Floated off at 2:15 p.m. and tied up in pond—between Gill and *Wanderer*. Clara came over, and we played Chinese checkers. Ina invited us over Sunday evening—Mert's birthday. (I'll bet Carl won't go.) My first daffodil came out today.

Hazel with two friends (probably Clara and Sophie, The Pest).
Note the Olympic *behind Hazel.*

3/13—Mon.

Miserable day. Rain and wind. Clara was sick all day—too much from last night maybe. Carl went to K. to see the doctor about his *itch*. Doctor gave him a shot, some pills, and a blood test and said come back in one week. Ina came over to borrow my tatting book. *[Tatting is lace made by hand using a small shuttle, used chiefly for trimming. It is pretty much a lost art today.]*

3/24—Fri.
Left Home for K.

Snow and wind, very cold. Got up early. Had an awful time trying to get something for breakfast—everything was on the boat. Found about 1 cup of cake-flour, so made some hotcakes, but no bacon. Carl went out to boat, and I cleaned up the place and got everything ready to go on the boat. Of course Sophie had to come up and stay and stay. Carl came home at 11 a.m., and we began to load things in the skiff—2 skiffs full, including me. Left the pond about 12—cold and snowing—went to Standard Oil for gas, oil, and water. Tied up at "C" float. Carl went to get some ointment from the druggist for his *itch*—$.75. Letters from Mother, Zellah, Ella. Bedspread from Mother. Knife for Carl from Rex.

3/25—Sat.
Ketchikan

Beautiful day. Had a finger wave and shampoo at the Colonial Beauty Shop. After lunch, went up town and bot groceries. Carl met me half way home and helped to carry things to the boat—then we both went up town. Started to use coal-oil for our *itch*.

3/28—Tues.

Horrible day—<u>poured</u> all day. Never left the boat, it was so wet. Carl went back to the doctor for a report on the blood test—OK. Never came home till after 3 p.m.—then left again at 4 and didn't come home till 8 p.m. Nothing to eat all day, and went to bed. Blackout tonite from 7:15 to 7:45. Made a devil's food cake. 2 ½ inches of rain the last 24 hours!

3/31—Fri.

Left shack week ago today. <u>Bright sunshine</u> when I got up! So decided to do some washing. Carl worked on generators. Wouldn't work, so he went over and got Paul Gilmore to look at it, and he couldn't make it work either. So Carl took it up to Bob Burn's shop, and it has to be re-wound—$10.00. And it was the one we bought from Sears 2 years ago and have never used! Finished washing dishes when Mrs. Smith *Lornty* came over and wanted me to go to the bank with her for identification so she could get a check cashed. Did some shopping because tax doubles tomorrow. All our clothes got dry except Carl's underwear and overalls.

4/1—Sat.

And Snow! And rain. Made a devil's food cake for the dinner tonite, also an apple pie for us. Went up to Federal Drug for Carl's itch—but drug-gist couldn't recommend anything. Clara came and played checkers in afternoon. Went to wanigan at 6. Pouring rain.

4/4—Tues.

Nice day, so I went up town about noon. Ordered some crochet thread at Sears. Saw Carl, and he just came from the bank with $100.00. Went up to Newmann and got me a pair of stockings and pajamas. Got Carl 4 pair sox. Stopped at cold storage and got some herring from *Pirate*. Bill Wright on the *Ada* borrowed a cup of sugar. He about died when I took out the sack of sugar. He wanted to buy it, but Carl told him we had already traded it for a friend's canned peaches. *[Sugar was rationed during the war, and people bartered with it.]* Carl helped me clean the rest of the herring. The fish buyer we spoke to on the dock this afternoon dropped dead late today. He looked healthy to me. New generator—$26.00; asbestos—$.25.

4/5—Wed.

Nice day all day. I took down all our charts and made a list of all bays, harbors, etc. Had some more fried herring. Went to 7 p.m. show at Revilla @ $.65 each—*Forever and a Day*. Carl painted the stove and pipe on the downstairs stove—so smelly we had to turn it off and use the galley stove.

4/6—Thurs.

Carl is in his cups again and didn't get home till after midnight.

4/7—Fri.

Rained and blew all day. Was eating breakfast at 11:30 when Danny came. He stayed till after 1 p.m. and was back again at 2. Stayed for supper and all night. Slept on the floor. Too ruff and wet for him to go home. Carl was drunk again all day. Kept us both awake nearly all night with his nonsense.

4/8—Sat.

A beautiful day; should have washed, but Danny was here, and he stayed and stayed. Carl left and went up to the Shamrock about 11 a.m. Danny stayed till about 1 p.m. Then I went up town and had only been back a few minutes when Danny came back again—and still no Carl. So when Danny left, I went up to Shamrock and dragged Carl home. He was with Charlie Craft. Put Carl to bed, and I got dinner—he ate and went back to bed. I went to the Revilla. Carl was still in bed when I got home at 10 p.m.

4/9—Sun.
Easter Sunday

Horrible day. Rain and wind. Carl was in an awful mess, sick, couldn't eat. He went for long walks in the rain. Spent a lot of time on the *Faithful*. Asked Smiths over for the evening. Carl had to have some whiskey, so he got some from a boot-legger for $8.00 a pt.! He sure acted awful when Smiths were here. Smiths are leaving Tuesday morning for Duke Island. Guess we'll go too, but don't like that part of the country.

4/10—Mon.

Rained and blew most of the day. Weather permitting, we will leave in the morning. Bot $10.00 worth of groceries at Piggly Wiggly. Carl is getting good and drunk. Brot Stringer home with him—and 2 steaks, so big we'll never eat them all. After dinner, Carl insisted on going up town, so I went with him. We went to the Stedman and had 2 Tom Collins. Carl met a Coast Guard man and had to have him over to our booth—and asked him down to the boat, too. I think his name was Myers.

4/11—Tues.
Ketchikan to Naha Bay

Nice day, but windy. Carl is pretty drunk. Had a hard time to get him up and to the Income Tax Man—had to pay $25.00. Bot some groceries, and left at 1 p.m. with *Lornty* for Standard Oil. Got water and 22 gals.gas with 3 gals.oil for stove. Reported to Tower at 1:55—tied up at Float beyond Loring at 5:30. Carl was a mess all day—went to bed as soon as we arrived. Four other boats came in tonite—*Lila A*, *Sonny*, and 2 No. *[numbered]* boats. Carl was up several times in the nite.

4/14—Fri.

Rained off and on all day. Carl still sick—can't eat anything. I made a lemon pie about 9 a.m. A man and his kid came in a rowboat and took the little powerboat that is tied up here and went to Loring. He came home about 4 p.m. with his wife and another boy—simple minded. They live on a farm 2 or 3 miles from here and asked us to come up. Smiths came over for news at 7 and Chinese checkers.

4/16—Sun.
Loring to Ketchikan

Not such a good day. Cloudy and some wind. Got up
early, and Carl worked on the tag lines. At 11:25,
we left for Ketchikan. Good weather all the way.
Arrived in Thomas Basin at 3:15 p.m. Had to tie
up to *Sonja*, making us the 4th boat from float. I
went after mail—one letter from Zellah. Smith came
by and told us there was an opening at foot of
ramp where we were 2 years ago, so we went over.
John (watchman) told us we were too big—only No.
boats allowed. But as we were only in for a few
days, we could stay this time.

4/18—Tues.

Nasty day. Blew and rained all day. Made an apple
pie and some jello. Gus was here, and told us to
use soda paste for our *itch*. He had it and that
cured him. So we both took a bath and used it.
Coast Guard came and did their annual inspection
today. Walked on float for a while—then we took
our Chinese checkers and went over to *Lornty*. Will
go over to the cabin tomorrow if weather allows.
Boiler plate—$4.50; asbestos—$.50.

4/19—Wed.

Sunshine! We both took a soda bath before we dressed.
After breakfast, we went up town and bot grocer-
ies. Had a hair cut ($1.00) and bot some charts.
Had our lunch and pulled out for the Standard Co.
Then rowed across to the cabin. Rowed back to the
Oil Co.—then to Thomas Basin. Took a soda bath and
to bed—and *itched* all night! No mail. 2 charts @
$.75 = $1.50; hose = $1.80.

4/21—Fri.
Meyers Chuck

Horrible day. Rained and blew all day. At hi tide (noon) we bounced and rolled, almost like out in a storm. At mid-nite (hi-tide), it was so bad I had to get up and put the slats in the cupboard shelves. Carl started to put the iron plates on the bow, but too wet. I scrubbed the floor downstairs and crocheted. Never left the boat all day.

4/24—Mon.

Beautiful sunshine, but cold in the wind. Should have washed clothes. Made a lemon pie and cleaned the boat out. Mrs. Smith and I sat in the sun all afternoon and crocheted. Carl lengthened the cleaning troughs and put the iron plates on the bow. Took baths and doped ourselves in Purex—for *The Itch*.

4/26—Wed.

Another nice day—so I did some more washing, as Carl put on the last of his clean clothes this morning. About 9 a.m., we went clam digging with Smiths. Couldn't find any. We rowed up to Jimmie's shack and peeked in. Talked to *Vag*, who was on the grid. On our way back, we stopped at the reef and got a washtub full of clams in about 20 minutes. Came home and made a chocolate cake. Put hot applications of Epsom Salts on Carl's arms and legs for *The Itch*. Sent our Post Office key in with Gus on the *Taku Jack*.

4/27—Thurs.

A beautiful day—about the nicest we've had. *Lornty* went on John Egan's grid at 4:45 this morning.

At 8 am., Carl went over to help him scrub the hull and copper paint. They were all thru at 12 noon. I made bread and cinnamon rolls. Went to bed early as we expect to go on the grid at 4:30 in the morning. Two Coast Guard boats anchored here tonite, and the crew—2 in one boat and 4 in another—had a water fight.

4/28—Fri.

Cleaned and fixed all the clams—what a job! Up at 4 a.m. Rain and wind. We would pick a horrible day to go on grid. Almost decided not to go on grid but went on anyway. As soon as possible, Carl started scrubbing from the rowboat. Clay came over about 8 to help. Carl discovered that our keel was just about worn thru, so he had to take it off, turn it around, and drill new holes. Carl Entuit let him use his drill press. By this time, it was raining hard. I helped to scrub and copper paint. Old Captain Hanson wanted Clay and me to come over for carrots, and we had to listen to his sailing days in Siberia. He gave us carrots and rhubarb. I gave him ¼ of my cake. We tried to get off at hi tide, but the bow was stuck. Carl moved a lot of heavy things out on back deck, but no good. So we went to bed at 9 p.m.

4/29—Sat.

Dull gray day, some wind and showers of rain. Up at 5 a.m. and thot for a while we would not be able to make it off the grid. Pulled the skiff up on back deck and moved a lot of lead, too. Finally Carl could push us loose. Came thru the gap, too. Made clam chowder. Felt too miserable to do much. Doped Carl again with hot salt applications for his *itch*. Tom came in the store, very peeved. He took a bath last nite and washed his clothes and then discovered it was only Friday!

4/30—Sun.

Sunny day—with showers in between. Did some house cleaning, woodwork and doors, etc.—scrubbed both floors. Carl has a bad cold and went to bed about noon. He aches all over, and his *itch* seems to be worse. Broke out all over his chest and arms and back. I put hot towels on him; it seemed to help some. We have a bad leak in the stern, under the trolling hatch. Will have to go on the grid again.

5/1—Mon.

Not a very good day. Showery and blowing. Was up a lot last nite with Carl's *itch*; he had a fever and couldn't sleep. Put hot packs on his back, chest, arms, and legs. I had a bad headache, and after I made a pudding, took two aspirin and went to bed for a while. Carl went after water again, so I went too. Bot some curry powder, some cocoanut, and Blue-It *[for use in rinse water to preserve the whiteness]*. Put more packs on Carl, for *itch*, before we went to bed.

5/3—Wed.

My 44th birthday, and it sure was a flop! Carl was sick all night with a cold and *The Itch*. Rubbed him with sulphur and lard. That didn't do any good, so I washed it off and used a 50% solution of Sloan's liniment. It was too powerful, so washed it off and rubbed him with cold cream and then talcum powder. Began taking sulphur and molasses.

Went up to Otto's and put his grocery shelves in order. Made myself a whip cream birthday cake and gave no one any of it!

5/5—Fri.

A beautiful day. Sunshine and nice and warm. Hung my clothes again. Still wet from yesterday. Cleaned up and did some crocheting. At 11:30 a.m. we went on Jimmie's grid. He went with us and worked all day with Carl. Fixed the leak near the keel and put in more cement in the bow. Went ashore and looked at Jim's cabin and got some water. They finished the work about 5, then we had dinner. Carl was so cross today. He feels bad from his cold, but I don't think he has to be so bonooz. Played checkers and waited till 10:30 before we could get off.

5/12—Fri.
Wrangell

Nice day. Put the fish in the cans; Carl sealed and Clay stacked the boiler. Then they re-smoked the fish that we didn't can. At 1:30 the first batch was done, then we started the next. All the men left us. We crocheted till 5—when the other boiler was done. Took our smoked fish out of smoke house and left it to cool before we took it home. Gladys gave me some tatting samples. My cold is much worse.

5/13—Sat.

Raining. Scrubbed floors. Walked up to Gladys' house and divided the fish. Union meeting—voted to start fishing the 15th but will wait for word from

Ketchikan. Gladys and Janet came over after supper
and we crocheted till 9:30. Carl didn't get home
till 12:30. He and McDonald were beer drinking.

5/15—Mon.

Rained in the morning. I wrote letters and made
a bread pudding. Carl cleaned out the ice-hold,
all ready to take off. After lunch Gladys, Janet,
and I walked to town. Walked around the bay and
got some Devil's Club leaves for Carl's *itch*. *[The
indigenous devil's club plant is used by Native Americans both as food and
medicine. The Tlingits steep it into teas, mash it into salves, and chew, sip,
and steam it. They turn to devil's club to treat coughs and colds, stomach
ulcers, tuberculosis, hypoglycemia, adult-onset diabetes, etc. They call the
plant the "Tlingit aspirin."]*

5/16—Tues.

Another rainy morning, but by noon it had cleared
up. Gladys, Janet, and I went for a walk out to
Dibbles' and back. Picked more Devil's Club leaves.
Guess Carl will go to work with Herb at the gravel
pit @ $1.00 per hour. Birthday card from Zellah
with $1.00.

5/17—Wed.

Rained off and on all day. Telegram came this
a.m. that we could go back to fishing at 8 p.m.
tomorrow. Jack could hardly get away quick enough.
Went and got gas and oil and ice and beat it for
Kindergarden. Carl and Clay decided not to leave
till tomorrow morning. Took Carl up to see Dr.
Clements about *The Itch*. He said it was cedar
poisoning. Gave him some pills and said to use
carbonated Vasoline and to not wear wool next to

his skin. Carl went to work at 7:45 with Herb; at 8:05 he was home again. They had all the help they needed for now. Had whip cream on our gingerbread for supper.

5/18—Thurs.
Wrangell to Quiet Harbor

Up at 6:30—and raining and wind blowing. Went right over to Cold Storage and got in line for ice. We had our breakfast, and by 9:30, we had 3,300 lbs. of ice and one cake of bait. Went to Standard Oil and filled water tank, then back to float. Carl put the canvas roof back. After lunch, we left for Quiet Harbor. Kind of sloppy, and cold. Made some ice cream on the way. Got to Quiet Harbor at 4 p.m. Jack Brindley had 29 "hot" fish and Neimeyer had 33. *[I assume "hot" fish are those taken before the legal season starts.]* Horrible rain and williwaws, so we anchored by ourselves. After supper, Jack and Gladys came over after spark plugs. Jack said he thot that the strike was over at 8 a.m. instead of 8 p.m.! Went to bed at 9:30. About 18 boats in harbor, and all fished before 8 p.m. except *Lornty*, Bennett, and us.

First Official Day of Fishing

5/19—Fri.—4:45 a.m. to 9:30 a.m.
Quiet Harbor

First day of fishing. Only caught 4 kings, and 3 were too small—so our first day's catch was one 8 lb. red! Tied up to *Lornty* till about 3 p.m. Then anchored by ourselves. About 20 boats in harbor tonight. Today's fish = 1.

5/20—Sat.—5:30 a.m. to 2:45 p.m.

Cold. Rain. Wind. A miserable day. Only caught 4 fish all day & the largest was a white. Tied up to *Lornty* till after supper. They are having engine trouble. He only caught one fish today. Only 7 boats in harbor tonite. Total fish so far = 5 (4 +1).

5/22—Mon.—5:20 a.m. to 8:30 p.m.
Wrangell

Beautiful day. We left an hour or so before *Lornty* did. Our anchors were wrapped together, but it didn't take long to untangle them. We got one fish in Steamer Bay then started towards Quiet Harbor. Got one more on the way. About 3 p.m. *Lornty* decided to go to Wrangell and get his engine fixed. So we trolled toward Wrangell till 6:20. Had 4 fish. Had our supper about 9. So tired, went to bed at once—left all the dirty dishes. Saw 4 PT boats go by about 4 and in about 30 min. two more. Awful roar and huge swells. Today's fish + 5 (total 14).

5/26—Fri.
Wrangell to Snow Pass

Bad day. Wind and lots of rain. Had breakfast and went over to Standard Oil to get water and pay for the gas we got just a few days ago. Had to wait till 8 before he opened up. Went to ice dock for ice. Almost hit the reef at the far end of the dock. Had an awful time landing; Carl made about 4 trips. *Ella C* was selling and had a skiff dragging. It was in our way, so we had to wait till he was thru selling before we could get close enough to the ice bucket. By this time about 3 other boats had tied to us. Went around to the float, and a Coast Guard boat was taking up all the space. The plane float was on the other side—so we hung on to the end while I went up to pay for ice and collect for our 2 fish of yesterday. Cold Storage office was too busy, so we will pay next time (1½ tons ice—1 cake bait) and got $4.02 for our fish. At 9:10 left for The Nose and to meet *Lornty*. Fished there till noon—no fish, so ran to Quiet Harbor. Fished a while—no fish. So decided to run to Snow Pass. Anchored at 5:30 in Snow Pass.

5/27—Sat.—4:50 a.m. to 5:30 p.m.
Snow Pass

World's Worst Day. Just poured down all day, and the wind blew a regular gale all day. Tried to cook a pot roast on the oil stove and every time we turned, Carl had to go up on roof and turn stove pipe. Fished till 5:30 p.m. and only had 8 fish. *Lornty* was already anchored, so we tied to him for a while. Then anchored alone later. Many halibut boats went thru today.

5/28—Sun.—4:35 a.m. to 5:15 p.m.

A nice sunny day. Left at 4:35 and trolled till 5:15 p.m. Only had 4 kings and one halibut. Lots of boats arrived today—Jack Brindley, Herb Zieski, Kelsey, and *Sharkey*. I did some washing and scrubbed floor below. Carl and I tried to halibut jig on the back of the boat after supper, but no luck. Had to tow an Indian boat into the harbor. He had ignition trouble and had drifted all nite. We had heard a gunshot, but thot someone was shooting fish—it was him trying to draw attention. The Indian boat had a man, woman, 2 young girls and boy, and a huge dog in a little boat. After we towed him in, we tied up to *Lornty* for a few minutes, then off again.

5/30—Tues.—Memorial Day—4:35 a.m. to 12:05 p.m.

Fair day. Blew off and on all day and rained in spells. Fished till noon, had dinner all ready when Carl decided to quit. Hadn't had a bite for hours. *Wanderlust* came in late this evening and brot us some venison. Started on a crocheted tablecloth—for myself!

5/31—Wed.—5:15 a.m. to 12:50 p.m.

Last day of May, and what a day! Regular December weather. Rained all day, and about noon, a Southeaster blew up. So we quit and came in—with 2 small fish, and one of those was white!

6/2—Fri.—4:55 to 11:15 and 1:10 to 6:50
Snow Pass to Steamer Bay

And another beautiful day, but not many fish. Got 3 fair-sized ones—and lost one. Decided to go to Steamer Bay. Tried to find *Lornty*, but they were gone. Started fishing at 1:10 p.m. *Ann* and *Jerry* followed us across. Got 3 nice big ones and lost a big one—Carl was mad, as usual. A self-powered barge came in the bay about an hour after we got here. Anchored where we usually do—so we had to go over nearer Happy's place. Two of the boys off the barge came over in evening. Carl gave them some herring for bait, and they gave Carl a pack of cigarettes. Carl and *Jerry* got drunk.

6/4—Sun.
Wrangell

The only morning we could sleep for over a week, and Carl wakes me up at 6:30 and will not let me go back to sleep. So I washed clothes. After dinner I asked Carl to go up to first store with me to help carry milk. Because I would not give him a bottle of beer, he wouldn't go—so I had to go alone. As I was ready to leave, he came in and bot a case of beer ($5.75)—so I had no help on the groceries. Rained as soon as I had my washing on the line.

6/5—Mon.

Horrible day. Poured all day. Carl is an awful mess and getting worse. *Benny* and *Sharkey* don't help much. Carl came home with 2 huge steaks. He went off again as soon as he ate, so I went to the show—*Mayor of 44th Street*. Stove was flooded with oil when I came home.

6/6—Tues.
Europe Invasion!

[The Allied invasion of Normandy on the northern coast of France took place on the morning of June 6, 1944. The D-Day invasion was directed by the American general, Dwight D. Eisenhower. It involved troops from a dozen countries and about five thousand boats, the largest war armada ever assembled.]

Mailed Father's Day card to Dad with $1.00. Went to Standard Oil Co. early (in the rain) for gas, oil, and water. Then to get ice—and such a time we had. Carl was too drunk to do much, and I couldn't do it all, so the cold storage man came down and helped. Took 1½ tons and 2 cakes of bait. By this time it was getting ruffer and ruffer and raining, too. Tied up to inside float. Carl went up town and got more oiled up and brot some booze back. He and *Sharkey* had some, and then we went back to float. Carl wouldn't even cover his ice. He went to bed and slept most of the day. I poured most of his whiskey out and re-filled the bottle with water, and he never knew the difference. I'm sure disgusted with this drink business.

6/8—Thurs.—Carl's birthday
Point Baker to Cape Pole

Good weather, so we left early. No sunshine but smooth water all the way. Lots of boats here at

Pole. Not much fish. Carl broke 2 doz. eggs—fell into the hold! *[The icehold is used as a refrigerator, as well as for icing fish.]* Everyone's talking about D-day in France on Tues. We lost so many of our boys—it's a shame. Sure hope the "higher-ups" know what they're doing.

6/12—Mon.—4:30 a.m. to 7:55 a.m.

Began fishing at 4:20—fished all the way to Cape Decision—no bites. Saw Charlie Coe—no fish. He had been here for a week, too. So we pulled up and came in here *[Wrangell]* to wash clothes. Carl skiffed 40 gals. water, then he went hand trolling—only got one small rock cod. Janet Smith made ice cream in afternoon, then Carl and I went rowing and trolling—got nothing. This has been a beautiful day. Sunshine and no wind. Hope we get a few more of them.

Trollers near Wrangell.

6/14—Wed.—5:15 a.m. to 8:30 a.m.
Pt. McArthur to Malmsbury

Left McArthur with 6 boats ahead of us and 4 in the rear. But too foggy at the Cape, and we all came back. *Lornty* and us started to fish, but all the other boats went back to harbor. John Egan stopped to talk to us, but before he got into the harbor, the fog all lifted. So we picked up our lines and ran for it. Punch Board John was ahead of us, and about 7 or 8 behind us. No fog around the Cape, but dirty tide rips and ocean swells. We rolled and tossed, and I got sick and had to go to bed for about one hour. *Lornty* and *Motion* tied up to us, and 5 other boats anchored out. John came over for breakfast. I made ice cream for us all; also a bread pudding for tomorrow. Another beautiful day—3 in a row. Something will bust open in a day or two, I betcha!

6/15—Thurs.—5:15 a.m. to 6:05 p.m.
Malmsbury to Gedney

Another beautiful day. Left M. at 5:15. All the other boats went across to Pt. Alex. but *Lornty* and us. Trolled up to Gedney—no bites—pretty ruff and rolly, so we pulled up the lines and ran up to *Lornty*, all ready to go to Alex. But he had 2 fish, so we decided to stay. Then pretty soon he pulled up and came over to us, and we just got a big one, so we fished all day between Pt. Ellis and Troller Islands. Got some nice big ones—2 were white. One was so big Carl could hardly haul it in—66# 4 oz.! I took a picture of Carl with it.

Carl with king salmon—66 pounds 4 ounces.

6/18—Sun.

Fog-bound. Rolled and bumped into *Lornty*, so at 10:30 p.m., they untied from us and anchored by themselves. Carl got up at 4:00 a.m.; we had drifted out toward the entrance, to the place about where Reichwein had his scow last year. Evidently our anchor hit a high spot, as we were not drifting when we got up. After we had our coffee, we noticed a can that did not move with the tide. We discovered that it was a herring net, and we were on top of it—but our anchor line had not gone thru it. We pulled up and went ahead—never touching the net. As we went by *Progress*, he commenced to bawl Carl out for stealing herring out of his net! We didn't even know it was his net, let alone bother it. Carl tried to talk to him and ask for an explanation, but he went down in his boat and wouldn't come out. So we went back and made him come out. He was so wild and unreasonable—wouldn't let Carl explain—just kept accusing us of stealing his herring. Finally he got in his skiff and went over to his net, and we stayed and watched him. His net was not torn, and he had some herring—but not much. Carl was very much upset all day. Too foggy to go out, so I washed clothes, and Carl got 20 gals. of water.

6/22—Thurs.—5:45 a.m. to 11 a.m.
Gedney

Rain and fog—but decided to go out anyway since we have been fog-bound for two days. I had a terrible headache. It began to get ruffer and ruffer, and I got good and sick and went to bed. Finally at 8 a.m., I did manage to get some breakfast for Carl, and then I went back to bed. All this time, we never had a strike, so Carl said we had better go in. Carl started to get rocks, as our ice is just about all gone. I went to bed and stayed there all day. Carl didn't feel well either. Lorntys came over for the news.

6/25—Sun.—6:45 p.m. to 8:30 p.m.
Gedney to Malmsbury

Another beautiful day but we can't fish—even if there were some fish—because there is no buyer. But Carl got up at the crack of dawn, as usual. I didn't get up till 7. After breakfast, I made a chocolate cake and a bread pudding. Then at low tide (11:00), we all went ashore—*Alice E* and *Lornty* and us—and dug some clams. Came home, and I cleaned them all (awful job), then cooked dinner. Carl made Jimmie a slingshot. Then we all decided to go to Malmsbury so we could be there for the early morning fishing. Anchored at 8:30, and the two other boats tied to us. Had steamed clams and hot muffins for supper at 9 p.m.!

6/26—Mon.
Gedney

Rain and fog, but smooth water. Fished at Pt. Ellis till 12:30—when the fog got so bad we could not see Baranoff Island, we picked up. The whole bay was full of schools of herring—we trolled thru several of them—but got no fish. Dropped our lines again in front of Gedney—but no luck, so came in. Carl made a mistake and put gas in the fuel-oil tank!

6/28—Wed.

No one went out today—so we didn't either. I cleaned, steamed, and ground up all the clams and canned them using the pressure cooker. Only had 3 pints. Jimmie Travis came over several times. He likes his slingshot. Carl got some more rocks for the hold. Janet Smith borrowed our magnet to get her crochet hooks. *[Metal objects dropped overboard in shallow water could be retrieved with a magnet tied to a line.]*

7/1—Sat.—4:45–3:30 and 4:00–6:00
Trollers Island

Left Trollers Island at 4:45 and followed *Alice E* out thru the rocks—a short cut. Fished at Pt. Ellis all day. <u>Got a halibut that weighed 147 lbs.</u> dressed—and $3.60 for the liver. Had an awful time getting it on deck. Carl shot it 3 or 4 times and dragged it behind for about an hour. It chewed thru 2 ropes! *[This was one aggressive old halibut! Seemed as tough as the large shark they caught earlier. Interesting that they sold its liver, too. Apparently fish livers from different fish varieties were of value.]* In afternoon, when it was dull, we went into Gedney and sold—about 3:30. The first day of July—hope this is the beginning of better luck for us.

7/2—Sun.—4:30 a.m. to 1:15 p.m.
Trollers Island to Explorers Basin

Left T.I. at 4:30 and fished at Ellis Pt. Another dull gray day. Broke 3 tag lines, lost 2 leaders and one spoon. Hit a 10-fathoms place twice! I had a nap and so did Carl. Began to blow about 11, and by 12 it was good and ruff. Couldn't find Jack to tell him we were going into Gedney—so-o-o had to turn around and run all the way back to Pt. Ellis.

He was on his way then to Gedney—but it got ruffer and ruffer, so we went into Explorer's Basin. We were following Jack from a distance, and we ran right onto a <u>reef</u>! Hit on the port side—not too bad, but scared me silly! We watched all day for leaks, but none showed up.

7/8—Sat.
Elena Bay

Another beautiful day. Up at 7:00. Made hot biscuits and fried fish for breakfast! Jack and George got some meat last nite, so all the men went over and skinned and cleaned. Brot it back to our boat and we cut and divided it into 7 parts (for the 7 boats). Had fried liver for lunch. Had more fried fish for supper. Put our meat in a sack in the hold, covered with pepper to keep the flies off (so Janet said) but inside of an hour, I had flies on 2 pieces! Cleaned it all up and wiped it all off again. Saw a huge bear on the beach.

7/9—Sun.—8:40–11:00 and 12:15–3:50
Elena Bay—Pillar Bay—Red Bluff Bay

Up early. Beautiful sunny day. I ironed and made a pudding. We all decided to go to Warm Springs, so we all left at 8:40. George Collins went back to Gedney for gas, but all the others came along—McDonald, Dan or *Dock*, Kelseys, Zieskis, Brindleys, Lorntys, and us. Smooth till we got to Pt. Ellis, when it got worse and worse. White caps, and we rolled so Jack went into Pillar Bay, and we all followed him except Herb and Kelsey—they kept right on going. We ate lunch and then started out again. Pretty good all the way across till we got near Baranof, when a West wind blew and it

really was ruff. Jack went into Red Bluff Bay, so
we did too. Tied up to *Ruth* at some pilings. Went
ashore and picked some salmon berries. Beautiful
scenery—snow and waterfalls.

7/10—Mon.—3:45 a.m. to 7:10 a.m.
Red Bluff Bay—Warm Springs

Left Red Bluff Bay at 3:45. Cloudy and foggy. A
bit lumpy now and then, but it smoothed out before
we got to Warm Springs *[therapeutic hot springs]*. Hope the
Springs will help with Carl's *itch*. Arrived at
7:10. Carl took a bath in the Springs immediately. I washed clothes, got dinner, and then took a
bath—so hot I nearly passed out. Went to bed for
a while. After supper Gladys, Janet, Carl, and I
went for a walk to the falls, across the swinging
bridge, and to the lake.

7/14—Fri.—10:00 a.m. to 9:30 p.m.
Tyee

Not very good weather, so we stayed in till 10
a.m. It was nice all the rest of the day, so we
stayed out till 9:30. The cannery here will not
buy after 8 p.m., so we will have to sell tomorrow. Got 16 salmon. The 3 from *Lady Alyce* came
over and stayed for coffee and didn't leave till
11 p.m. Carl and I were so tired and sleepy. Carl's
itch is much worse—guess Warm Springs didn't help
much. Might have made it worse.

7/16—Sun.—6:00–1:00 and 3:30–9:00

Nice day. Didn't get up very early. Most of the
boats didn't leave till we did. Carl started
using plugs today, and we began to get fish right

away. Plugs are a mess—lots of strikes and lose lots, but they seem to get more fish here than the spoons. Fished till 12:00 noon. No bites, so we went in. Had 17 salmon—sold, but as it was Sunday could not get our money.

7/17—Mon.—4:20 a.m. to 3:15 p.m.
Tyee

Dull, gray day—misty. Still using plugs. Got about 15 more kings today. As I was about to dish up the Malt-o-meal this morning, the glass bowl fell out of my hand onto the stove and smashed all to pieces—glass over everything. So I had to throw the mush overboard, and we ate corn flakes. Very foggy by 2:30, and no fish—so we came in. Yesterday and today we made $123.00.

7/23—Sun.—4:30 a.m. to 4:00 p.m.

Fog, wind, mist, and ruff water. But we fished all day anyhow. Fished down to Malmsbury and in the harbor, then back. Only made $50. Others made $60 to $100. We rolled and tossed all day. I'm so tired tonight—just from rolling—couldn't cook much. Corn flakes and toast for breakfast. Warmed-over scalloped spuds and fresh tomatoes for lunch. Had to hang on to the teakettle while it boiled. Got sort of sickish and had to go to bed for an hour. Cleaned all but 7 fish today (44 in all). No money at the scow tonite.

7/26—Wed.—4:00 a.m. to 5:00 p.m.

Dull gray day. Fog and mist. Many, many boats came in from Alexander, Tyee, Security, etc. *Lady Alyce* came and tied up to us about 7 p.m. and stayed till

I sent them home at 9:30. Walter gave me a bear's tooth from one that he had shot up at Sitka. They want to follow us in the morning as he has never fished here before and has no harbor charts.

7/27—Thurs.—4:00 a.m. to 4:30 p.m.
Gedney to Malmsbury

Got lost in the fog with *Lady Alyce* following us, and we were following *Lindora*. Turned around a couple of times and finally trolled towards Malmsbury and ran out of the fog. Got into a school of cohoes and got about 15 all at once. Had a sea lion chasing us too. Carl shot at him, but we rolled so, it only scared him. Went in early to sell, had our dinner, and then left for Malmsbury. Picked up *Lady Alyce* outside of Gedney and took them with us.

This is a photo Hazel had of Lady Alyce. *She was new to the area. As the tide was going out, she got hung up on a local rock that was a hazard well known to the old-timers. So the old-timers found her situation very humorous, especially since* Alyce *did not tip over, which could have been a disaster. The text on the back of the photo says everyone got off safely and re-boarded when she floated free at the next high tide.*

7/30—Sun.

Too ruff to fish, so we stayed in. *Lady Alyce* was out for 3 hrs.—only got one small fish. About 7:30 a whole bunch decided to go trout fishing and left, but we didn't go.

8/2—Wed.—5:15 a.m. to 9:30 a.m.

Dull, gray day. Fished in front till 9 a.m. and only had 5 fish, so we came in. *Alice E* tied up to us. About 11 a.m., *Lady Alyce* came back from trout fishing and tied to us, too. Brot us some trout. Had fried trout and hot cornbread. Carl cleaned out the oil stove—it sure was full of soot. We sold to Reichwein and paid the $3.00 for the chicken. He was so drunk he couldn't figure our slip. Overpaid us about $3.00, but we returned it. Many, many boats in the harbor tonight.

8/6—Sun.—4:30 a.m. to 11:30 a.m.
Malmsbury to Gedney

A nice day. Fog till about 9 a.m. but no fish. Didn't get a bite till about 8:30, so we picked up and came in. Only had 7 cohoes. Carl started to get drunk while gassing up—and went back for more as soon as we ate. He stayed out till 9:45. Russell and *By George* were with him. Bud on the scow had to kick *By George* off, he got so mean. Russell came over after me, but I wouldn't go. Carl came home very much polluted.

8/8—Tues.
Gedney

Carl is still on a binge. Got up at 4 a.m. and yelled at Russell. He and Carl tied the boats together. Then Carl went over to his boat and the 2 of them drank whiskey till I got up and called Carl home to eat breakfast at 6:30. Then Carl and Russell went over to Hansen's Barge and stayed and stayed. I washed clothes. Had to go after Carl to help me take the clothes ashore to the creek, so I could rinse them. We were short of water, and Carl just won't get any for me. Genevieve and Russell parked here most all day; she even brot him a bowl of soup while he sat here. Then back to the scow went Carl and Russell. Stayed till 5:45 when I called him home to eat, but he didn't come till 6:30. He had 2 qts. of beer and 3 pints of whiskey. *[Whew!]* They wanted to go to Teb. deer hunting. I wouldn't go as Carl was too drunk—so I hid the key.

8/15—Tues.
Security to Petersburg

Left Security at 5 a.m. on our way to Petersburg, followed *Lady Alyce*. Smooth water all the way. Ran into fog just beyond Cape Bendal and had to run by compass for about 2 hrs. Went up to see Dr. Benson—examined Carl and gave him some drops and some soap to use each nite for his *itch*. Have to stay here for a few days.

8/16—Wed.
Petersburg

Sure seemed good to sleep late. But "The Pest," Russell Dowell, was here before we had breakfast and stayed and stayed. I get so fed up with him I could scream! *Alice J*, *Ella C*, *June*, Brindleys, *Essu*, and *Beacon* all came in today. *Service* came over and beat his wife, and while they were here, in walks Russell and Genevieve! They left for Wrangell about 11 a.m. and expect to see us there in a few days! Carl got some more soap pads from the druggist (for *The Itch*). Bot groceries. Went to the show—*China Girl*.

8/17—Thurs.

Rained some in the night, also today, but nice in afternoon. Went to see Dr. Benson again for *The Itch*, and Carl is to go back again on Saturday. Went to the show again to see *Big Street*. We took our last sulphur bath tonight. Tomorrow we take a soap and water bath. We went on the grid.

8/19—Sat.

Most of the trollers left today—*Tonto*, *June*, and Brindley. Carl went back to the doctor. He gave us some salve—thinks we might have **7 yr. itch**! *[Seven-year itch, also called scabies, is an odd term for a small mite that lives under the skin. It causes severe itching, beginning in the wrists and feet. They call it the seven-year itch because it is very difficult to get rid of.]* Carl is drinking too much. Forgot all about the show, so I went alone. Many more halibut boats came in today, all loaded up again with booze.

8/21—Mon.

Beautiful day. Did some washing. Bennett tied up to us when he got off the grid at hi-water. Carl went to see doctor about *The Itch* again. He can't do anything more for us. Said we had better go to Seattle and see Dr. Ollund. (Can't do that for a while.) Gave us some more drops and pills. We bot rubbing alcohol, poison ivy lotion, and Epsom salts.

8/22—Tues.

Expected to leave today, but Carl felt too rotten. I bot some more groceries, and Carl bot more whiskey. I went to the show, but Carl stayed home and drank. Bennett and *Christine* met me after the show, and we had a malted milk. While we were in there, Carl came by. Came home, and Bennett came in and stayed till 12:30. Hid Carl's bottle, and he got mad at me.

8/23—Wed.

Carl got up at 4 a.m. and went over and woke Bennett up. Then he went back again at 5 and wanted to leave for K. Bennett came over for breakfast. (I didn't know Carl had asked him.) Carl slept most all day. Bennett left us at hi-tide to tow *Christine* off the grid. I went to Coast Guard and bot a Wrangell Narrows Chart. Carl bot 2 more bottles of whiskey, came home, and slept till dinnertime, got up and ate, went back to bed, and stayed till Bennett and *Christine* came by at 11:30. The old fish prices still prevail—thot new schedule was for the wholesalers only. Carl wanted to leave at hi-tide, but I hid the key as he is in no condition to drive a boat. I don't know what to do about his drinking. I even threatened to leave him, but that doesn't work. *[Not surprising; true alcoholics are addicts and often are not susceptible to logic.]*

8/24—Thurs.

Rain. Carl left the boat early this morning and didn't come home till 11:30, so drunk he could hardly walk. He was soaking wet from the rain or maybe from falling off dock—who knows? He went to bed and slept all afternoon, got up and ate

supper, then went back to bed. I took a long walk
out toward the mouth of the Narrows. Pat Devinity
and wife came over, and we made ice cream, but
Pat and Carl were too drunk for any use. Carl got
sick and had to go to bed—so I had to sleep on
the floor till 2 a.m. when I couldn't stand it any
longer and made Carl give me half the bed.

8/25—Fri.

Rained hard all day. Carl has been gone most of
the day. Bennett brot him home at 6:30—he had been
asleep on Bennett's boat for 2 hours or so. Bennett
left as soon as he ate, and Carl went to bed, so
I went to the show. Mrs. Devinity flew to Wrangell
and back today ($15.00) to get their mail. Wrote
letters to Mother and Zellah. Niemeyer came by
and said he bot the *Sydney* for $1,500.

8/26—Sat.

Carl is in a worse mess—went to Pat's boat and
stayed all day. I did some washing and had to pack
water as we have been out of water for a week or
more. *Essa* and *Alice E* came in with 5,000 lbs. of
kings. A couple came over to look at our boat—to
buy it. Carl told him $5,000. (Of course Carl
didn't talk to me about selling the boat.) Don't
think the people had $5.00 anyway. Took Carl for
a long walk all over town tonite. Made myself a
reservation for the Ketchikan plane for Sunday,
3:30 p.m. If Carl is still in his cups, I'll go
to the shack; if he sobers up, I'll stay.

8/27—Sun.

Raining. Rained hard all morning, but by noon it
cleared up, and the sun came out. Carl is beginning

to sober up, so I cancelled my plane reservation. He is pretty sick, but since it's Sunday, he can't get any beer or whiskey. Went for a long walk. Mr. and Mrs. Pat and a friend came over—all pretty drunk. Carl went to bed, and I went to the show. Bennett, *Christine*, and his gal friend took me for a malted milk after the show. Bennett brot me home and stayed, and I made coffee. Carl is getting sicker and sicker. At 12 noon today, we went over to Union Oil and got gas, water, stove oil—<u>expect</u> to leave early tomorrow.

8/28—Mon.

Raining. Horrible day, poured all day. Carl is too sick to travel so will have to stay another day. Made a batch of brown sugar cookies. Looked at *Hansen's Handbook* [Captain Farwell Hansen's Handbook for Piloting in the Inland Waters of Southwestern Alaska]—$10.25—too much, so I did not buy it. About 2:30 p.m. Pat D. came back! Carl saw her in a beer parlor, very drunk, so we did not talk to them. Saw Mrs. Harry Race come in on the plane.

8/30—Wed.—8:20–3:15
Snow Pass to Meyers Chuck

Never woke up till 8:00. Beautiful sunshine—all the boats were gone, and we were all alone. Started out as soon as we got dressed. Carl was pretty sick most of the day and had to go to bed. When we were opposite Ratz Hbr., Carl said to steer for Ship Island, and he pointed across. So I did, and we ended up going to Union Bay Cannery! Went around Misery Island and into Meyers Chuck. *Lornty*, Stan, *Vag*, and *Jim K* were all here. Jim had 200 lbs. and so did *Vag*. Traps closed last night, so we should get a few fish now. *[The traps must have closed for the season as, otherwise, they were required to be closed only on Sundays.]*

9/3—Sun.—5:55 a.m. to 3:40 p.m.

First day of fishing since 8/14. Nice day and smooth water. Fished till 3:40. *Lornty* and Stan left for Ketch. 12 cohoes and 1 hump. After supper, Lonesome Pete brot his accordian down to *Duchess*, and I took my mandola over, and we played and sang till 9 p.m. Carl began to *itch* again today so took some more drops.

9/5—Tues.—5:45 a.m. to 11:30 a.m.
Meyers Chuck

Beautiful day—smooth water and bright sunshine. Caught 9 cohoes. Carl got two 5-gallon cans of water, and I washed clothes after lunch. Then he got 2 more cans. It's pretty brown *[silty]*, but soft. *Echo* came in after dark tonight and tied to us, of course—made Carl so mad! Carl talked to West today, and he wants $4,500 for his place and boat. *Vag* brot me a pail of ice for ice cream, then when I got it made, he didn't want any. End of fishing season.

Totals for 1944 season: 7,563 lbs. = $1,054.76.

9/8—Fri.—6:00 a.m. to 11:00 p.m.
Meyers Chuck to Ketchikan to Home

Got up and decided to go to Ketchikan. Beautiful day, smooth water and sunshine. *Knickerbocker* was behind us all the way. Wind started to blow when we were opposite City Float. Got pkg. at Sears;

mail; deposited $450.00 in bank. Blodt has a new float house—all done, right on our beach. House was in good condition.

9/9—Sat.
Home

Beautiful day. Took all the clothes out of the trunk and hung them on line to air. We seem to have *The Itch* again. Wrote letters to Mother and Zellah.

9/10—Sun.
Home to Ketchikan

Nice day. I started to make an apple pie. My oven wouldn't get hot, so Carl cleaned out the lower oven and I had to bake the pie at Clara's. Went to town. Got the film of Carl's hands being scrubbed by me. Letters from Orie and Zellah. Went for a walk, had a malted milk, and went to Coliseum to see *Something about a Soldier*. I won $45.00 playing Bingo! *[Interesting that Bingo was offered at the Coliseum—the local movie house.]*

9/11—Mon.
Ketchikan to Home

Very hot day. Went to town and bot me a pair of gray wool slacks, a blue-green silk blouse, yellow wrap-around for my hair, and $6.50 of kitchen gadgets. Came home in our skiff at 3 p.m., loaded with stuff. Boat leaked and floor got wet, and we lost most of it on the porch steps.

9/13—Wed.

Carl got up early and went to town before breakfast. Said he had to see *Jay M* about boat lumber—but he never did. Said he'd be home at noon, but it was 9 p.m. when he got here. Got mad at the outboard and threw it overboard! *[Not only a stupid thing to do, but also expensive.]* What am I going to do with him?

9/22—Fri.
Ketchikan to Home

More rain and wind. Paid P.O. box rent; *Fish News* for 6 mos.; and had deed for shack recorded. Had a bad thunder and lightning storm in late afternoon, and poor Champ was so scared. Carl made a nice bed for him out of canvas, and he stayed quiet all nite till 4 a.m. when I had to let him out. Then he went back to Clara's. Lots of robins and bluejays around this afternoon.

9/28—Thurs.

Rained all day, and still my clothes are on the line. Carl went to town early again and didn't get home till 4:30. I made a nut bread and crocheted an edge for my dresser scarf. Didn't feel so good, so stayed quiet. Carl talked to Everett Hudson about this boat that is for sale in Metlakatla. He expects to go back to Met. in the morning and will take Carl with him and will keep him over night if necessary.

9/29—Fri.—My first "Hen Party"

Beautiful day, first one since Tuesday. Carl went to town again today. Clara, Hannah, Ina, and Ruby came about 1:30. We sewed and talked till about 4 p.m. I served coffee and tea, nut bread sandwiches, vegetable salad (jello), and strawberry jam. Had the table all set and ready when in walks Sophie! I sure was sore—as I only prepared for 5.

10/1—Sun.

Horrible day. Just poured down all day long. All water barrels are over-flowing. Washed and ironed all my summer's crocheting. Ruby and her "child," Paul Scott, were over right in the middle of *Charlie McCarthy*.

[Charlie McCarthy was a wildly popular radio program for two decades— 1936 to 1956. Edgar Bergen, a vaudeville performer, actor, and comic-strip writer, developed a talent for ventriloquism at a young age. When Bergen asked a local carpenter to create a dummy, the wisecracking Charlie McCarthy was born. The puppet became Bergen's lifelong sidekick, even though other characters were later added to the program. The fact that Bergen was widely popular for a ventriloquism act on radio (when the trick of "throwing his voice" was not visible) indicates that his appeal was primarily the personality he applied to his characters.]

Blodts floated off their scow house, so now they are gone, and we won't have them around any more— thank heavens. Heard some good programs on the radio: *Jack Benny*, *Gildersleeve*, *Kate Smith*, and *Bumsteads*. Started another doily set.

10/4—Wed.
Ketchikan—Home—Ketch.

Clara's Hen Party. Weather bad, so Carl thot I had better not row over to Clara's. As I was washing the dishes, Mr. and Mrs. Katz came by on their way to Clara's—so I threw my clothes on, wrote a note to Carl, and went over with them. They came back at 5 p.m., and I came too. Clara served apple pie and cheese and cake. Carl got drunk today—brot Jack Tavis home with him. Carl nearly set the boat on fire trying to lite the lamp—has a big burn on his finger. I went to see *We Are the Marines*.

10/5—Thurs.
Ketchikan

Another horrible day—just poured all day. Carl wouldn't stay home for breakfast even, left before I got up. About 12:30 I went up town. Tried to get my shoes repaired, but they wouldn't take them. Carl left again after dinner and stayed away for hours. Tried to use our lantern (lamp) again, but it wouldn't work. Had to get the watchman to connect the electric lights, and he was mad! Katzes took their gas boat over to Wilsons' and put it on the grid, borrowed our skiff to come home in—but never came back. Guess it was too stormy, and they stayed overnite.

10/7—Sat.

Party at Tavis'. Horrible day. Rained hard and wind blew all day. Lillian, Mrs. Frank, and I went to Rummage Sale at Dug Out. Nothing there I wanted. Carl brot home an Ex-Prize fighter from the Shamrock, both <u>so</u> drunk! He was supposed to be a chiropractor and gave us both an adjustment. Went up to Lillian's and Jack's at 8 p.m. Joe Somuck and wife (Filipino Indian mix) were there. Carl got so drunk he passed out. Jack had to help me get him home.

10/8—Sun.

Carl is so drunk, he never got out of bed all
day. The sun came out for a while, so I went for
a walk. Came home and got dinner. Katzes didn't
bring our skip back till this morning. I went to
Coliseum to see *Road to Happiness*, bot Carl some
cigarettes and some ice cream. Was planning to go
home today, but too stormy.

10/9—Mon.

Blodts' party tonight. Carl was so drunk he couldn't
get out of bed. Has drunk 1 quart of whiskey since
noon yesterday. Jack Tavis came in about 2 p.m.
Carl left while Jack was still here and went to
the Shamrock and never came home till after 6—so
drunk he just fell on the bed—and another quart
in his pocket. I'm at my wits end to know what
to do! He won't listen to me, and I've begged,
threatened, and even got mad and bawled H—— out
of him, and it all runs off just like rain off
a roof. Blodt came over at 7:30 p.m. and wanted
to know why we were not at the party—had to tell
them that Carl was sick with a <u>cold</u>! Hansens,
Tavises, Clara, Betty and her boyfriend, and me
were there. I was too sick with worry to enjoy
it. Jack and Lillian brot me home—11:45—Carl was
gone. Came home at 12:30—some other drunk had to
help him home. Fell on the deck and nearly fell
overboard. I'm going back to Pennock tomorrow.
From there I don't know what to do. Can't sleep
nights; he snores so and sprawls all over the bed.
Tried to sleep but had to get up at 2 a.m. Had
a long crying spell—couldn't stop. Will go home
alone as soon as it gets daylight. Maybe if I'm
not around, Carl will be better.

10/10—Tues.

Left the boat at 6 a.m. Just as I was leaving, Carl came out and wanted to know where I was going. I told him I was going home *[to the shack—by skiff]*. He said, "How will I get home tomorrow?" I said, "That's your hard luck; you can get home the best way you can." Got home at 6:45. Clara had stayed all nite with Hansons, so she wasn't home either. I went to bed and slept till 10:30. When Clara came home, I had to tell her why Carl wasn't home too. She left for K. before noon and took our skiff back to the *Olympic*. She said there was no one at home on the boat when she got there. No sign of Carl all day, so I guess he thinks more of his drinking than he does of me. I cried a lot again today.

10/11—Wed.
Hen Party at Hannah's—1 p.m.

Beautiful day, so we all walked up to Hannah's. She served sandwiches and cookies. Carl didn't come home today, either.

10/12—Thurs.
Home to Ketchikan

Still no Carl. Didn't sleep very well—cried a lot. Lots of fog. Clara and I left at 8:15 and rowed to Union Oil. While Clara went to Katy's apartment, I went to the *Olympic*. Carl was all locked in and very sick! I sure had a sweet mess to clean up. Clara came back to boat, and we had dinner. Carl bought the little speedboat for $112.00. Called Chris Hanson to see about New England Fish Co. job—he told us to call the Chief Engineer (Minnick), which I did, but he knew nothing of it and said to see Mr. Johnson, the manager.

10/14—Sat.
Ketchikan

Poured all day. Went to see Mr. Johnson at New England—was busy, so we went back in afternoon. Seemed to be much interested in us, talked about the job and showed us pictures of the place. Said he would call us tomorrow. It pays $8.60 a shift, and we pay $15.00 a month for house, with electricity furnished.

10/16—Mon.

Waited all day for New England to call. About 2 p.m. we walked up town and bot some magazines. From 4 p.m. Friday till 10 a.m. today, we've had 10.17 inches of rain! *[This is yearly average rainfall where I live in Escondido, California.]*

New England Fish Company (NEFCO).
(Photograph from Ketchikan Museums.)

10/17—Tues.
Ketchikan to Pennock *[Home]*

Rained some, but didn't pour down. Came home with Wilsons, and they toured our Putterer. Carl <u>rowed</u> it home, and all the neighbors came over while he propped it up on the beach. Sure seems good to be home again. Never heard a word from Johnson at New England.

10/19—Thurs.
Home

Another nice cold day. Clara and I went to town in her skiff with the outboard. Too ruff to go to Basin so went to Union Oil. Note in door of boat to call Mr. Johnson at New England. He wanted to see Carl, but as Carl didn't come over, he said to come tomorrow afternoon. Bert Stone said his wife wanted to see me at Alaska Sportsman, so I went down. They wanted me to go to work at $.70 per hour, but with this New England job pending and living on Pennock, I just couldn't. However, I did ask for a job at Christmas.

10/20—Fri.

Beautiful day. Made some cocoanut macaroons and washed clothes. Carl took out old motor and Jack helped carry it up to the shed. Lots of grease in boat. Carl cleaned it all out with gas. Borrowed Danny's boat and rowed over to New England to see Mr. Johnson. <u>Carl gets the job</u>! (Only no place for us to live at present, as the house is rented). We could live with one of the crew in a house, or live on the *Olympic* till the house is vacant. Mr. Johnson was too busy to talk much. We are to phone him tomorrow afternoon, and if he is not busy, he will take us out to Herring Cove to see the layout.

Powerhouse (Powerplant) for the New England Fish Co. where Carl worked. It is located at Herring Cove, approximately seven miles out of town. (Photograph from Ketchikan Museums.)

10/21—Sat.

Rain, Rain, Rain. Louis Johnson came over and brot us a fish. Carl took the shaft out of the boat, and it had to be straightened, so we decided to go to Ketch. with Ina and Clara. Left at 12:15—in the rain. Carl went all over town trying to get a new pipe; called Johnson at 3 p.m.—too wet and cold, so will meet him at 9 tomorrow morning. Went to *Days of '98* with Lillian and Jack. Carl won $1.15 at Bingo. Danced a few, had lunch, and went home. Bot some new rubbers *[soft flexible shoe covers]*—men's—to go over my new flat-heeled shoes.

10/22—Sun.

Nice day. Went to New England at 9 a.m., but Mr. Johnson was busy, and Mr. Minnick was off, so would we come back at 8 a.m. tomorrow. We walked back to the *Olympic* and gathered up our stuff and rowed home. Very ruff till we got to Hansons'. Cold wind, too. Took us 45 minutes. Clara invited us over for dinner at 1 p.m.—venison chops. Carl worked on the Putterer all day. Took baths. Carl went over to Wilson to get the corrugated tin for the roof—that Wilson said he could have for $.50 a sheet—but now Wilson wouldn't let him have it. (Some of Ina's meanness showing up.)

10/23—Mon.—Zellah's birthday

Nice day. Rowed over to New England at 7:30 a.m. Had to wait a while for Mr. Johnson and Minnick. Finally left and drove out to Herring Cove. Small Powerhouse, only 2 dynamos. "Our house" was occupied, and no one at home (or up), so we couldn't go in. However, it seemed to be 4 large rooms. Our little dab of furniture will rattle around in there. Mr. Johnson said he wrote them to vacate. So it will be Nov. 23rd before we can move in. As there isn't a good place to anchor the *Olympic*, we will leave it in the Basin and live on it, and Carl can go and come on the bus ($.35 round trip) till the house is vacant. Came back to New England about 10 and went to the *Olympic*—had lunch and then rowed home. Carl and I painted the Putterer; it sure looks nice. Carl is to begin at New England Nov. 1st, so I traded with Ruby and will house the sewing club this Wed. instead of Nov. 1st.

10/26—Thurs.

Rain—wind—rain—wind. Spent most of the day in bed and running to the Johnny with the back-door trots. Have bad cramps off and on. Carl went to town at 10:30 and got back at 1 p.m. I ate boiled rice and hot milk all day, but it didn't do much good. Bad wind storm in night. Letters from Ella and Katy.

10/27—Fri.

Rained and blew all day. I went to see Dr. Stagg. Gave me 3 prescriptions to take—$3.50. Carl installed the engine in the Putterer, and it is all ready to go—on tomorrow's hi tide.

10/30—Mon.

Rain and wind. Went to Ketch. twice in the Putterer and took lots of our stuff over. Also 30 gallons stove oil. All in the rain! The Putterer stopped several times both ways, and finally on our way home the last time, the steering wire broke. So Carl is very much disgusted with the whole business. Now he is going to take the propeller off and put on the one we bot in Seattle, and also the new shaft—but it has a kink, and will have to be straightened.

10/31—Tues.

Rain. Got up early (before daylight). Carl rowed over to see Minnick, and he told Carl to come to work at 10 a.m. tomorrow. At hi tide Carl towed the Putterer over and put it on Danny's grid. Took the wheel off and the shaft out; now he has to install the new shaft and wheel. I had a sick headache and stayed in bed most of the day.

11/1—Wed.—Carl's first day at New England.

[Carl's job at the Powerhouse is seven miles out of town.]

Fog. Carl left for town before 8 as he took the shaft in to get straightened. Packed his lunch in a paper bag and gave him a pint fruit jar with milk in. I washed clothes, then went over to Ruby's for sewing club. She had tuna fish salad, Ritz crackers, olives, cheese, jelly, and coffee cake. Expected Carl home by 7 p.m., but he never came home all nite. Clara had me over for supper. Then she came over for the evening, and we sewed and listened to the radio till 11 p.m. and still no Carl. He had to work till 7 a.m. Thurs. morning. He tried to call Hansons, but they were not home.

11/2—Thurs. 11 p.m. to 7 a.m.

Carl got home at 8:30 a.m. Had to work from 1 p.m. Wed. till 7 a.m. Thurs. He went to bed and slept till 1 p.m., then worked on boat till dark. At 9:30 p.m., he left for New England. A minus tide, and we had to drag the skiff miles. Beautiful night, smooth water and moonlight. Clara came over and stayed till 11:30, and I sat up till 5:30 a.m. so I would be sleepy when Carl came home and could sleep too while he slept. It is so hard to keep quiet while he sleeps in this little house.

11/3—Fri.—7 p.m. to 2 a.m.

Cold wind—no rain. Carl got home about 9:30—very much disgusted; he has to go back to work at 6:00

p.m. tonite and gets thru at 2 a.m., and no bus
to town till 7:30 a.m. Went to bed and slept till
noon. Had our brunch and rowed to Ketch., and I
went with Carl to work so I could see our furniture and the house. Took the 5:30 bus from town.
Met Ray Bowling as he left for town, also Mr. and
Mrs. Lewis (the renters) and their 2 kids. Visited
with them and had cake and coffee with Ray when
he came home on the 10:30 bus. At 1:30 a.m., Bob
Lewis drove us to town. Got to bed about 2:30—so
cold we shivered ourselves to sleep. Lewis' are
leaving at 7:30 a.m. Friday, Nov. 10, so we can
move in on Friday.

11/4—Sat.—4:30 to 11 p.m.

Nice day. Slept till 10:20 a.m. After breakfast,
Carl went to Northern Machine to get his skiff.
Clara came over with Champ. Entwitts couldn't
keep him; he was too ruff with the baby. She
wanted to give him to us, but Carl wants a baby
pup that he can train. So she called Crafts, and
Danny was glad to get him. So Carl, Clara and I
and Champ got on the bus. Carl went to work, and
Clara and I went to Crafts' (6½ mi. from town).
They insisted that we stay for dinner. They made
me call up Carl at Powerplant for him to stop on
his way home. At 1:30 a.m., Charlie drove us to
town. Clara stayed all nite with Crafts. When we
got to the boat, we decided to row home—got there
at 2:30 a.m.

11/5—Sun.—4:30 p.m. to 11:00 p.m.

Rain and wind. Didn't get up till 10 a.m. Carl
worked on the Putterer till 2 p.m. Had dinner, then
Carl left for work. Terrible wind and rain; drove

him almost to Thomas Basin—lots of white caps. Carl came home at 12 midnite. Al Bernhoft told Carl tonite that they were going to get a raise of $1.50 per day. $8.16 + 1.50 = $9.66 per day.

11/6—Mon.

Carl's first day off. More rain and wind. Cold and wet. At 4:30 p.m. (hi tide), Carl floated the Putterer, but he couldn't get it started, so I had to row him (and it) over to the pond. Rope got caught in the wheel. Tied up to Louis for the nite. Went home and started to pack up—ready to move to Herring Cove.

11/8—Wed.—7 p.m. to 11 p.m.

Up early and went to Whiskey Cove before breakfast. Beautiful day, cold, smooth water. Made two trips from shack to New England. Packed everything up in the warehouse. Started to rain. Came back to Olympic for breakfast, then took a load from Olympic to New England. Came back to Olympic and went up town and made a date with Ireland Transfer to move our stuff from NEFCO to Herring Cove Friday morning. Came back to Olympic and got dinner for Carl, and he caught the 4:00 p.m. bus. Melvin came over just before we ate—and hinted around for Carl to take him home—but Carl didn't take the hint!

Moving to Herring Cove (Near Pumphouse)

🐟

11/10—Fri.

Cold and frosty. Carl went up to Ireland Transfer, and I met him and the truck at the Basin
at 8:15. Picked up all our stuff at New England.
Carl rode in the back so he could watch things,
and I rode with the driver. Carl was nearly froze
to death when we arrived. A man was there waiting
to disconnect the phone. By 9:15, the truck was
ready to leave. The house was horribly dirty—especially the kitchen and bathroom. I started in on
the kitchen today. Carl fixed the spare room. Ray
came over to see how we were getting along. Poor
radio reception. Very cold—frost on everything
at 9 p.m.!

11/11—Sat.—4 p.m. to 1 a.m.

A good night's sleep; our new bed is very comfy.
Snow on all the tree tops this morning—so pretty.
Still working on the kitchen. Walls, cupboards and

floor are just about as dirty as you can imagine. Ray went to town on the 6:30 bus and came home on the 10:30 bus with Ted Brown. He had a 10 lb. turkey and asked me to roast it for their dinner tomorrow! It is frozen stiff and not even cleaned! Gave them lemon pie and coffee.

11/12—Sun.—4 p.m. to 1 a.m.

Got up about 9. After breakfast, I wrestled with the turkey for 2 hrs.! Cleaned, picked, singed, and made dressing. Roasted it from 11:30 to 3:30—and it really was good. Used Mother's "Rag" method. *[Wonder what this method was.]* Made gravy and took it all over to Ray's. Boiled spuds, asparagus, celery and olives, bread and butter, cookies and cherries. Came home and finished scrubbing the bathroom.

11/13—Mon.

Horrible day. Rained and blew a horrible gale all day. After breakfast, Carl began to carry boxes, suitcases, and what have you, up to Mac's. Finally got it all there, then went to Progress to buy groceries. At 12:30, we loaded up, stopped at Mac's for our other things, and then started for home. Carl drove slow and got along just fine. *[They were in a borrowed vehicle.]* Unloaded, and Carl drove back to town and got the 4 p.m. bus back home. Carl bot 2 pair of white-dotted organdy curtains at Sears @ $3.95 pair. I fell on slippery walk in front of house and hurt my sore arm. Spent $63.00.

11/16—Thurs.—12 noon to 7 p.m. and 7 p.m. to 2 a.m.

Rained all day. Carl had to go to work at noon for Ray. Carl washed the ceilings in kitchen, bathroom, and living room. *[Ceilings get dirty from soot.]* The kitchen was pretty awful. I washed clothes and hung them in the Powerhouse, and some were dry before I went to bed. About 4:00 p.m. Ray called Carl and said he wouldn't be home till 10:30 bus—but he never came at all so suppose Carl will have to work his shift tomorrow, too. I'm all stiff and sore from the fall I took on Tuesday.

11/17—Fri.—7 to 2

Sunshine—but cold. Carl walked across the marsh to look at a log for a float for the Putterer. Ray did get home last nite—at 4 a.m. in a taxi—so Carl didn't have to work his shift after all. But he did go to town at 6:30. Bergseth stopped in on his way back from town about 10:15. At 11 when Carl went over to Powerhouse, Bergseth's car was on fire in the garage! We put water on it and finally got it out, but it sure wrecked the insides. Put curtains up—same ones I had in the cabin with sugar sacks for the bottom sashes.

11/20—Mon.—Carl's day off

Caught the 7:25 a.m. bus in rain and wind. Had breakfast on the *Olympic*. Bot some curtain material (10 yards) at Mrs. Abercrombie's @ $.45. Met Al Bergseth at Progress, and he said that New England had a turkey for us—for Thanksgiving. So I asked Tavises to come out for dinner.

11/21—Tues.—7 to 2

Horrible day. Rain and wind. Got up late. After breakfast, Carl pumped out both boats and did some odd jobs. Then we took our things up to Progress and bot some more groceries. Got bus and home about 1:30. After dinner I started in on the curtains and made the ones for kitchen, spare room, and front door before I went to bed. Just got in the house from town, when Mrs. Steiner came over and asked us to dinner on Thanksgiving—but we already had asked the Tavises.

11/22—Wed.—4 to 7 and 7 to 2 p.m.

Had to go to New England to get the turkey. Took the 1:30 bus. Stopped at New England and got the turkey. Checked on the *Olympic*. Got the 4:00 bus home. After dinner, made a cake and a pumpkin pie, took a bath, and went to bed. Carl worked for Ray—from 4 to 7, then his own shift from 7 to 2.

11/23—Thanksgiving Day—7 p.m. to 2 a.m.

Nice day, but cold and frosty. Carl worked on his canal all day. I fixed turkey and put it in the oven at 12:30. Cleaned up the house. Tavises came on the 4:00 bus. Had dinner at 5. Bergseth asked us over for "movies" at 8:45. Came home at 10:00 p.m. and had lunch. Tavises got the 11 bus; it was full when it got here. Last Thanksgiving we were at Mother's and went home with Zellah and Rex. Menu for today: roast turkey, dressing, gravy, mashed potatoes, stewed tomatoes, carrot sticks, olives, cranberry sauce, mustard pickles, bread and butter, and pumpkin pie.

11/24—Fri.—1 to 7 and 7 to 2

Wet and cold. Carl did more digging in canal. Minnick came out and talked to Carl about cutting down the brush along the power line from Herring Cove to Ketchikan. He and Ray will be paid for their time. I washed clothes all day. When I went to hang them up in the Powerhouse, Mrs. Steiner had her clothes on the line, so I had to pile mine in that bathtub. Carl is to get a raise, which will include all of November. Also, the Union has made a change in their schedule—40 hrs. in 5 days instead of 6 like it is now. This is to take effect Dec. 1st. Carl will probably have to fill in one or two days a week at the main plant in Ketchikan.

11/26—Sun.—4 p.m. to 1 a.m.

Still cold and a little snow on the ground. Finished my washing—so now everything is clean. Ruth and Harvey drove out for a while, but they left early, as it was beginning to freeze. Ruth wants me to make a "basket" for her to take to the Legion Basket Social Saturday nite. I'll work on it tomorrow afternoon, and then we'll have dinner there with them.

[Basket Social Auctions were a popular means of raising money for various organizations in the '40s and '50s. The ladies packed a special homemade lunch and placed it in a basket or box (usually a shoebox) decorated lavishly with ribbons, lace, and flowers. The men, not knowing who had made the lunch, bid on the baskets. Great care was supposedly taken to keep the decorations secret, but in reality, the women always told their husbands and boyfriends how to identify their creations so they could bid on the right box when the auction began. After all the baskets were paid for, the high bidder for each basket shared the lunch with the one who prepared it. The organization, of course, collected the money. I participated in several of these auctions as a teenager in the '50s.]

11/27—Mon.—Carl's day off

Cold! Still some snow on the ground. Went to K. on the 7:25 a.m. bus; Ray went too. *Olympic* was cold and damp. Made fires in both stoves. About 11 a.m., went to Pennock in the Putterer. Towed Jones' skiff. Got the ¾ mattress and a few other things. Went over to Ruby's to see our kittens. Clara insisted that we stay for lunch. Then she went to K. with us, and we towed her skiff. Bot groceries at Progress, borrowed his truck, and picked up the two boxes of apples and box of pears that Zellah sent. Stopped at winter yard for some lumber, stopped at New England, and loaded the mattress on the truck, and drove out to Herring Cove. Unloaded, and just as we were about to leave, Ray arrived with his lumber for the "bus depot." When we got back to Progress, Carl delivered groceries to Model Café and went up to Ruth's. I went up to Ruth's and worked on her basket. After dinner, we left so we could go to the 7:30 show—*Song of Russia*. Very good—especially the girl, Susan Peters. Took the 10:30 bus for Herring Cove. Ray came over about 11:30 and stayed till nearly 1 p.m. He and Carl are to work on the "clearing" job tomorrow.

11/29—Wed.—Overtime 8:30 a.m. to noon. Worked 7 to 2 also.

Rained. Up at 7:30—pitch dark. Ray and Carl left at 8:30 for work. Made a coffee cake and forgot to put in the B.P. *[baking powder]*. First time I ever did such a stunt. It sure was awful. About 10:30 Chris Hanson called from New England—too much power! So Carl had to slow down the machine. Chris called about 4 times—very excited. Bergseth came home about 11, and Carl had him come in to see if he had done the right thing, and he had. Ray wasn't home at 2:30 a.m. when we went to bed.

11/30—Thurs.—7 to 2, 2 ½ hours overtime

Up at 7:30. Waited and waited for Ray. Finally at 8:30, Carl went over and woke him up. He was suffering from a hang-over and didn't want to go, but Carl insisted, so at 9 a.m. they were on their way. It was a bad rainy day, and at 11:30 they came back. He and Carl and Bill Bitzell had a few drinks, and Carl got pretty sick. I had to get after him to go out to the Powerhouse on the hour. Bergseth came home at 11 p.m. and came in and told Carl about the new schedule! Carl has to go to work at 5 a.m. tomorrow! Sun. 5 a.m.-2 p.m., Mon. and Tues. off, Wed. and Thurs.—4 p.m. to 1 a.m., Fri. and Sat.—5 a.m. to 2 p.m.

12/1—Fri.—5 a.m. to 2 p.m.

Long, hard day for Carl. Went for a walk after 2 p.m. Ray went to town with Bill Bitzell and came home with him at 4:30—½ hr. late and drunk! And with a pup. Came over here and made such a fuss; we pulled all the shades down and turned lights down low.

12/5—Tues.—Carl's day off

Cold, clear day. The policeman came down on the float while we were talking to Danny and Nicholas. He asked if we knew anyone who wanted a dog. I went up to Patrol Car and looked at him. Black and white long haired—part Collie and part "Ketchikan Special." He gave me "that look," so we took him home with us—on the bus. He has been pretty good so far. Not very much pup, and I think he has been mistreated. Named him Dopey.

[Dopey became Hazel and Carl's constant and loving companion. He barked every time the bells on the fishing lines rang in case they didn't hear them. I knew and loved Dopey, too!]

Hazel with Dopey.

12/6—Wed.—4 p.m. to 1 a.m.

Rain and wind. Washed clothes. Ray went to town on the 1:30 bus and Bergseth on the 4:30. About 7:30, a taxi brot Ray home with 2 girls. He pulled down all the shades, and the place was lit up like a church. I had to get up at 4 a.m., and he still had all the lights on. Carl painted all 4 chairs a lettuce green. Carl made a "house" for Dopey.

12/8—Fri.—5 a.m. to 2 p.m.

Rain and wind and a southeast wind. Carl covered Dopey's doghouse with oilcloth. Ray came home on the bus at 1:30. Hasn't been near us since last Sat. night when he was so polluted.

12/10—Sun.—5 a.m. to 2 p.m.

Rained. Finished all my letters. Took a bath and got ready to leave on the 4:30 bus. Took Dopey with us. Walked to Thomas Basin in a soaking rain. Too wet to go to a show so we stayed home and read. The 6:30 bus went off the road and smashed all to pieces—the driver was scratched and bruised. Just heard about Mrs. Frank shooting her husband. Don't blame her one bit—he's such a mess.

12/11—Mon.—Carl's day off

Took Dopey for a walk, and everyone had to stop and talk. Saw Clara, Wilsons, Gene, and Ruby. There was something queer up in the sky that we all were looking at. Didn't quite look like a blimp. Went to Lillian's for supper, and then we went to see the *Seabees*. Mailed Xmas cards.

[What Hazel and her friends saw in the sky may have been a fire balloon or balloon bomb. This was an experimental weapon launched by Japan during World War II. It was called the Fu-Go Weapon and supposedly was a revenge bomb for the 1942 Doolittle raids on Tokyo. Hydrogen balloons with incendiary devices attached were designed as cheap weapons intended to make use of the jet stream over the Pacific Ocean and wreak havoc on Alaskan, Canadian, and American cities, forests, and farmlands. Between November 1944 and April 1945, the Japanese launched over nine thousand of these fire balloons. They were found in Alaska, Washington, Oregon, California, Arizona, Idaho, Montana, Utah, Wyoming, Colorado, Texas, Kansas, Nebraska, South Dakota, North Dakota, Michigan, and Iowa, as well as Mexico and Canada.

[The balloons were relatively ineffective as weapons, causing only six deaths and a small amount of damage, and they survive in memory mostly as an ingenious and dangerous curiosity. The Office of Censorship sent a message to newspapers and radio stations asking them to make no mention of balloons and ballon-bomb incidents, lest the enemy get the idea that the balloons might be effective weapons. Cooperating with the desires of the government, the press did not publish any balloon-bomb incidents. Perhaps as a result, the Japanese only learned of one bomb's reaching Wyoming, landing and failing to explode, so they stopped the launches after less than six months.

[A non-lethal balloon bomb was discovered in Alaska in 1992.]

12/12—Tues.—Carl's day off

Carl worked most of day on Putterer. Put in a new steering system. Bot me a green felt tam and pair of black gloves. Mailed package to Arlene and Alan. After supper went to Coliseum to see *Murder on the Water Front*.

12/13—Wed.—4 p.m. to 1 a.m.

Cold, frosty day. Carl walked down to New England to get wire for re-wiring the house. I went up to Lillian's and phoned about the buses. Only 2 buses a day—one at 7:30 a.m. and one at 5:30 p.m. Ben Rasmussen said we could have his truck, but he wanted it back by 3 p.m. So we drove out with all our junk (plus Dopey). I drove the truck back alone and took the 5:30 bus for home.

12/17—Sun.—5 a.m. to 2 p.m.

Dull, gray day—but cold. Wrapped candy and salmon for Mother and Dad and Zellah. Wrights came about 1:30. After dinner, went to end of road for Christmas trees and greens. Put up the tree and trimmed it before we went to bed.

12/19—Tues.—Carl's day off

Got up late. Went over to Pennock *[to their shack]* about 1 p.m. with Clara. Got 2 kittens from Ruby. Came back to *Olympic*; gave the female to Flo Wright and took the male home. Got myself a job at Alaska Sportsman for 60 cents per hour. Start tomorrow at 8:30. Awful cold on the boat all nite. Dopey was cold too.

12/20—Wed.—4 p.m. to 1 a.m.—5 hrs. overtime

My first day at Alaska Sportsman. Took the 7:25 bus. Stopped off at the boat—Ruth had not picked up the Xmas tree. Started work at 8:30 till 12:00 and 12:30 to 5:15. About 15 or 20 women work there. Stopped at Post Office—huge package, guess it's from Mother—no name on it. Took the 5:30 bus for home. Carl worked on pipeline and sprung a leak in the pipe; had an awful time getting it stopped. Unwrapped package—a beautiful green wool blanket—from whom? Letter from Zellah.

12/23—Sat.—5 a.m. to 12 p.m.

I worked from 8 to 12. Bot some groceries, shaving lotion, perfume, and tobacco. Got the 1 p.m. bus for home. Very cold and snappy, but sunshine. Carl and Ray and Bill started to imbibe; Ray and Bill got pretty polluted and ran the car off into the ditch. Had to get a wrecker to drag it out—then they went to town in a taxi. Carl bot a pint of gin from Ray. Drank too much, and I got mad at him, and he got mad at me! Swell way to celebrate Christmas. Carl was going to work Ray's shift, but Al told him to go to bed at 10:30 and he would finish the shift.

12/25—Mon.—Christmas—Carl's day off

Cold, dull, gray day. Started to rain about noon, but it didn't melt all the snow. We left for K. on the 1:30 bus with 2 pies, Dopey, and the cat in my knitting bag. Warmed up the boat, and about 4 p.m. went up to Lillian's. They gave us presents. Was I embarrassed when we didn't give them anything. Carl got a yo-yo and an ashtray, and I got a sharp knife holder, a doll clothesline, and a pair of silk stockings. We came home at 11:15, warmed up the boat, and fed the animals.

12/26—Tues.—Carl's day off

I worked from 8:30 to 5:30. Carl had lunch ready for me when I came home at noon. Got a package from Mother—my old plaid coat made into an afghan [*resourceful*], peanuts, soap, calendar, kitchen pad, and dishtowels. After supper, went to see Wallace Berry in *Rationing*. [*Most movie themes seem to be war-related.*]

12/27—Wed.

I worked from 8:30 to 5:00. Carl had lunch ready when I got home at noon. Got the *National Geographic* today. Carl went home on the 1:00 p.m. bus with Dopey and Tuffey. I came home on the 5:30 bus, and the road was real slippery. The driver drove so fast I was scared to death. I'm not going to work tomorrow on such roads.

[Interesting that the dog and cat rode on the bus. I don't think Hazel's father, my grandfather, allowed animals on his buses. My grandfather was Superintendent of Public Transportation for the City of Seattle. I remember watching him work at the large dining room table, charting numerous bus routes and schedules. As Hazel grew up in a "charting" home, this may account for the detailed fishing records she kept so diligently. They remind me of my grandfather's long lists and charts.]

12/28—Thurs.

Didn't get up till 8:30. Called Peggy at Alaska Sportsman and told her it was too slippery to come in on the bus. Today is the last day anyway. Went for a walk in afternoon, and three dogs followed us, including Dopey. Minnick's truck was here when we got home; he was up on the pipeline repairing a hole that he told Bergseth to fix last summer. Wrote 5 letters.

12/31—Sun.—5 a.m. to 1:30 p.m.

Snowed again today—so deep around the house Dopey got lost in it. Snowplow came by twice before we went to town on the 1:30 bus with Dopey and Tuffey. Snowplow also came around the house twice. Had some trouble on the road—too much snow to go up the Roosevelt Drive—slipped a couple of places. Went to show to see Laurel and Hardy. Carl got his last check—$643.41. *[A windfall! Compare that to the measely amount they earned from fishing fourteen-hour days, making endless repairs on their boat, and putting up with frigid cold and drenching rain.]* Powerhouse sink was froze up. Carl had to thaw it out with hot water.

Another year endeth!

Part VI
1945

The Lost Year

These are the remains of the 1945 diary. Numerous pages are missing and many entries are incomplete or not in shape to be transcribed. The pages were partially destroyed by silverfish—not silver fish (salmon) but silverfish (insects)—and I never discovered the outcome of The Itch.

1/1—Mon.—New Year's Day

Had a horrible night—was too cold to sleep, and the New Year's whistles woke me up. So we didn't get much sleep and got up late—10 a.m. Carl pumped out the Putterer and cleaned the snow off the roof. Walked around town—most stores were closed. Bot eggs and butter ($1.30) at Alaska Meat Co. and donuts ($.70). Walked up to City Park and watched the ice skaters—came home and took a nap. Al Bergseth came aboard and said he was leaving Tues. for Seattle; his wife is worse at Leavenworth. *[A mental hospital was located at Leavenworth, Washington, in the 1940s. As a child, I remember hearing stories/jokes about the facility]*. Carl will have to be at work at 3 p.m. Tues. and will work till 1 a.m. every day till Bergseth gets back. Jack Ickles came in about 6 p.m. and had coffee with us. He got back from Seattle last Thurs. He said some fisherman friend told him that Gills are going to sell out *[their shack next door to Hazel and Carl's]* on Pennock Island to him for $400.00—and after Clara always said we were to have the first choice of buying it! We went up to her hotel to see her, but she was working at the Blue Fox. Went to show.

1/3—Wed.

Rained hard all day. Carl walked over to the sawmill. The log that Carl had such a time tying up belongs to the owner, so Carl will have to give it back to him. Made a lemon pie.

1/4—Thurs.

Got up at 5:30 a.m. to go to bathroom, and no lights in Ray's house—also when we got up at 7:00 a.m. Ray overslept 3 hours. Tried to make Carl believe he was up all the time and that he blew a fuse! Carl told him off. Cleaned house and wrote letters to Mother and Grace. Carl fixed an egg crate for a sewing cabinet, and I'm covering it with oilcloth. Minnick was out today to patch a leak on the pipeline. So much is going on with the war these days. I have a hard time focusing on it since I have my own war going on right here with Carl all the time.

1/6—Sat.

Another wet, cold day. Went for a walk. Carl got mad at Ray and bawled him out, so now he'll be mad at us. Carl went up to the dam—was only gone 45 min. He is much worse today. I've talked to him and even got real mad and bawled him out, but it just doesn't make an imprint. I'm so disgusted with him. This is a good job, and he'll never get one like it again. And he will get fired just as sure as anything if he doesn't stop drinking. Ray is just aching for a chance to knife him. Covered the sewing box and washed green material for the sides. Pictures of Alan and Arlene came today—cute.

1/7—Sun.

And still Carl is indulging—what can I do or say to make him quit? I've tried everything I can think of. If he lets himself get fired on account of this boozing, I don't think I could stand it. Everyone in town will know about it in 24 hours. Walked up to the bus wreck and back. Dopey was so dirty; I gave him a bath. Tuffy is sick today—won't eat. Ray came over after supper to play Chinese checkers. He went home about 8 p.m. Carl was so sick he went to bed early.

1/8—Mon.

[This entry is barely readable. Hazel's diary says it was a rainy, windy day made much worse (for her) because, while she was working around the shack, Carl went off to town to buy yet another bottle of liquor. As best I can make out, he came back drunk and (still) sick from his on-going intoxication. Hazel tried to get Carl to eat, but he was too drunk and had to go to bed. He snored so much that Hazel had to sleep in another part of the room on a cot. She writes that she was so disgusted with the situation with Carl that she'd join the WAC (Women's Army Corps) if she weren't too old.

[Originally called the WAAC (Women's Army Auxiliary Corps), over 150,000 American women served in the WAC during World War II. The WAAC was established in 1941 to work with the Army. It wasn't until 1943 that the WAAC was converted to the WAC, which became part of the Army itself rather than merely serving with it. Members of the WAC were the first women other than nurses to serve in the Army. Both the Army and the American public initially had difficulty accepting the concept of women in uniform. However, it was realized that women could supply the additional resources so desperately needed in the military and industrial sectors. The Army could not afford to spend time and money to train men in essential service skills such as typing and switchboard operations when highly skilled women were already available.

[Hazel would have been a valuable asset to the WAC if she had been serious about joining. She was highly adept at typing and shorthand and qualified for other clerical positions. But she was just a few months too old. Applicants had to be U.S. citizens between the ages of twenty-one and forty-five. They also had to have no dependents, be at least five feet tall, and weigh a hundred pounds or more. Hazel qualified on all other counts at the time.]

1/9—Tues.

Rain and wind. No buses today. Went to town with Anna and Ray. Rained and a heavy gale all the time I was in town. Letters from Zellah and kids.

Went up to tell Clara about the buses, and she had already made arrangements with Charlie Craft to drive them out. I was so upset because I owe Crafts a dinner but can't have them now as that would make 9, and I don't have room or dishes for so many. It sure will look swell for Craft to dump the Gills and then go home for his dinner and come back at 11 to take them to town. Also called Hanna. If weather is too bad, they won't come. Got home at 3:30. Carl is too drunk and drinking more all the time—so sorry I asked this bunch out for dinner. Clara keeps a secret like a sieve, and Chris isn't much better. All Ketchikan will know about Carl by Thursday noon. Alaska Sportsman called tonite and wanted me to go to work tomorrow—but no buses. They are supposed to be running tomorrow, but you can't depend on it. Carl phoned for a taxi to bring out a quart of whiskey (to his work)—$20.00!! He left it sitting in the office right where Ray could see it. I took it home and hid it, and now he is mad at me.

1/10—Wed.

Got up to go to bathroom at 2:10 a.m. and heard a funny sound in Powerhouse. Lights went low and then bright. *[Much of this entry is bug-eaten, but from what scraps of text I can read, it seems as if Ray was supposed to be tending the plant but failed to do so, allowing the generators to run low on fuel. Hazel awoke Carl, who went over and fixed the problem and then got into a verbal fight with Ray for being irresponsible. The fight was bad enough that even Hazel joined in, telling off Ray.]*

1/29—Mon.

Didn't get up till nearly 10. We packed and repacked junk. Was washing dishes when old man Russell came in. He stayed and stayed. I sure can't stand that man. Went for a walk with Dopey. Stopped at Sears, and Maggie said they wouldn't need me to work, because the girl came back from her vacation sooner than expected. Wrote a card to Anna Pengra asking for the directions for the crocheted tablecloth. Stayed home after supper and listened to the radio. Read and crocheted till after 1 a.m. New England Co. wrote Carl for his Social Security number. *[This apparently was part of the process of firing Carl from his Powerhouse job. Whether it was Carl's drunkenness, the fight with Ray, or both that caused the firing is not clear.]* The bridge is closed, and we have to go around on Creek Street.

1/30—Tues.

Beautiful sunshine all day. A lady across the float (Mrs. Owens) lost their dog, and they left today for Horn Arm and asked us to look for it. Sewed at Red Cross from 2 to 5. Was asked to help at Alaska Sportsman, and so I am to start work at 8:00 tomorrow. Went to see *Major Minor* at Revilla.

1/31—Wed.

Mrs. Owens advertised their lost dog over the radio and gave us as people to contact, but no one ever called. Still have to crawl over the fence across the bridge. Wages at Alaska Sportsman—$.70 per hour, and time-and-a-half over 40 hours in each week. Carl went down to New England and got his check for $177.17—his last check. *[Carl has been fired.]*

2/9—Fri.

Rained hard all day. Nearly drowned coming home at noon. Had to borrow Cecilia's rain hat and

Pearl's umbrella. Wore a dress to work, but it was so cold I'm going back to wearing slacks. Carl has started in drinking again—has been at it for 2 days now.

2/10—Sat.

Horrible day—raining and blowing a gale. Carl was too sick (hangover) to eat breakfast and was still in bed when I left for work at 11:45. He came by the office and suggested we have lunch at the *Knickerbocker*. He was late meeting me and drunk, too. Worked till 5 p.m. New floatbridge across the creek completed today. Carl was not home when I arrived, so I ate alone and took a nap. At 8:30 he came home—staggering drunk. I worked at the Officers Club till 2 a.m. Very tired when I got home.

2/11—Sun.

Never went to bed at all last nite. Carl was sprawled all over the bed and snored, so I couldn't sleep. I sat up in the chair all nite. Carl stayed in bed till late, never ate any breakfast, then left the boat, and was gone for hours. Came home just as I was eating dinner—wouldn't eat anything and went to bed and stayed there all day and nite. Dopey and I went for a walk. Carl sweat so in bed, I just couldn't stand to be with him—had to sleep in the chair again.

2/12—Mon.

I sure felt embarrassed when Carl came into the office this morning and asked me what I wanted for lunch. About one hour later, Gen Dowell came in and said Carl was at their place, and I was to come up for lunch. Not a very good lunch, either. It is now 9:30 p.m., and I haven't seen Carl since lunch—and no word from him, either. Carl left his overcoat some place—can't even remember where. Also, he has no idea how many checks he wrote, so I went to the bank and put all our money in my name.

2/13—Tues.

At 10 p.m. last nite, Gen came down to the boat and said Carl and Russell were at her place, so drunk they were nearly out, and she wanted me to go home with her and see if I could do something about Carl. When we got there, Carl and Russ were in bed, together. I tried to take Carl home with me, but he was too drunk. So Gen fixed a bed on the daveno, and I came back to the boat. At 7:55 a.m., I went past their house (on way to work), but no lite—so I didn't go up. At 9:30, Gen came down to the office and told me that she was taking care of Carl and I was to come up for lunch. Went home first, got Dopey, and took some food up to the Dowells. Carl and Russ were sure a mess—just disgusting,

2/14—Wed.

Very cold—snowed, then froze during the nite. At 4:25 a.m., the fire alarm sounded. The roller skating rink was on fire—burned pretty badly. Got up at 6:00 to make a fire in the oil stove, but we were all out of oil. So no heat in the oil stove—only the gas stove. Carl never got up all day—stayed in bed and drank more whiskey. Wouldn't even go after fuel oil. I had to order it from Old Dad at

noon; when I came home at 5 p.m., had to put it
in the tank. Carl just stayed in bed and refused
to do a thing. And this is Valentine's Day!

After 2/14

*[In terms of diary entries for the year 1945, the brief note for Wednesday,
February 14, 1945, is the last one I have. The rest of Hazel's 1945 diary is
missing and presumed destroyed (either accidentally or on purpose).*

*[I have no doubt that other entries did exist; Hazel wrote in her diaries
almost every day for her entire adult life. But for this particular year I
have only these first few weeks. And even these diary pages are incomplete.
Portions of the pages were ravaged by the silverfish. I have, nonetheless,
transcribed as much as I could of what I found.*

*[It's regrettable that 1945 should be—in diary terms—"The Missing Year."
This was such an historically significant period in terms of both U.S. and
world history. I would have liked to know what news filtered up to Alaska
about the progress—and ultimately the end—of World War II. And I'd
have liked to know the reactions of Hazel and Carl and other fisherfolk
to the war news during this end-of-war era. How did the closing months
of the war impact the local community?*

*[As life transitioned—and, for the most part, improved—for residents of
the continental U.S., what happened in isolated Alaska? Did the winding
down of the war effort make their economic condition worse by collapsing
the demand for fish and by reducing military expenditures in Alaska?*

*[I'd also like to know how the relationship of Hazel and Carl evolved—or
more likely devolved—during this critical year. It appears that Carl was
drinking more than ever, and it's likely that his health was on the verge
of collapse (though neither Carl nor Hazel knew that at the time).*

*[Did Hazel or Carl (or both) do something they later regretted during
those missing months? If so, that could be the reason that most of the
diary entries are gone. I know that Hazel deliberately destroyed some of
her diary pages, though I do not know which ones.*

*[These questions were never answered completely in Hazel's entries, but,
reading between the lines, there are clues.*

[Up to this point Hazel's story is told entirely from her diaries. Stitching together the remaining entries, and based on my personal insights, I have filled in the blanks and merged different parts of the story to create a conclusion.

[I was very young (eight years old) at the time Hazel and Carl's fishing odyssey ended. The final chapter of their story is written here close to what I remember and in the approximate order and dates in the following diary entries.]

Part VII
1946

Early 1946

[Hazel and Carl spent a large portion of the winter of 1945/1946 on their boat at the Fishing Terminal in Seattle. Hazel's dad (my grandfather) needed some serious surgical procedures performed, so perhaps that was one reason they took the Olympic back to Seattle. Hazel worked at her old job at the State Game Department, located in the Smith Tower. The Smith Tower at that time was the tallest building west of the Mississippi River. It was built in 1914 by Lyman Smith of typewriter fame.

[Carl continued with his drunken escapades—always an embarrassment to my aunt. Carl was hospitalized for several days with stomach and chest pains while in Seattle.]

2/14—Thurs. *[Still in Seattle]*

Valentine's Day. Gave Carl a big valentine. He sure was surprised. *[Hazel's love for him wasn't always reciprocal.]* Carl went to town to buy pipe for the toilet vent, but it didn't fit when he got it home. Ran out of oil last night—about 8 p.m. Had to get 10 gals. from Pritcher. It was our own oil to begin with anyway. At 7:20, we had an earthquake; it shook the boat and scared us silly. *[This earthquake was 6.1 magnitude. Must feel strange to be on a boat during an earthquake—maybe like being in a storm.]*

4/23—Tues.

Carl and I went up to see Dad. *[He was still in the hospital.]* He seems well. Won't see him again for months. *[Hazel and Carl were about to return to Alaska for the fishing season.]*

4/24—Wed.—1st day
Left Seattle for Alaska with *Sea Wolf* and *Doris K*

All three of our boats have a dog aboard. Left Ballard at 6:15 a.m. Got thru the locks at 7:10. Went by way of Mukilteo and Columbia Beach. Beautiful day, smooth water and sunshine. *Doris K* had a leaky gas tank and had to stop and pump gas into a drum. Then we got stuck in the mud just before we reached Deception Pass. *Doris K* got stuck first, and we went to help him, and then we got stuck. We got loose again, but a flat-bottom scow had to pull *Doris K* off. Got to Deception Pass too late—tried to go thru but couldn't make it *[low tide]* so turned around and anchored in a bay near the pass.

4/25—Thurs.—2nd day
Deception Pass to Friday Harbor

Good weather all the way to Port Townsend. Went thru the Canal. *Laxen* had to pick up his skiff. Left right away for Friday Hbr. As soon as we poked our noses out into the Straits of Juan de Fuca, we began to roll. Dopey and I got sick. Arrived at Friday Hbr. at 2:30. Mailed letters to Mother and Dad.

4/26—Fri.—3rd day
Friday Harbor to Departure Bay

Nice day, good weather. Went thru Dodds Narrows rite on the nose; didn't have to wait for the tide. Went on to Departure Bay and, as the weather was good, went across the Straits of Georgia. Smooth water all the way. Arrived about 7:30. We anchored, and the 2 boats tied to us. Rowed Dopey ashore.

4/27—Sat.—4th day
Departure Bay to Squirrel Cove

Nice weather. As soon as we started, we heard a terrible rumbling noise—our exhaust pipe had burned off. Had to shriek at each other all day, and the pipe was so hot you couldn't touch it. Nice weather. Had to wait at Stewart Island from 10-12:30 for the tide. Carl bot some hooks; case of milk $5.25; case of eggs @ $.48—but *Surplus* took half. Went thru Yuculta Rapids with no trouble. Carl fixed the exhaust.

4/28—Sun.—5th day
Squirrel Cove to Shoal Bay

4/29—Mon.—6th day
Shoal Bay to Port McNeil

Left in the dark and followed John into a blind bay and had to come back—lost 1 hour. Rained all day. Followed some gill-netters across Mibank. Pretty ruff, too. Couldn't see our poles sometimes. Saw the *North Sea* abandoned on the rocks—wonder what happened. Over-took *Sea Wolf* and *Rande A* before we got to Jorkins Point. Stopped at Klemtu, had

breakfast, and John got gas. Went on again and
once more over-took *Sea Wolf*. Arrived at Buttedale
at 3:30. About 5:30 *Sea Wolf* and Co. arrived—with
about 25 more boats. We got 10 gals. gas; 3 loaves
of bread and chili con carne.

4/30—Tues.—7th day
Port McNeil to Cascade Harbor

5/1—Wed.—8th day
Cascade Harbor to Bella Bella

Left at 4:20. Foggy and misty. Good weather till
6 a.m.—then it began to rain and blow. We rolled
and tossed till we got across. Still pretty ruff
till we got to Namu. Had to take our shoes off—too
slippery on the linoleum. Got to Bella Bella about
4:30. Mailed letter to Mother.

5/2—Thurs.—9th day
Bella Bella to Buttedale

5/3—Fri.—10th day
Buttedale to Meville Island

Some birthday! Mrs. Howard gave me a wooden bowl.
Made myself a birthday cake. Also bot a chicken
for the occasion. Still raining. Left at 4:30—and
so did *Sea Wolf*, but we soon left them far behind.
Surplus broke a turnbuckle, and we went back for
them, but they got it fixed OK. Pretty choppy thru
Arthur Passage. Got to Melville Island (God's
Pocket) at 7:30. We didn't know the way in—but
took it slow. Three Canadian trollers were there,
too. We anchored and the 2 boats tied to us. Had
trouble with the oil stove all day, wouldn't get

hot. Carl drained it tonite, and it was half full of water.

5/4—Sat.—11th day
Melville Island to Ketchikan

Left early. On our way out, saw about 12 boats anchored in a little pocket. Several boats were behind us all the way across Dixon's Entrance—it was rolling but not too bad. Got to Ketchikan at 3:30. Went to P.O. and got our mail. Total running time 88 hrs.—7 and 9/10 miles per hr.

5/6—Mon.
Ketchikan

Horrible day. Wind blew all nite, and it just poured all nite and all day. *Sea Spray* came down to see us. Chris and Leonard helped Carl fix up his gear, so I had them stay for lunch. After supper, I walked up to P.O. and back. Letters from Mother and Zellah, and also several cards. Carl started drinking today.

5/7—Tues.

Walked up to see Mrs. Burnett. She sure looks awful, so thin. Charlie was there too, on his way back to the hospital. Saw Ina Wilson. She has sold everything and is leaving for Everett tomorrow a.m. Carl is worse—hasn't been home all day. At 1 a.m., he was still out when I went to bed.

5/8—Wed.

At 10 a.m. I went up to the City Jail, and there was Carl—had been there all nite—drunk, with a

big gash on the side of his head! Cost $15.00 to
get him out. Got home, and as soon as he could,
he went back to the Shamrock. Dragged him home,
and at 4 p.m. he was back there again! Once more
I dragged him home—but not much use.

5/12—Sun.—Mother's Day

Horrible day, rained and blew all day. *Sea Wolf*
and *Rande A* came in about 10 a.m. with 14 fish for
5 days fishing. Had to can them as no buyers would
buy them. About 4 p.m., Carl and I took Dopey for
a walk. Standard Oil man gave us a ride to the
P.O.—had a malted milk and walked back to the boat.
Made 3 doz. donuts. Wrote to Ruth Iffert asking
her to forward our mail to Petersburg.

5/14—Tues.

Dad had another operation—Swedish Hospital. Called
Mother on the phone at 8:30 p.m. ($4.75). Washed
my hair, and then I commenced to feel sick; had to
go to bed, again. Got up at 2 p.m.; felt a little
better. After dinner we went for a walk to Thomas
Basin and saw the gang.

5/15—Mon.

Showered all day. Washed clothes. Carl went fishing on the *Surplus*—from 11 to 5:30. Got 9 fish.
Will have the *Totem* can them and we'll get 1/3,
Surplus 1/3 and *Totem* 1/3. *[They can't sell their fish yet since
the official fishing season hasn't begun.]*

5/16—Tues.

Went fishing today—first time this year. Left at 5
a.m.—fished till 3:30 p.m. Got 8. Rainy day and

cold. Sun came out a few times. The *Totem* will can our fish and furnish the containers for ½ of the total canned. So *Surplus* and us put our fish together, and they will can it tomorrow. They already had ours done from yesterday.

5/23—Thurs.
Ketchikan to Meyers Chuck

Nice day. Good weather all the way. Arrived about 9 a.m. Dopey rolled in some rotten fish, and does he stink! Cleaned and polished all our old spoons *[fishing lures]*. Carl had to make a hole in the floor around the exhaust pipe as it was getting too hot.

5/27—Mon.
Meyers Chuck to Wrangell

Left at 5:30. A beautiful day, water smooth as glass. Arrived about 1 p.m. Lots of boats here—*Betty K*, *Narmata*, *Sequoia*, *Surprise*, *Yitka*, and many others. Old drunken Bennett stopped to say hello.

5/28—Tues.
Wrangell

Three big boats tied on the outside of *Surplus*— and we were on the inside. Began to blow, so we pulled out and went across to the Oil Dock Side. Found a place on the inside, next to Joe Lawton's boat. Walked up to see *Quester* in drydock. Asked him down for evening, but he never came. Made a cake too, so Carl and I ate half of it before we went to bed.

5/31—Fri.
Salmon Bay to Point Baker

Point Baker to Louise Cove. Left Sal. Bay at
4:10 a.m. Carl changed oil in the engine. Dopey
had a flying squirrel to play with. Fun watching
them. Left Point Baker at 1:00 p.m. and got to
Louise Cove at 3:30 p.m. Rained hard all nite.
Lots of driftwood.

[A flying squirrel is a small squirrel that has skin joining the fore and hind limbs for gliding from tree to tree. The Northern flying squirrel is one of only two species of flying squirrels to be found in North America. Its range is from as far south as North Carolina across the northern part of the U.S. from Nova Scotia to Alaska, and to the West Coast.]

Official Fishing Season Begins

6/2—Sun.
Malmsbury

Fished from 4:30 to 6:30 but got no bites. Dopey and I both got sick—ruff water. Our gear didn't work so good. Came back to the harbor and washed clothes.

6/3—Mon.
Malmsbury to Gedney

Cracker Box Mack and his pal were anchored in the bay when we got up—so he came over and visited for a while. Left at 9:30 for Gedney. Woollerys are the buyers for Bill Mullens. Peck and Pete were there, and we five were all the boats there. Woollery is making a float to go from the scow to the shore. Carl and Pete are drinking and getting drunk.

6/5—Wed.

Fished from 5:30 to 10:30. Got 2 fish, one large red and one white. Carl was too drunk to put the gear out—wanted to go to bed, but I wouldn't let him. I canned the white king—got 12 cans.

6/6—Thurs.

Bennett and Patterson arrived this morning from Wrangell, and Carl got drunk with them. Pat gave me a rib roast, cauliflower, and asparagus, so I cooked dinner for them all. Wind started to blow very hard, so we all had to move from the float. Carl wouldn't move—tied the bow to the scow, and when we broke a line, he wouldn't even come aboard and anchor. So I had to start the engine and literally drag Carl aboard. Then he tied up to Al Rhymes till we both dragged anchor, and had to re-anchor. Carl slept on the bench and kept the radio on all nite. I had another crying jag—Carl didn't even hear me.

6/7—Fri.
Gedney to Pt. Alexander, 2 hours and 30 min.

Alarm went off at 3:00 a.m., but Carl wouldn't get up, so I shut it off. Finally at 5 a.m., Carl started the engine and went to the scow and tied up so he could get a pt. of whiskey—which he left at the scow last nite. I wouldn't get up and slept till 8:30. At 10:00 a.m., Carl decided to go to Pt. Alexander; got there at 12:30. Letters from Mother, Zellah, Peggy Wilgus, and the office gang. Carl and Bennett drank all day, and Carl stayed up town for dinner—while I stayed home, waiting for him to come home and eat supper!

6/8—Sat.

Got gas, oil and water. Carl's birthday, and I'm not doing a darn thing about it, either. The way he has acted ever since we came to Ketchikan, he doesn't deserve a thing. He wouldn't eat any breakfast, so I ate alone. Carl got up in a drunken stupor and drank some ammonia that I was using to wash windows! He hollered and screamed. I didn't know what to do. Gave him a lot of warm soapy water, milk of magnesia, castor oil, Wesson oil, lots of milk and orange and lemon juice, also dry mustard in a glass of hot water. He heaved twice, and then I gave him an enema too. His mouth and tongue were badly burned. What a disgusting mess! *[I can't understand how Hazel put up with this. She must have really loved Carl. Why, I don't know.]*

6/9—Sun.

Carl is still pretty sick, but was able to go up to the liquor store and get Mrs. Mullens to get him a pint of whiskey. *[Liquor stores were supposed to be closed on Sundays.]* She came back with Carl, had a drink, and then stayed for breakfast. Bennett came in from fishing and had dinner with us; then Carl had him buy another quart! I was up all nite dishing whiskey out—in 2 tablespoons in a glass of milk. Carl is feeling better from the ammonia, but now he is so drunk he doesn't know what he's doing. Fish buyer from Sitka came in today.

6/18—Tues.

Dull, gray day. Cashed my income tax check and bot groceries. I puttied all the cracks on the forward deck, and then Carl painted it, so now we shouldn't have any leaks. Tom and Jerry jumped on

Dopey tonite and had a bad fight. Poor Dopey. Carl is complaining of stomach pain all the time. He needs to see the doctor.

6/19—Wed.

Rain. Washed clothes all day. Battery on fan for the stove ran down, so Carl had to buy a new battery for $10.75. Our old one is being recharged, but it isn't ready yet. Cooked a pot roast in my pressure cooker in 45 minutes. Patterson and his squaw plus Bennett and another drunk all came over to listen to the Prize Fight. Went for a walk with Dopey and found a whole bunch of 4-leaf clovers. (Maybe that means my luck will change—fat chance!)

6/30—Sun.
Gedney

Carl was all in and went to bed most of the day—I had to do all the fishing. He bot a case of beer last nite, and it's nearly all gone now. His stomach hurts all the time. Complains of indigestion. Doesn't sound so good to me.

7/1—Mon.

Fish prices went up to $.26 on large reds. Carl was too drunk to go out, so I hid the ignition key. He drank beer and slept all day. Our forward deck leaks like a sieve, and he will not do a thing about it. He bot another case of beer today.

7/2—Tues.
Gedney

Carl is still a mess. Would not go out with him today so kept the ignition key. He slept most of the day and drank beer in between. Gave spoons and hooks to everyone that came by. I made some doughnuts and gave Woollerys 1 doz. Carl got up at 9 p.m. and went on the scow and stayed till 11:30 when he brought some Native aboard and gave him 1 doz. fishhooks. Rained hard most all day. Bennett gave us 2 deer steaks.

7/3—Wed.

Another rainy day. Most of the boats came in about 8 a.m. No fish. Carl was in no condition to fish again today. He went visiting to all the "whiskey" boats and drank beer all day—never ate one mouthful of food. Came home late tonite with another case of beer.

7/4—Thurs.

A horrible day. None of the boats went out. Carl couldn't fish if he wanted to—he's in such a bad condition. I took a bath and packed my things, all ready to leave on the packer tonite. Carl found it out and made an awful scene and promised he'd behave himself—so I fell for it again! Hoping that he really means it this time.

7/5—Fri.

Carl is too sick to fish. I helped Irene unpack her groceries—then she asked me to clean and cut a chicken for her to fry!

7/6—Sat.

Went fishing today—but Carl was so sick he spent most of the time in bed, and I did all the fishing.

So we came in at 12:30. All the other boats made over $100.00 today. We never caught one fish.

7/7—Sun.

Did not fish today. Carl was so sick he stayed in bed all day. I washed clothes till 3 p.m. Hung them on the roof of the scow, and they were all nearly dry at night. A very good fish day but not for us—some boats made $214.00.

8/14—Wed.
Snow Pass

Fair day, mostly cloudy. Carl and Laurel went fishing with Tex and Irene and her 2 kids. Dopey and I went calling on the woman in the float house—such a mess! Stove propped up with chunks of wood, rusty and rickety, dirty floor—and the baby didn't look too bright. The fishermen only got 2 fish. *Ella C* and *Harrigan* are here, icing fish. Made a lemon pie. Carl cleaned out the soot in the stove.

8/16—Fri.

Fished from 6:15 to 12:45—only got 5 cohoes and one king. Rained most of the day, caught some rainwater. Carl and Woollery are still working on plugs. Carl still not well. Wrote letters all afternoon.

8/17—Sat.

Neptune came in at 1 a.m., and Irene Woollery and her 2 kids went to town. Didn't fish; too windy. Many boats arrived today. Had Laurel over for lunch. Carl too sick to eat.

8/21—Wed.

Another awful day—such rain and wind. Big swells and wind blowing. Got worse as we neared the harbor entrance. Carl thot it would be smoother after we got out. We rolled and dived pretty bad till we got to another bay, and it smoothed down some. Only 5 boats made it—*Surplus*, *Dot*, *Chemp*, *Velera*, and us; all the others had to go back. It got pretty nasty—cold wind and rain. I got sick. Broke all my glass baking dishes. Couldn't cook. All the dishes were dirty. Sold to Einktors in Malms. He was paying $.32 for mild cures and $.18 for cohoes. *Surplus* tied up to us. Sold for $72.00.

8/22—Thurs.

Still stormy. *Questers* came over for breakfast. I cooked hotcakes and sausage and their eggs. Made a devil's food cake (out of Irene's sour milk) and had her and Laurel in for coffee and cake. Washed a few clothes—scrubbed floors—made ice cream. Caught rainwater. Too stormy to fish. Carl has been drinking all day.

8/26—Mon.
Wrangell

Another beautiful day. Went on the grid at noon. Cleaned off barnacles and washed the port side, and Carl copper painted. Didn't get thru till 8 p.m. Carl had to sit up most of the nite to watch the ropes. *[Since the tide was especially high, the boat would rise (perhaps quickly). If it were tied to a fixed point—like a solid pier—it could pull on the anchor ropes and either break them or tip over the boat if it held.]* High tide was at 1:30 a.m.—17′-1″. *Lee Ellis* is on the grid with *Beilby*.

8/27—Tues.

We scraped and scrubbed the hull. I helped scrape barnacles, and while Carl worked on rudder, I cop-per-painted the starboard side. We finished by 10 a.m. but had to wait till noon to get off. Went for a walk after supper. Met the *Princess Nora* and saw all the tourists. Harrington stopped us and took us for a ride to end of highway and back to their place for a drink.

8/29—Thurs.
Wrangell to Brownson Island

Beautiful weather still. Started washing clothes early. Carl got some linseed oil and painted forward deck. *Sea Wolf* and *California* decided to leave at 11 a.m.—so we went too. Got our laundry, 2 cases of salmon cans, and two 50# sacks of sugar. *[Ration-ing of many items came to a welcomed end in 1946.]* Then stopped for gas, oil, and water—left Wrangell at 11:45. Smooth water all the way to Brownson Island where we saw Stan Hausman and his girlfriend. Picked currants and salal berries.

8/31—Sat.
Ketchikan

Got up at 5 a.m. Carl took main poles off and left them at the cabin. Sawed off bow poles and dropped them overboard. Went to Union Oil Co. at 7 a.m., and Carl changed oil while we waited for them to open at 8 a.m. Got oil, gas, and water and waited for *Sea Wolf*. Finally at 10:30 we left oil dock for Thomas Basin to see what was wrong with *Sea Wolf*. Then our oil pressure left—all the oil went in the bilge. Met *Sea Wolf* and turned back to Oil Co. Then *California* broke his rudder chain—and it was 2 p.m. before we all got fixed up. Too late to leave, so we all went back to Thomas Basin for the nite. Mrs. Burnett stopped in. She looks very bad. Saw *Sea Wolf*, and he said *Rande A* was in and would be going too. Went up town and bot groceries; mailed letters to Mother and Zellah. Also received one from Mother. Stopped to see Flo Wright, and she told me that Jack Tavis was on a binge, and Lillian had left for Chicago. While we were eating supper, *Janie* came over and wanted to go south with us. Carl told them they would have to see *Rande A* as he would be the leader. Was so mad at Carl I slept on bench—all he does is bawl me out and correct and criticize all I say. Sure will be glad to get to Seattle and be by myself for a while.

9/1—Sun.
Ketchikan—near Hump Back—4 a.m. to 2:45 p.m. and 4 p.m. to 7:30 p.m.

Left Ketchikan at 4 a.m. with *Janie*, *California*, *Rande A*, *Sea Wolf*, *31A102*, and us. Fog at Hog Rocks till Mary Island. We all followed *Rande A*—fog all the way to Dumdas Island. Stayed there from 2:45 to 4 p.m. Went into a small island at 7:30, and 2 Canadian fisherman were there. *Janie* tied to us. Dave took all 3 dogs ashore.

9/7—Sat.

A horrible day. Wind and rain in sheets. So bad I never left the boat all day. Didn't get up till after 7 a.m. *Surplus* was tied on outside of *Chemp*, and *Chemp* was next to us, and we were next to the float. *Surplus* had to move as the wind was blowing us all into the shore. *Chemp* stayed with us till Jim and Carl got the engine going.

9/10—Tues.

Stayed in all day. Horrible day. Wind and rain. Rained in torrents and so misty could hardly see shore line. Hailed so hard it bounced off the waves. Rowed Dopey ashore and picked a few cranberries.

9/14—Sat.
Coffman Cove—Ketchikan

Left hbr. and all was nice and smooth till we got to Ratz Hbr. when it began to blow and get ruff. Went across to Meyers Chuck to get out of Ernest Sound swells, but it began to smooth down so we went right on to Ketchikan. Passed the *Salvor*, and George Porter gave us our mail. *Dot* had to stop twice en route on account of dirty gas line. Got to Ketchikan at 3 p.m. Carl went to town to drink. I had supper alone.

9/15—Sun.
Ketchikan

Carl not well, so he slept while I picked currants and salal berries. Mildred Kaetz gave me a jar of strawberry jam and some turnips. Ruby Johnson gave me a qt. of currant juice and some beet pickles to take to Mother, cabbage, turnips, and spuds. Also some magazines. Spent the rest of the day fixing the berry juice.

9/16—Mon.

Horrible day. Rained and blew hard all day. Scrubbed floors and did a little washing. Carl and Dopey walked to Union Oil Co. and back in the rain. They were gone a long time. Think Carl stopped to drink. *Tonto* came over and marked our charts for harbors. Got lights from the watchman.

9/17—Tues.

Wrote to Mother and Zellah that we will be leaving in the a.m. Carl changed oil and filters, and Dick helped him. I canned the berry juice for jelly. Then at noon we went to Union Oil Co. and got gas, stove oil, and water, ready to leave in the a.m. if the weather is OK. After we came back, I went up town and bot groceries and stopped to see Ruth. She wanted us to come for dinner and play cards, but Carl wouldn't go. Think he has been drinking again. So cancelled the whole works. The whole bunch was here for the evening—till 2:15 a.m.: George, Dick, Duward, Mildred, Leonard, Chris, and finally Al from *Linda Joe*. Made coffee twice! The weather report was too bad for traveling, so we will not leave in the morning. Made an apple pie.

9/18—Wed.

Horrible day. Rained and blew all night and all day. Made cinnamon rolls. Waited all day for the rain to stop so I could go to the store—finally at 4 p.m. had to go anyway. Carl is off on another of his binges. He wasn't home when I went to bed. Dopey is very restless tonight. Guess he misses Carl. I don't. Left Carl's supper on stove. Cold tonight. Might freeze. Serves him right.

9/19—Thurs.

Carl is dead! Can't believe it. Police officers came to the boat to tell me. Said he died in the bar. Pals thought he was drunk, as usual—propped him up in a booth and left him. Bartender found him while cleaning up before closing. No other details yet. Sick to my stomach. Didn't sleep—cried all night. What will I do?

9/20—Fri.

Talked to police again. They say Carl probably died of heart attack—coroner's first guess. It doesn't really matter if he died of drinking or heart attack or just falling off stool. Have to decide what to do now. Many decisions to make.

9/24—Tues.

Heart attack is official ruling. Don't really care at this point. Talked with Mother and Dad. Decided to sell boat and shack and return to Seattle. Think I can get old job back at Fish and Game Department. Have to make burial arrangements tomorrow. Local funeral parlor arranging details.

9/30—Mon.

Sold *Olympic* to local dealer for $3,800. Think *Sea Wolf* will buy shack. Plan to leave for Seattle Thursday on the *Prince Rupert*. End of fishing, now and forever. Never was my dream, but did not expect it to end this way.

[In an interview for the Seattle Times *in the '60s, Hazel stated: "The experience was worth a million dollars. Except: I don't think I would do it again for a million dollars!"]*

Epilogue

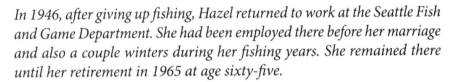

In 1946, after giving up fishing, Hazel returned to work at the Seattle Fish and Game Department. She had been employed there before her marriage and also a couple winters during her fishing years. She remained there until her retirement in 1965 at age sixty-five.

Hazel at the typewriter at her job at the Fisheries Department.

Hazel at her retirement.

Besides her job, the Order of the Amaranth was a major factor in Hazel's post-fishing life. Amaranth was a social and philanthropic organization that promoted the practice of truth, faith, wisdom, and charity. Hazel engaged in these activities for many years, becoming the Royal Matron and Grand Lecturer (a state office). She traveled to various chapters throughout the state to give instruction. I'm sure she was happy, once again, to wear formal ball gowns like the ones she had enjoyed wearing as a young socialite. (I remember that at age eighty-two she had an entire closet stuffed with beautiful, long gowns.)

Hazel and friends in formal attire.

During the forty-six years after she finished fishing, Hazel involved herself in our families' lives as much as possible. My mother, Zellah (Hazel's younger sister), died at age sixty-five, so Hazel became the mother and grandmother figure for our families.

Hazel stayed with us over the Christmas holidays of 1977. The phone rang almost every night, and a male voice asked for Hazel. We all questioned her about her caller, but she wouldn't say much—just grinned. Below is the first part of a letter I received from her a few months later.

> *May 6, 1978*
>
> *Dear Arlene:*
>
> *Well, suppose I had better tell you all about this!!! Homer and I have known each other for about a year. We met at the Senior Citizen dance in Woodinville. He has been a widower for over 4 years and lived alone up here in Marysville. He would come down and visit with me and I would drive up to see him once in a while. He wanted to get married before Christmas but I said no. So finally we decided to get married. We were married in the Memorial Baptist Church in Everett, the church that all his family attended.*

In 1978, at age 78, Hazel married for a third and final time—to Homer Knight of Everett, Washington. With this marriage, she became part of a large family. That was important to her because she never had children of her own. Homer's extended family welcomed Hazel warmly, and they were wonderful to her. Hazel and Homer were happily married for several years before Homer's death.

In the meantime, my parents and brother and I (in our teenage years) had moved to California. We made the trip in a converted U.S. Army troop-transport trailer. We lived in it four years prior to moving south and continued to live in it, all four of us, for four additional years after our migration.

Hazel was still driving to California from Washington for holidays and visits with us when she was in her eighties. In 1984—at age eighty-four—she drove down to help with our daughter's wedding! She was quite a woman.

Hazel died in 1992 at Everett, Washington, at age ninety-two.

Glossary

Alaska Day—*a legal holiday observed on October 18. It is the anniversary of the formal transfer of the Territory of Alaska from Russia to the United States, which took place at a flag-raising ceremony at Fort Sitka on October 18, 1867.*

ballast—*heavy material, such as rocks, gravel, sand, iron, or lead, placed low in a vessel to make it more stable.*

bilge—*the lowest internal portion of the hull.*

bite (bight)—*a curve or recess in a coastline, river, or other geographical feature.*

blackout—*war-time requirement; no lights visible from outside houses so that enemy planes could not see where cities or buildings were.*

bow pole—*trolling pole mounted on the bow of a fishing vessel.*

bulkhead—*a dividing wall or barrier between compartments on a boat*

chuck—*Chinook jargon for a saltwater body that fills with high tide.*

coho—*a deep-bodied North Pacific salmon with small black spots. Also called silver salmon.*

cradle—*see "ways."*

divinity—*a fluffy, creamy candy made with stiffly beaten egg whites and sugar.*

fathom—*a unit of length equal to six feet.*

fathometer—*electronic instrument for measuring the depth of water.*

fiddler—*a type of small fish.*

forecastle—*part of boat forward of the foremast.*

foremast—*mast of a ship nearest the bow.*

gaff—*hooked tool used to club and lift fish into the boat.*

galley—*area of a boat designed for cooking.*

gill netter—*fishing boat which uses a fishing net that hangs vertically in the water so that fish get trapped in the net by their gills.*

grid—*see "ways."*

gurdy—*a winch; a mechanism to help bring up the fishing line (which can be very heavy if fish are hooked).*

hatch—*the cover over the cargo hold opening of a boat.*

herring spoon—*a bait-shaped metal jig used to attract salmon and other fish (see jig).*

jig—*a very large fishing lure with one or more hooks, used to catch salmon and other large fish.*

mandola—*a stringed instrument; large tenor or bass mandolin.*

marker—*stop attached to trolling wire at four- or five-fathom intervals to indicate depth of the water.*

nertz (nerts)—*slang for nuts.*

Nucoa—*early brand of margarine.*

packer—*a boat that moves among the fishing fleet when many miles from a cannery and buys fish from the fishermen and ices it. The packer also brings the mail, gas, supplies, etc.*

pinoche—*a candy made with brown sugar.*

plug—a *lure with one or more hooks.*

purse seiner—*a fishing boat that fishes using seines (nets) that are drawn up into the shape of a purse to encircle the fish*

salmon

> *Chinook*—*largest species of salmon; also called king. Some have red flesh, some white. White brings a third less in price. Usually sold fresh, frozen, or mild-cured.*

> *chum*—*cheapest grade of salmon; also called dog; usually canned or smoked.*

> *coho*—*also called silver or medium red; usually canned or smoked.*

> *pink*—*most numerous and smallest; also called humpback; most all is canned.*

> *sockeye*—*most valuable commercial species; also called red.*

scupper—*hole in a boat's rail to allow water on deck to drain overboard.*

Seward's Day—*a legal Alaska State holiday. It falls on the last Monday of March and commemorates the signing of the Alaska Purchase on March 30, 1867. It is named for then-Secretary of State William H. Seward, who negotiated the purchase for the price of $7,200,000. That figured out to be about two cents per acre. Seward's Day should not be confused with Alaska Day.*

skiff—*a shallow, flat-bottomed, open boat with sharp bow and square stern.*

Skippy—*brand name of an oil-burning stove.*

spoon—*lure for catching salmon.*

steerage—*part of a ship providing the cheapest and least desirable accommodations for passengers with tickets.*

tag line—*wire or line attached to end of trolling pole.*

trawler—*boat that fishes with a trawl net or seine.*

troller—*boat that fishes by trolling a baited line along behind.*

trough—*the hollow between two swells in the sea. A ship "in the trough" has its side to the sea and is in danger of rolling over.*

union suit—*a single undergarment combining shirt and pants.*

wanigan—*a float house.*

ways—*a grid structure that supports a boat in order to repair, paint, clean, etc. the hull; a form of drydock; used in the expression "on the ways."*

wellies (also known as wellington boots)— *a knee-length waterproof rubber or plastic boot.*

williwaw (willy)—*a sudden violent squall that blows offshore from a mountainous coast.*

About the Author

Arlene Lochridge holds a BA degree from San Diego State University and an MA degree from California American University. Retired from twenty-seven years as a teacher and consultant, she now devotes time to many community organizations, as well as her church. When not in their hometown of Escondido, California, Arlene and her husband spend their time in BayView, Washington.

The manuscript for this story won Editor's First Choice Submission award at the San Diego Writers' Conference in January 2008.

For further details of A Fish Out of Water, visit www.arlenelochridge.com.